WHAT IF THE AMERICAN POLITICAL SYSTEM WERE DIFFERENT?

Herbert M. Levine

Neil B. Cohen

Joy E. Esberey

Thomas H. Ferrell

Judith F. Gentry

Glen Jeansonne

John J. Pitney, Jr.

M. E. Sharpe, Inc. • Armonk, New York • London, England

For Michael Weber

Available in the United Kingdom and Europe from M. E. Sharpe, Publishers,
3 Henrietta Street, London WC2E 8LU.

Library of Congress Cataloging-in-Publication Data

What if the American political system were different? / edited by Herbert M. Levine.
    p. cm.
Includes bibliographical references and index.
ISBN 1-56324-009-2 (cloth)
ISBN 1-56324-010-6 (paper)
1. United States—Politics and government.
I. Levine, Herbert M.
JK21.W43   1992
320.973—dc20
91-26730
CIP

Printed in the United States of America
The paper used in this publication meets the minimum
requirements of American National Standard for
Information Sciences—Permanence of Paper for
Printed Library Materials, ANSI Z 39.48-1984.

BB   10   9   8   7   6   5   4   3   2   1

Contents

Preface

The bicentennial celebrations of the Constitution in 1987 inspired many Americans as well as foreign observers to assess the American political system anew. The United States Constitution is the oldest working written constitution in the world. Its political institutions and processes—whether provided for directly in the Constitution, such as separation of powers, checks and balances, and federalism, or accepted later as part of that document, such as judicial review—have become a model for many other constitutions.

Some bicentennial commentators hailed the achievements of the framers of the U.S. Constitution in establishing an enduring political order based on principles of self-government, limited government, and the rule of law. Others praised the framers for their judgment about human nature and individual liberty.

But other commentators expressed dissatisfaction both with the original document and with subsequent historical developments that have shaped the political life of the nation. Civil rights proponents pointed to the moral blemish of slavery and the lack of equal opportunity for African-Americans. Feminists deplored the absence of women among the framers and the lack of concern for women's rights. Conservatives condemned the "imperial judiciary," which, they claimed, had usurped the powers of Congress.

Still other analysts wondered whether structural changes should be made in the American political system. Some called for the United States to adopt certain features of a parliamentary system to allow for greater accountability and more effective government, and others recommended a strengthening of the federal system to restore the powers of the states. Still others thought that it was time to rewrite the entire Constitution to make it more suitable for America's needs in its third century.

The bicentennial of the Constitution also generated discussion about the character of contemporary public policy. The role of government in managing the economy and providing for social services was debated anew. Liberals called for more governmental control, while conservatives argued for less. Foreign policy seemed to be at a particularly critical juncture. The cold war between the United States and the Soviet Union was reassessed, with some arguing that the arms race should be tempered now that the cold war had ended. Others said that the Soviet Union could not be trusted and that the United States should not cut back on defense spending.

As I read the articles and books of writers, social scientists, and political figures and listened to speakers reflecting on the great issues of the American political system, I wondered what the United States would be like today if its course of historical development and political system were different. What if the nation had started out with radically different institutions and political structures? What if it had never enacted the major welfare legislation of the New Deal? What if it had never had to contend with the cold war?

Consideration of different political outcomes was not a new experience for me. As a teacher of American government for twenty years and as an author or editor of several books used in college American government courses, I have been keenly aware of speculation about political change. I recognize that nearly every argument about the structure, processes, and policies of American government includes speculation about the future. Take such and such a position, advocates contend, and these benefits will follow. Take the same position, critics argue, and the results will be catastrophic. Whether the issue involves a constitutional power (such as the authority of the judiciary to invalidate legislation), a political process (such as how parties choose their candidates), or a public policy (such as whether a particular welfare program should be expanded), each side claims that its vision will contribute to a better society.

Stimulated by the discussions accompanying the Constitution's bicentennial, I considered preparing a book that would speculate on how the American political system would be different if it had taken some alternative course over time. As I investigated the literature in the field, I looked at some excellent books that pondered different historical and political outcomes. But none comprehensively addressed the most central questions of American political life.

And so I asked some political scientists, historians, and a legal scholar to join me in speculating about a different America. Some wrote chapters describing a different American political order. They hypothesized as to what the United States would be like without a written constitution and bill of rights, without judicial review, with a parliamentary system, with a unitary structure. Others assessed how the system would be different if the character of political participation had been different. They wondered: suppose there had been no slavery; suppose women had been guaranteed the same rights as men in 1787; suppose the United States had a three-party rather than two-party political system; suppose there were no television. Still others writers focused on public policy, contemplating what the United States would be like if it had rejected welfare programs or if there had been no cold war between the United States and the Soviet Union.

Each author wrote independently. As a group, they reflect no single ideological or partisan point of view, and, as will be evident, there are clear differences of opinion among them. Some authors feel the alternatives they describe would be improvements; others do not. The only requirement was that each speculate and present a vision of a different America. The authors well understand that their efforts are akin to science fiction, since they can never be sure that their visions of "what *might* have been" are equivalent to "what *would* have been." All agree, however, that this exercise presents a way of looking at some of the great features of the American political system in a manner that produces new insights.*

Readers will no doubt agree with some conclusions and disagree with others. Where there is disagreement, the authors hope that readers will be encouraged to think seriously about what was wrong with the analysis and to do some informed speculating of their own. If the book stimulates readers to think about these important issues and present new ideas about old subjects, it will have served its purpose.

Herbert M. Levine

---

*A book somewhat similar in approach to this one is Nelson Polsby, ed., *What If? Explorations in Social-Science Fiction* (Lexington, Mass.: Lewis, 1982). It contains articles not only about American government and history but about other historical figures as well. A book considering different outcomes in American history is Morton Borden and Otis L. Graham, Jr., *Speculations on American History* (Lexington, Mass.: D.C. Heath, 1977).

Acknowledgments

I am indebted to the numerous people in the academic and publishing world who helped me at various stages in the editing and production of the book. The contributing authors were forthcoming in ideas and were responsive to suggestions for changes in their chapters. Robert J. Spitzer of the State University of New York–Cortland read the manuscript in draft form and made superb critical comments and recommendations for modifications of the final draft. Ann Hofstra Grogg copyedited the manuscript with extraordinary and inspiring expertise and diligence.

The contributing authors and I worked closely with Michael Weber, social sciences editor for M. E. Sharpe, Inc. We all appreciate the impressive contributions that he made to the book—contributions that include ideas for chapter topics, insights about content, and attention to style. Always helpful, he is a most constructive, imaginative, caring, and patient editor.

Herbert M. Levine

About the Authors

Neil B. Cohen is professor of law at Brooklyn Law School. He is a specialist in constitutional law and frequently writes for law reviews. Professor Cohen has also published a treatise on commercial law.

Joy E. Esberey has taught political science at the University of Toronto since 1970. She is the author of *Knight of the Holy Spirit,* a biography of Canadian prime minister Mackenzie King. Professor Esberey is especially interested in the comparative study of political systems in the western democracies.

Thomas H. Ferrell is professor of political science at the University of Southwestern Louisiana. His research and writing have been mainly in state, local, and urban politics.

Judith F. Gentry is professor of history at the University of Southwest Louisiana. She has served as president of the Southern Association for Women Historians and of the Louisiana Historical Association. Professor Gentry's major research interest is the public finance of the Confederacy; she is also an expert on the problem of eliminating sex bias in vocational education.

Glen Jeansonne is professor of history at the University of Wisconsin–Milwaukee. He has written more than forty articles and four books, including biographies of Leander Perez and Gerald L. K. Smith. (The latter was nominated for a Pulitzer Prize.) Professor Jeansonne was awarded a John D. and Catherine T. MacArthur Foundation fellowship.

Herbert M. Levine taught political science at the University of Southwest Louisiana for twenty years. In addition to scholarly work, he has published numerous texts on introductory politics, American government, and international relations.

John J. Pitney, Jr., teaches government at Claremont McKenna College. He has been a Congressional Fellow of the American Political Science Association and has served as a senior domestic policy analyst in the House of Representatives and as the deputy director of research for the Republican National Committee.

Introduction

What if the American political system were different? From the earliest debates among the framers of the Constitution at Philadelphia in 1787 to the present, Americans have had profound differences over the character of American government. The discussions and compromises at the convention centered on the power of the central government with respect to the states, the relationship among the different branches of government, the importance of protecting individual liberty against government, and matters of public policy. The Constitution crafted by the framers had no sooner been written than it was criticized for its lack of a bill of rights—a criticism answered by the adoption of the first ten amendments.

But Americans continued to ask questions about the structure of government that the framers created, the political institutions that developed outside of the written constitution, and the wisdom of government policy on foreign affairs, finance, internal improvements, slavery, the economy, and welfare. Although the United States has grown from a small, agricultural country on the periphery of world power in the eighteenth century into a big industrial power with security interests that span the world, the debates over American government have been constant and serious.

The framers believed that concentration of power is dangerous to liberty, and so the political system they created included a number of devices to ensure that power would not be concentrated. Most notable of these features are separation of powers, checks and balances, and federalism.

The separation of powers allocated power among three branches of government—the legislative (Congress), executive (presidency), and judicial (courts). The system of checks and balances ensured that each branch of government exercised some power—some check—over the actions of the other two. Federalism recognized the existence of a central, or federal, government and a series of permanent regional governments—the states.

Over time, additional political structures and practices not specifically mentioned in the Constitution came to have a vast impact on the American political system. Most notable among them are the power of the Supreme Court to declare acts of Congress unconstitutional—known as judicial review—and the formation of political parties.

In the course of two hundred years, moreover, the character of national public policy has changed. In the early years of the Republic domestic policy was guided by the notion that that government is best which governs least. Today, however, the federal government plays a major role in managing the economy, regulating industry, and providing welfare services. Two centuries ago, the United States relied principally on a navy and a divided Europe for its military security from foreign threats. Today, it is a military superpower that is the dominant actor in the global arena.

The focus of power has also changed. Today, the power of the president as commander in chief and chief diplomat is more formidable than it was in the eighteenth century. Today, also, the central government has taken over functions previously held by the states.

Still, for all the differences, much in the American political system remains the same. The basic structure, based on separation of powers, checks and balances, and federalism, continues. And, as in the eighteenth century, the president and Congress are often at odds over the conduct of foreign policy as well as the limits of executive powers.

An examination of what the American political system is, how it has evolved, and the policies it has pursued inevitably leads to differing conclusions. Indeed, some people say that the system has been either a failure, or, if not quite a failure, then an impediment to effective government and sound public policy. They make a variety of charges, for example: (1) The separation of powers has made it difficult for the executive to conduct foreign policy and so has been harmful to U.S. security interests. (2) The distribution of power has impeded the country's ability to secure the welfare of its people. (3) For all its emphasis on liberty and equality, the system has failed some groups, most notably African-Americans and women.

But defenders of the existing American political system find much to praise, for example: (1) The separation of powers serves the conduct of foreign policy well, as the success of the United States as a world leader demonstrates. (2) The distribution of powers has not prevented the United States from providing welfare programs at both the federal government and state government levels. (3) For all its weaknesses, the system allows minority groups and others to participate and exercise real power that benefits their interests.

Whatever appraisal one makes about the American political system, one can profit from speculating how the American political experience would have been different under a different kind of political system. We already know what has actually happened; we cannot be sure what might have happened. Still, such speculations can offer insights that not only influence the way we think about the past but also shape our prescriptions for a better future.

We know that political processes affect outcomes. The very large majorities required to ratify constitutional amendments resulted in the failure of the Equal Rights Amendment, for example, which would have prohibited discrimination based on gender. The fact that the American governmental system was designed to make strong, positive government difficult created obstacles to the federal government's adopting welfare programs and enacting legislation regulating business interests.

Would the Equal Rights Amendment have failed, would welfare programs have been enacted earlier, if the American political system were different? The authors contributing to this volume consider these and other developments in a political fantasy that speculates about a different America.

Neil B. Cohen (Chapter 1) contends that without a written constitution and bill of rights the United States could still have constitutional government based on laws, customs, and judicial decisions. But he sees important changes in how representative democracy and civil liberties would affect the social fabric and how the different system would shape the powers of each branch of government, the relations among the branches of government at the federal level, and the strength of individual liberty.

According to Thomas H. Ferrell (Chapter 2), a unitary system would still have had to establish relationships between a central government and regional units. But a unitary government would not have created the electoral college as a means of choosing the president. At the same time, it would have made the president a more effective legislative leader, unified the judicial system, strengthened political parties, changed the character of interest group behavior, increased voter turnout, and enforced more uniformity in laws.

John J. Pitney, Jr., (Chapter 3) devises a scenario in which the United States has three major political parties—the Democrats, Republicans, and Populists. He sees this three-party system characterized by a great likelihood that losers of the popular vote in presidential contests would win in the electoral college. He describes new problems between the House and the Senate, changes in the political behavior of state governments, an increase in voter turnout, and more diverse choices among issues and policy alternatives.

If the United States had no television, according to Herbert M. Levine (Chapter 4), the character of political campaigns and the social composition of elected members of Congress would change. But he doubts that people would be less cynical about politics and that political participation would increase. He contends that other media, such as books, newspapers, and radio, have had effects similar to that of television on political leadership, domestic legislation, foreign policy, and war.

Joy E. Esberey (Chapter 5) considers an America with a parliamentary system. Central to her view is that Americans would thereby regard government as an instrument for effecting economic and social change rather than a threat to individual liberty. She sees major consequences for the character of political parties, the political behavior of interest groups, the relationships among key government policy makers, and the power of individual legislators. With a parliamentary system, the United States would have developed a strong welfare state. Its foreign policy would have led to increased expansionism in this hemisphere and affected world history in other important ways.

In Chapter 6, Neil B. Cohen considers what the United States would be like without judicial review. He sees possible benefits in terms of the seriousness with which the president and Congress would regard their oaths to obey the Constitution, a greater openness in constitutional decision making, and a greater likelihood of interpreting the Constitution according to present-day concerns. He contends, though, that the detrimental effects would outweigh the benefits in both structural and legal ways. The Supreme Court would no longer be the arbiter among the branches of the federal government or between the federal government and the states. Most serious of all, Cohen notes, is that legitimate minority rights would be curtailed.

Of all the immigrants coming to the United States, only black people arrived as slaves. In considering an America without slavery (Chapter 7), Glen Jeansonne sees important consequences not only for African-Americans but for the rest of American society as well. In his view, an America without slavery would have developed a much more efficient economic and educational system. Black people would have been considered as another ethnic group, subject to a less intense racism. There probably would not have been a Civil War, and the Fourteenth Amendment, which in the twentieth century served as the basis for expanding civil liberties, would not have become part of the Constitution. Jeansonne considers the impact of a slave-free America on the development of political parties, the importance of race as a factor in politics, and civil rights for other groups.

Judith F. Gentry (Chapter 8) asks how American politics would have been different if the 1787 Constitution had guaranteed equal rights for women. She notes that with such a guarantee, the United States would have adopted welfare legislation sooner and more women would have held elective posts, served on juries, and become members of the armed services. In her view, an equal rights provision would have changed the character of government programs, government employment, and public educational institutions. It would also have had an indirect impact on the private sector. Both civil and criminal law would be quite different, too.

In the twentieth century, the United States developed government programs in health, education, and employment as a means of promoting opportunity and benefits for people of limited income. These programs assumed that government had a role in encouraging social and economic equality and produced what has been described as the welfare state. In Chapter 9, John J. Pitney, Jr., imagines the United States without a welfare state. He considers the consequences to American society, taxation, education, social security, health care, and poverty programs. He then discusses the political impact on the size and cost of government; elections; legislative, executive, and judicial authority; and the political agenda.

In Chapter 10, Herbert M. Levine speculates about an America that did not have to contend with the cold war—the intense competition between the United States and the Soviet Union in the decades following World War II. He finds that the United States would still have been a big power in world politics and that, in some ways, it would have faced a more dangerous world. He assesses the impact of the absence of the cold war on budgetary priorities, relations among the three branches of government, the growth of a military-industrial complex, civil liberties, and civil rights.

Throughout its history, Americans and other observers have had lively discussions about ways the American political system should be reformed. The reform tradition continues, as befits a vigorous democracy debating the character of political institutions and the direction of public policy. In the past few decades, for example, reformers have proposed features of a parliamentary system, changes in the two-party system, the adoption of the Equal Rights Amendment, the expansion of the welfare state, and measures to end the cold war.

Although this book does not deal directly with reform, by implication the subject is very much present. Those proposing changes in American governmental structures, processes, and policies might usefully consider the fantasies fashioned by the contributing authors. Such a consideration might serve not only to strengthen or modify their own proposals for change but also to stimulate their speculations about "what if the American political system were different."

WHAT IF THE AMERICAN POLITICAL SYSTEM WERE DIFFERENT?

NEIL B. COHEN

1 | What If There Were No Written Constitution and Bill of Rights?

We have all grown up knowing that one of the most important political documents in this country is the United States Constitution. Yet it is not entirely clear to many people what this document is and why it is so important. Indeed, it would not be surprising if most people thought of the Constitution as merely one of those old, important pieces of paper like the Declaration of Independence that are on display at the National Archives.

The original copy of the Constitution is, in fact, on display at the National Archives, but that museum exhibit, impressive though it may be, does not represent the true importance of the Constitution. The Constitution is, simply, the most important document of American government.

What is a constitution? And why is ours so important? It is critical to examine these questions before imagining what life would be like without a written constitution.

What Is a Constitution?

Dictionaries typically contain several definitions of *constitution*. Some definitions deal with the physical makeup of someone or something. It is from these definitions that, for example, we understand President Harry Truman's habit of referring to his regular, early in the day walk as his "morning constitutional." The remainder of the definitions, however, are much more relevant to an understanding of the term in the context of government.

These definitions speak, variously, of the act of establishing something, the organization of a state and the distribution of sovereignty within it, the basic principles of a society that determine the powers of the government and the rights of the people and, finally, a written instrument embodying these rules.

These definitions, while all relating to government, have quite different emphases. Yet all contribute to our understanding of the United States Constitution. Indeed, our Constitution has functions that fulfill each definition. For purposes of simplicity, the functions served by a constitution can be described in three broad categories: philosophical, political and structural, and legal.

Philosophical Functions of a Constitution

A constitution is said to embody the basic principles of a nation. It is a statement of "what we are as a people." Consider the preamble to the Constitution of the United States:

> We the People of the United States, in Order to form a more perfect Union, establish Justice, insure domestic Tranquility, provide for the common defence, promote the general Welfare, and secure Blessings of Liberty to ourselves and our Posterity, do ordain and establish this Constitution for the United States of America.

Not a word in the preamble sets forth any rules of conduct or organizing political principles. Yet it is a stirring statement of aspirations for the national government. The preamble sets out a list of the ideals that it is hoped that the national government established by the Constitution will fulfill. The six ideals listed in that short paragraph are, essentially, a philosophical statement of the functions of our government. As such, the preamble speaks also about that which the American people value in our government.

The text of the Constitution also reveals significant information about the philosophy of national government in the United States. Most particularly, it asserts a belief that the national government, while supreme within its areas of power, should have limited powers. Furthermore, it shows additional distrust of centralized power by dividing power among different branches in the now-familiar *checks-and-balances* pattern. In this pattern, each branch has some authority to control the actions of the other branches.

Of course, the preamble, as eloquent as it is, was written to introduce the original Constitution and cannot therefore be considered a source of all the values embodied by today's Constitution. Indeed, the preamble was written before the *Bill of Rights*—the first ten amendments to the Constitution—were adopted in 1791. The Bill of Rights provides a series of individual rights, such as freedom of speech, press, and assembly, the right to a jury trial in criminal cases, and guarantees of due process, which the federal government cannot deny. In extracting a philosophy of government from the Constitution, it would be remiss not to consider the Bill of Rights. Even more clearly than the preamble and the text of the original Constitution, the Bill of Rights evidences a philosophy of limited government. The limits put in place by the Bill of Rights are, of course, restrictions on the power of the national government flowing from a strong belief in the rights of individuals. In addition, the Fourteenth Amendment (adopted in 1868), as it is now interpreted, makes it clear that part of this philosophy is the belief that the rights of the individual ought to be protected not only from the national government but from *all* levels of government.

Political and Structural Functions of a Constitution

As the dictionaries indicate, a constitution determines the organization of a state and the distribution of sovereignty within it. The United States Constitution certainly fulfills this role. As all children in the United States learn at a young age, the Constitution establishes the three branches of the federal government—the executive, the legislature, and the judiciary. Together, these three branches embody the sovereign power of the United States.

Moreover, the Constitution allocates power among these three branches. Article I of the Constitution establishes the *legislative branch*—Congress—and defines its legislative power in an eighteen-paragraph "laundry list" of topics including, most notably, the power to regulate interstate commerce. Over the years, the *commerce power* has been held to encompass not only regulation of interstate commerce itself but also regulation of matters that have a significant impact on interstate commerce. While Congress cannot regulate commerce that is "purely local," there is very little in our national, interconnected economy that does not have an impact on interstate commerce.

Article II of the Constitution establishes and defines the *executive power*—essentially the power of the president. Despite the current perception that the president has enormous powers, the description of those powers in Article II is quite modest. The article tells us that the "executive power shall be vested in" the president but elaborates few details of that power.

Article III of the Constitution establishes and defines the power of the *federal judiciary*. This article creates the Supreme Court of the United States and authorizes Congress to establish the remainder of the federal court system. The article also sets out the powers of the federal courts. For the most part, the courts may resolve *cases* or *controversies*, involving questions of federal law (including the Constitution itself) or involving the United States or citizens of different states. Most important, it has been held that included in the power to resolve cases is the power of *judicial review*. Judicial review, the subject of Chapter 6, is the power, in a proper case, to rule that the actions of a state or local government or one of the other branches of the federal government have violated the Constitution and are, therefore, void.

Legal Functions of a Constitution

In addition to, and perhaps more fundamental than, its other roles, the Constitution is a legal instrument. That is, it is *law*—a set of rules binding on society that are enforceable by courts. Indeed, not only is the Constitution law, but it is a very special type of law. According to Article VI of the Constitution, the Constitution is the "supreme Law of the Land." In other words, other law, such as federal or state statutes inconsistent with the Constitution, is void. Indeed, it is this *supreme law* feature of the Constitution that spawned the concept of judicial review.

As law, the Constitution fulfills a very different function from the philosophical and political functions described above. The Constitution, not the government, is supreme. Consequently, it can be relied on by individuals in disputes with the government. If the government acts in a manner inconsistent with constitutional mandates, it is acting lawlessly. Therefore, a person injured by this lawless action can use the legal system to obtain redress. Of course, the prospect of judicial enforcement of the Constitution as *law* serves a deterrent function also:

the government is less likely to act inconsistently with the Constitution if it may be challenged successfully in those actions by an individual.

A Brief Tour of the United States Constitution

The 1787 Constitution

Today the United States is governed by a constitution originally drafted in the summer of 1787. As promulgated then, the Constitution consisted of the preamble (described above) and seven articles. The first three articles established the three branches of the federal government, setting forth the extent of their powers and establishing linkages among them. While the government thus established was one that had a limited number of powers, the government was generally supreme when acting within the sphere of those powers.

The remaining articles deal with a variety of subjects. Article IV contains a variety of rules concerning federal-state relations. Each state must, for example, give "Full Faith and Credit" to the laws of the other states and must extradite those accused of crimes in another state. The national government, for its part, guarantees each state a "Republican Form of Government" and must protect the states against invasion and domestic violence.

Article V describes the process of amending the Constitution.

Article VI of the Constitution is most famous for its *supremacy clause*:

> This Constitution, and the Laws of the United States which shall be made in Pursuance thereof; and all Treaties made, or which shall be made, under the Authority of the United States, shall be the supreme Law of the Land; and the Judges in every State shall be bound thereby, any Thing in the Constitution or Laws of any State to the Contrary notwithstanding.

Perhaps more than any other part of the Constitution, the supremacy clause gives the document its character as law, and it is the notion of constitutional supremacy that would be most harmed by the lack of a written constitution.

Article VII of the Constitution sets forth that the Constitution would be deemed established when ratified by nine states, which it was by the middle of 1788.

The First Ten Amendments to the Constitution:
The Bill of Rights

During the debates concerning the ratification of the Constitution, much criticism centered on the lack of a Bill of Rights similar to that in effect in some of the states. While the proponents of the Constitution as originally drafted took the position that protection of individual rights was unnecessary because the national government, being a government of only limited enumerated powers unlike state governments, would not have the power to encroach on such rights, it was eventually agreed that a bill of rights would be proposed.

A proposed bill of rights consisting of twelve amendments to the Constitution was transmitted to the states in 1789. Of these, ten were ratified in 1791. These ten amendments constitute the Bill of Rights as we know it today and establish a wide array of individual rights against encroachment by the federal government. It is important to note that these amendments, by their own terms, do not limit the power of the states to encroach on individual rights. Such rights against the states were left (at least until the passage of the Fourteenth Amendment) to the protection of the individual states, in their own constitutions or otherwise.

The protections provided by the Bill of Rights include, in the First Amendment alone, freedom of speech, press, and religion, the right to peaceably assemble and to petition the government for redress of grievances, and the prohibition of an establishment of religion. The Second Amendment protects the right to bear arms; the Third Amendment concerns quartering of soldiers in civilian homes. The Fourth Amendment protects the "right of the people to be secure in their persons, houses, papers, and effects, against unreasonable searches and seizures"; searches are allowed only with a warrant issued by a court.

The Fifth Amendment provides a series of rights. Pursuant to that amendment, one can be tried for a serious crime only upon grand jury indictment and can be tried only once for any particular offense. In addition, one cannot be compelled to testify against oneself. Furthermore, the federal government may not deprive anyone of life, liberty, or property without due process of law. Finally, private property may not be taken for public use without just compensation.

The Sixth Amendment provides several rights in the criminal process—the right to a speedy, public trial before an impartial jury, the right of the accused to confront witnesses and to subpoena witnesses, and the right to counsel. The Seventh Amendment protects the right to a jury trial in civil litigation. The Eighth Amendment protects those in the criminal process against excessive bail and cruel and unusual punishment.

The Ninth and Tenth Amendments, unlike the first eight, convey no specific rights. Rather, their purpose is to make sure that the rights of individuals are not interpreted too narrowly and that the powers of the federal government are not interpreted too expansively. The Ninth Amendment provides that the "enumeration in the Constitution, of certain rights, shall not be construed to deny or disparage other rights retained by the people." The Tenth Amendment establishes that powers not granted to the national government by the Constitution are reserved to the states or to the people.

Other Amendments

Since the Bill of Rights, the Constitution has been amended sixteen times. The most significant are the post–Civil War amendments—the Thirteenth, Fourteenth, and Fifteenth Amendments. The Thirteenth Amendment abolished slavery, and the Fifteenth Amendment assures that all citizens have the right to vote without regard to race, color, or "previous condition of servitude." The Fourteenth Amendment is the most far reaching of the three and, indeed, may be the single most important amendment to the Constitution since the Bill of Rights. That amendment contains the famous *equal protection clause* ("nor [shall any state] deny to any person within its jurisdiction the equal protection of the laws") and *due process clause* ("nor shall any State deprive any person of life, liberty, or property without due process of law"). Moreover, the Fourteenth Amendment has been interpreted by the Supreme Court to incorporate virtually the entire content of the Bill of Rights and make it applicable to the states.

Other notable amendments from a political perspective include the Twelfth Amendment (changing the method of electing the president and vice-president), the Seventeenth Amendment (providing for direct election of senators), the Nineteenth Amendment (giving women the right to vote), the Twenty-second Amendment (limiting presidents to two terms), the Twenty-fourth Amendment (abolishing poll taxes), the Twenty-fifth Amendment (providing rules for cases of presidential disability), and the Twenty-sixth Amendment (giving all citizens at least eighteen years old the right to vote).

What If We Had No Written Constitution?

No Constitution, or No Written *Constitution?*

Upon reflection, it appears that two issues are intertwined in imagining what American life would be like in the absence of a written constitution. Are we to imagine no constitution at all, or merely no *written* constitution? The distinction must be made, at least initially. After all, it is commonly said that Britain has an *unwritten constitution.*

That description of the British system is somewhat inaccurate, however. The story of the British constitution, such as it is, begins with the signing of the Magna Carta—a written document—in 1215. When King John signed that document, he accepted for the first time the existence of limits on the absolute authority of the monarch. While no other comparable written documents were adopted for almost five hundred years, a tradition of *constitutionalism*—that is, a recognition that even the sovereign powers of the monarch were derived from and subordinate to an established body of rules deriving from common law, custom and tradition—took root in Britain.

The seventeenth century saw further developments. The Interregnum (1649–1660—the period when England was a republic), the Glorious Revolution of 1688, and the 1689 Bill of Rights, established both parliamentary supremacy and limits on the powers of the monarchy. As Daniel A. Farber and Suzanna Sherry described in *A History of the American Constitution,* "The [resulting] British Constitution was both a description of existing institutions—including laws, customs, and traditions as well as the balance of power—and a declaration of fundamental principles."

Thus, the British constitution is more of a description of the British governing system and political philosophy than it is a governing document. Indeed, appeals to the British constitution have rarely been successful in limiting governmental power there.

In imagining American life without a written constitution, one must keep in mind the British model. Yet, the British constitution is certainly not a constitution in the same sense that the United States Constitution is. While in the absence of a written constitution something like the British model might have developed in a United States, it is unlikely that those whose experiences have been primarily with the American system would refer to the British model as a comparable constitution.

Could the United States have developed with no constitution whatsoever? This is really more of a semantic question than a political one. Whatever system of government we developed would be, de facto, our "constitution" in a sense, even if we did not label it as such. Indeed, it is not beyond the realm of possibility that our national governing structure, with its three branches, might have developed even in the absence of a written document. Whether our structure of *federalism*—that is, the interrelationship between the national government of limited powers and state governments (see Chapter 2)—would have developed comparably is more questionable.

A good way to imagine what the United States would be like in the absence of a written constitution is to look at the functions that the Constitution performs. As mentioned above, these functions include philosophical, political and structural and legal functions.

Philosophical Consequences

If there were no written constitution, there would be no broad, written statement of the American social/political contract. Two examples are illustrative.

Representative Democracy

The United States and the individual states themselves are governed, for the most part, by a representative democracy in which periodic elections are held to choose political leaders. With respect to the United States government, the particular method is set forth in detail in the Constitution. In the absence of a written constitution, our method of governance might, however impermanently, continue to be representative democracy; indeed, as in the British model, that method might well continue indefinitely. But would that method be as explicit a part of the social fabric as it is under our constitutional system? I think not. In the absence of a written Constitution, our method of governance would be a treasured part of the status quo, but I suspect that it would be less likely to be felt as a birthright. It would be "the system we have" rather than "the system we are guaranteed." The difference is subtle, but important.

Consider, for example, the way presidential candidates are nominated by the major political parties. The nominating process is not constitutionally mandated; rather, it has developed in evolutionary fashion over the years. The political parties have held nominating conventions for well over one hundred years, but the process by which delegates to those conventions are selected has changed dramatically in the last twenty years. Until those changes, the status quo was "the system we have." Had it been "the system we are guaranteed," the changes would have been unthinkable.

The Bill of Rights

Without a written constitution, the values underlying the Bill of Rights would no longer be exalted. The consequences flowing from the loss of such a central statement of individual rights would extend far beyond legal rights.

While the loss of legal protection against government interference with First Amendment freedoms would, for example, be devastating, the loss to the ideal of free speech would go far beyond the legal loss. First Amendment "values" percolate throughout our society even where the First Amendment does not, by its terms, apply. After all, the First Amendment, as augmented by the Fourteenth Amendment, places limits only on the ability of *governments* to abridge freedoms of press and speech. The United States government cannot, for example, constitutionally punish a *Washington Post* editorial writer for espousing socialism as the only solution to the nation's ills; the *Post* itself, however, is legally free to discharge that editorialist. Similarly, the state of Ohio could not constitutionally adopt a policy of refusing to hire civil service workers who do not contribute to the Republican party; on the other hand, the neighborhood grocery store, if it adopted the same policy, would not violate the Constitution. Yet, our internalization of First Amendment values goes beyond the legal jurisdiction of that amendment. In both situations described above, if the private entities penalized people for expressing their views, many would feel that there had been an interference with freedom of speech.

Another example of the internalization of First Amendment values beyond the legal reach of the amendment is provided by the development of academic freedom for faculty members in private universities. For instance, there is no constitutional impediment to Harvard University discharging a faculty member for advocating controversial views concerning the role of women in primitive societies. Yet such a discharge would certainly be perceived as an interference with freedom of speech.

In the absence of a written constitution, it is doubtful that such First Amendment values would be as internalized in our system as they are today. The result would be loss of tolerance, of respect, for the ideas of each individual, no matter how incorrect or odious those ideas may be. While this loss might not itself change any legal rights, it would represent a major philosophical shift in American society.

While there would certainly be losses flowing from the absence of a written constitution as a central philosophical document of American society, this is not to say, however, that there would be no national identity in the absence of a written constitution. An identity certainly would emerge, as has been the case in other countries, like Britain, without written constitutions. The character of our identity would likely be quite different, however. In our pluralistic society, a national unwritten philosophy of rights and government would probably be quite vague. Indeed, our self-image as a pluralistic society would be one of the first casualties of a constitutionless regime. At present, we tend to see our country as an amalgam of different ethnic and religious groups, some larger than others but all equally "American" under the Constitution.

In addition, any consensus as to a national philosophy that did emerge in a constitutionless society would be much more subject to change with transitory impulses. There is something about a written compact that is more stable and enduring than ideals carried forth through an oral tradition. Perhaps it is just as simple as the observation that the written word persists in its presence, even when temporarily unpopular, while the same idea not captured in writing is much more subject to being ignored or purposefully misinterpreted. It is unlikely, for example, that the Supreme Court would have held that burning the American flag was protected speech in the absence of a written guarantee like the First Amendment.

In sum, while the philosophical functions of our written constitution might be fulfilled, at least in part, in the absence of that document, if there were no written constitution our social compact would be more descriptive than prescriptive and, accordingly, less enduring.

Political and Structural Consequences

The lack of a written constitution would have a significant impact on the structure of the American government and the allocation of power within that government and between the federal government and the states. Assuming that somehow Congress and the presidency existed, at least temporarily, in a form analogous to that provided for in the Constitution, those two branches would be likely to take actions seriously inconsistent with current notions of federal power.

Most particularly, the structural features of the United States government and the federal-state matrix of relations would be impermanent and malleable. Without a written Constitution to limit the lawmaking power of Congress or the executive power of the president, those actors would be able to effect significant changes in the extent of their powers.

A good example of the ability of our written Constitution to thwart such changes is provided by recent attempts to alter the lawmaking process itself. The Constitution prescribes a very specific mechanism for creating federal laws. To become law, an act must be passed by both houses of Congress and presented to the president for signature or veto. If vetoed, the act may become law nonetheless if two-thirds of each house votes to override the veto. Over the last two hundred years, Congress and the president have, on occasion, felt that the lawmaking process is too inefficient to deal with issues Congress has no desire to regulate actively but does care about to some extent. Accordingly, in many cases from the administration of Franklin Roosevelt to the present, Congress has enacted statutes with legislative veto provisions.

In a typical statute with a legislative veto provision, Congress would give the president (or someone else in the executive branch) the authority to make a decision concerning some matter. That decision would be final unless one, or in some such statutes, both houses of Congress voted to override the decision. In this manner, Congress empowered the president to make decisions in an area in which it did not want to be bothered with individual decision making but did want to retain the ultimate power to overrule the president and decide in particular cases. An example of the application of the legislative veto is the reorganization of the Executive Office of the President or any executive departments or agencies. For more than forty years, the president submitted a reorganization plan to Congress that took effect if neither the House nor the Senate passed, within sixty days, a concurrent resolution disapproving the plan. The theory of these legislative veto statutes was that Congress could retain ultimate power but would not expend the time and energy to make the initial decisions.

While the legislative veto statutes may have been efficient, they were not constitutional. As the Supreme Court ruled in *INS v. Chadha* (1983), efficiency is not a constitutional criterion. The Constitution sets forth the method by which laws are made and only that method is allowed. The court observed that the veto decision by Congress is in the nature of lawmaking, yet the "law" would not be presented to the president for his signature or veto as provided in the Constitution.

If there were no written constitution, Congress and the president would have great leeway to select their own notions of efficient or appropriate allocation of lawmaking power without the limits applied in *Chadha*. Moreover, such allocations could vary from one substantive area to the next and from one time to another. For example, a Democratic Congress faced with a Republican president (not an unusual combination, certainly) might well pass laws concerning a popular subject such as consumer protection that give greater power to Congress and less power to agencies in the executive branch; on the other hand, Congress might abdicate responsibility to the president for a more politically dangerous subject like taxes. Later, with a Democrat in the White House, the pattern might change. The resulting allocation of power for any one subject at any one time might be beneficial but there would be a cost in structural stability. Would the gain outweigh the loss? Perhaps so, but it is unlikely.

If there were no written constitution, there would also be fewer limits on the substance of laws enacted. Federal lawmaking power would inevitably expand in scope and intrusiveness, at the expense of both the power of state and local governments and the rights of individuals. Let us consider scope first. While the powers given to Congress in Article I, section 8 of the Constitution are broad, they are far from limitless. Congress is not granted an all-encompassing police power enabling it to act generally in the interest of the nation or the citizenry. Rather, Congress is constrained to act within the enumerated powers granted in the eighteen paragraphs of Article I, section 8. If there were no written constitution, the extent of Congress's power would be essentially limitless. Congress would be able to pass legislation on whatever subject it wished—even those areas reserved for local decision making under our current system—setting forth whatever rules it desired. Congress would have jurisdiction over every aspect of life in the United States, and Congress, rather than the Constitution, would be supreme.

The laws passed by Congress in such a system would not necessarily be bad laws. They would, however, be laws of a sort different from those allowed under our current constitutional system. While the expansive reading courts have given to Congress's commerce power often suggests that Congress may legislate in any area it wishes to, as a practical matter Congress has felt constrained to demonstrate *some* connection to interstate commerce in order to pass regulatory legislation. Without the written constitution to limit it, Congress would be a national legislature of limitless, rather than enumerated and limited, powers. There would be no sphere of life over which Congress had no jurisdiction, and state and local lawmaking would exist only to the extent that Congress chose not to act. Traditional areas of local regulation, such as land use and public safety issues, would likely become subjects of federal regulation without constitutional limits on congressional power. Indeed, given our periodic national bouts of hysteria over criminal justice issues, the entire criminal law and justice system, now primarily local, would likely be federalized, with such unappetizing implications as a national police force.

In sum, if there were no written constitution, the allocations of power within the federal government, between the federal government and state and local governments, and between government and the individual would be likely to change. The changes might be more responsive to the issues of the day than they are to the allocations of power mandated by the Constitution, but the greater responsiveness would come at the cost of stability and fairness to unpopular causes and individuals.

Legal Consequences

Whatever question there might be about the degree of change in philosophical underpinnings and political allocations of power in the absence of a written constitution, it is virtually certain that substantial modifications would result from the lack of a written constitution that could be applied as *law* to redress wrongs. The Constitution is the "supreme Law of the Land." Without an enduring constitution as supreme law, we would be at the mercy of temporary fads and overreaching majorities. The British experience with an unwritten constitution is instructive here. Despite the eternal nature of the rights allegedly protected by the British Constitution, that constitution has not functioned well to limit parliament. Despite the lip service given to the notion of British constitutionalism, it is essentially Parliament, not the constitution, which is supreme.

The United States Constitution is, essentially, an antimajoritarian document. One of its primary functions, especially in the area of individual rights, is to prevent majorities from overreaching. It is not likely that, without a written constitution, majorities could be thwarted in their excesses. While an ethos might develop that discouraged majorities from unduly disadvantaging minorities, the absence of a constitution as a legal weapon to undo the excesses when they do occur would result, over time, in a society that works well for majorities, however temporary they may be, but is quite oppressive to legitimate minority interests. Even in our current system, it is not unusual for those holding the majority position on some issue to act without consideration for the rights of those in the minority.

The recent flag-burning controversy provides a good example. In 1989, in *Texas v. Johnson*, the Supreme Court decided that the state of Texas could not criminalize flag burning because such a prohibition would violate the First Amendment prohibitions on abridging freedom of speech. The Court's opinion made it clear that there could be no reason to prohibit flag burning other than to stifle the expressive nature of that conduct; the intent to stifle such expression is, of course, a cardinal violation of the First Amendment.

The outcry following the Supreme Court decision in *Johnson* was fierce. Indeed, while legal scholars tended to support the decision, the public at large did not. To the extent that there was a political debate following the decision, it concerned not whether the decision was correct but, rather, how best to reverse it. President George Bush and the Republican leadership proposed a constitutional amendment, while some Democrats supported a statute that would prohibit all flag burning, not just that which cast "contempt upon the flag," as the Texas statute had provided.

As anyone who carefully read the Supreme Court decision in *Johnson* knew, there was virtually no chance that the Supreme Court, if it followed *Johnson*, would uphold the proposed statute. As stated above, the opinion in that case indicated that there was no reason to prohibit flag burning except to stifle unpopular opinion. Nonetheless, many members of Congress proclaimed that the proposed statute was constitutional because of a cosmetic difference from the Texas statute.

The proposed statute was passed. To no one's surprise outside of Congress, in *United States v. Eichman* the Supreme Court in 1990 struck down the new statute by the same vote by which it had struck down the Texas statute a year earlier.

It is only the existence of an enforceable, written constitution that prevents majoritarian excesses such as the flag-burning statute from prevailing. When the majority actually enacts its position in contravention of individual liberties, the courts void it. More important, the specter of invalidation and the desire to act constitutionally usually encourage deference by the majority to the constitutional balance between governmental power and individual rights. Without the influence of a written constitution, it is unlikely that majorities would feel so limited.

Indeed, without the antimajoritarian strands of a written constitution, many aspects of our life would be very different. For example, the rights of those accused of a crime, never politically popular, would shrink to a tiny remnant of their current state. Can it seriously be imagined that a popularly elected legislature, unconstrained by the limitations of a written constitution, would robustly protect the rights of the accused? The entire concept of equal protection of the laws, one of the strongest defenses against overreaching political majorities, would also be weak or nonexistent in the absence of a written constitution. Finally, there is little doubt that unpopular speech and advocacy would be far less protected than under our current constitutional regime.

The antimajoritarian nature of our Constitution is even exemplified in the process provided for amending it. The Constitution provides that amendments need more than a simple majority. Indeed, the procedure is quite cumbersome. Either two-thirds of each house of Congress or two-thirds of the states are needed to initiate the process. Then approval of three-quarters of the states is needed for ratification of any proposed amendment. Without such roadblocks, even basic principles of American society, however they might exist in the absence of a written constitution, would be subject to emasculation by transitory majorities. In the absence of a fundamental document requiring supermajoritarian consent to amend, an unwritten constitution would be quite malleable.

Finally, without a written constitution to serve as law, the concept of judicial review would be largely empty. In our system the legislature and executive are not the final arbiters of their acts; rather, in a proper case, the courts can declare those acts as inconsistent with the Constitution and, therefore, void. Judicial review is not specifically mentioned in the Constitution, but it has been accepted as a fundamental principle of our constitutional system since 1803. In effect, the Constitution functions as if the principle were expressly contained in it. If there were no written constitution, however, the judiciary—the one branch insulated from majoritarian politics—would be essentially powerless to limit the acts of the other, majoritarian, branches that were inconsistent with the basic principles of the land. In the absence of judicial review to strike down constitutional violations by the other branches, the judiciary would not, for example, have been able to overturn President Harry Truman's seizure of the steel mills during the Korean War or the federal flag burning statute described above. Majority tyranny, at least at some level, would be likely.

Conclusion

If there were no written constitution, the American political system would be quite different in many respects. The Constitution serves philosophical, political and structural, and legal functions. Each function would operate quite differently in the absence of a written constitution. Philosophically, if there were no written constitution, our social compact might be more descriptive than prescriptive and, accordingly, less enduring. Politically, if there were no written constitution, the allocations of power within the federal government, between the federal government and the states, and between government and the individual would likely change. The changes might be more responsive to the issues of the day than they are to the allocations of power mandated by the Constitution, but the greater responsiveness would come at the cost of stability and fairness to unpopular causes and individuals. Finally, from a legal perspective, in the absence of a written constitution the judiciary would be largely powerless to limit the excesses of the majoritarian branches of government. The result would be, at least at some level, tyranny of majority interests at the expense of the rights of the individual.

If there were no written constitution, we might have a perfectly serviceable political system in the United States. The British do, although their system, it must be remembered, stands on the base of a much more homogeneous society than ours. We are spoiled in this country, though. A perfectly serviceable system falls far short of the system we have now and would represent a retreat. With all its faults, the American political system under the United States Constitution has done a remarkable job of providing an enduring political philosophy, structuring governmental powers, and protecting the rights of the individual. Anything less would be regression. Without a written constitution, we would certainly get something less.

Sources and Suggested Readings

Developing and expounding theories of constitutionalism is a flourishing cottage industry in the United States. There is no shortage of books and articles for the interested student. Indeed, winnowing the roll to a manageable few is a daunting task. The following is a brief, idiosyncratic list of helpful works.

Students interested in constitutional history should examine Daniel A. Farber and Suzanna Sherry, *A History of the American Constitution* (St. Paul, Minn: West, 1990); and Richard B. Morris, *The Forging of the Union, 1781–1789* (New York: Harper and Row, 1987).

Basic constitutional theory is explained and debated in Alexander Hamilton, James Madison, and John Jay, *The Federalist Papers*, ed. Clinton Rossiter (New York: New American Library, 1961). (Originally published in 1787–1788.); Bernard Bailyn, *The Ideological Origins of the American Revolution* (Cambridge, Mass.: Belknap Press of Harvard University Press, 1967); Charles A. Beard, *An Economic Interpretation of the Constitution of the United States* (New York: Macmillan, 1913); and Garry Wills, *Explaining America: The Federalist* (Garden City, N.Y.: Doubleday, 1981).

Structural issues are addressed in Daniel J. Elazar, *The American Partnership* (Chicago, Ill.: University of Chicago Press, 1962); Louis Fisher, *The Politics of Shared Power: Congress and the Executive*, 2nd ed. (Washington, D.C.: CQ Press, 1987); Felix Frankfurter, *The Commerce Clause under Marshall, Taney and Waite* (Chapel Hill, N.C.: University of North Carolina Press, 1937); and Herbert J. Storing, *The Complete Anti-Federalist* (Chicago, Ill.: University of Chicago Press, 1981), 7 vols.

Also worth reading for their perspectives on individual constitutional issues are Samuel H. Beer, "Federalism, Nationalism and Democracy in America," *American Political Science Review* 72 (March 1978): 9–21; Robert H. Bork, "Neutral Principles and Some First Amendment Problems," *Indiana Law Journal* 47 (1971): 1–35; Edward S. Corwin, *Liberty against Government: The Rise, Flowering and Decline of a Famous Juridical Concept* (Baton Rouge, La.: Louisiana State University Press, 1948); Charles Fairman, *Reconstruction and Reunion 1864–88* (New York: Macmillan, 1971 and 1987), 2 vols.; Learned Hand, *The Bill of Rights* (Cambridge, Mass.: Harvard University Press, 1958); Morton J. Horowitz, *The Transformation of American Law 1780–1860* (Cambridge, Mass.: Harvard University Press, 1977); Herbert Wechsler, "Toward Neutral Principles of Constitutional Law," *Harvard Law Review* 73 (1959): 1–35.

There are many anthologies of readings on constitutional theory. One of the best is John H. Garvey and T. Alexander Aleinikoff, eds., *Modern Constitutional Theory: A Reader,* 2nd ed. (St. Paul, Minn.: West, 1991).

THOMAS H. FERRELL

2 | What If There Were a Unitary Rather Than a Federal System?

Federal and Unitary Systems

Federal and unitary political systems are two of the ways by which governmental powers may be divided on the basis of geography or territory. These two types of systems provide for very different relationships between the central or national governments and lower level governments. The type of political system that a nation has profoundly influences both its governmental institutions and the political processes through which the system functions.

What Is Federalism?

Federalism can be defined as a type of political system in which significant governmental powers are possessed by both a national government and a number of regional governments. The regional governments have jurisdictions over smaller geographical areas and fewer people than the nation as a whole. The constitution of such a political system need not, although it may, spell out in specific language the precise powers that each level of government possesses. Nor does it necessarily have to prescribe an equal amount of power for the federal system's national and regional components. In fact, it can be argued that the distribution of powers between the levels can largely be left to the determination of the workings of the political process and to the people's elected representatives. From a practical standpoint, however, for a federal system to endure for an extended period of time, it is probably necessary that neither of the two levels of government have the power to abolish the other. The constitution should also provide ways in which the regional governments, as separate political entities, can participate in the political process.

What Is a Unitary System?

In a *unitary political system* governmental power is concentrated at the national level. Regional and local governments may exist, but whatever powers they possess are given to them by the national government and are exercised at the forbearance of that government. Thus, the central government at its discretion may enlarge or reduce the powers of its political subdivisions. Frequently in unitary systems the lower-level governments serve primarily as administrative arms of institutions that wield power nationally. They put into effect or implement the policy decisions that are made by the nation's political leaders. This is not to say that regional politicians or even bureaucrats may not have an influence on public policy through party or administrative channels, but the locus of ultimate political power or sovereignty is clearly at the national level.

There is a tendency on the part of many Americans, because of our two hundred years of experience with a federal system, to associate federalism with political democracy and unitarian systems with authoritarian or dictatorial governments. Such is not the case. A unitary distribution of governmental powers is completely compatible with political democracy as long as the system manifests the principles traditionally associated with democratic government: majority rule, popular sovereignty, and free elections. Great Britain is certainly a democracy; indeed a plausible argument can be made that in some ways it is more democratic than our own system, but it is also unitary—with power concentrated in national governmental institutions and leaders.

The American Federal System

While it is generally considered to be the first modern federal arrangement, the American federal system was not the result of a preconceived plan that the framers brought with them to the Constitutional

Convention of 1787. Rather it developed as a result of the compromises made at the convention that were necessary to settle numerous disputes among the assembled delegates. To some degree, the federal system that emerged was a compromise between those delegates who favored only a slightly more centralized government than was then functioning under the Articles of Confederation and those who wished to create a much stronger national government.

Although the Constitution that eventually emerged through the compromises made at the convention is virtually universally said to have created a federal system of government, there have been continuous differences of opinion since 1787 concerning the nature of that federal system. What relationship between the national and state governments did it mandate?

Different Kinds of Federalism

Until the Civil War one of the more commonly expressed "theories" was that the Constitution was a *compact* entered into by sovereign states, not by agreement among the people, and that the national government created by this compact had only those powers specifically delegated to it by the Constitution. This compact theory of federalism emphasized the primacy of the states and insisted that the powers of the national government were few and to be narrowly construed. Advocates of this position used the term *states' rights* to describe the theory. The Union's victory in the Civil War, however, left this theory in tatters.

In the second half of the nineteenth and early twentieth centuries *dual federalism* was a popular theoretical explanation for the constitutional relationship between the two levels of government. It posited a relationship in which each level of government functioned exclusively within its constitutionally mandated separate sphere of authority. It was argued that the Constitution delegates certain powers to the national government that it, and it only, has the responsibility for exercising and that all other governmental powers are reserved just as exclusively to the states. The constitutional justification for the separate sphere of state powers was primarily the Tenth Amendment, which states: "The powers not delegated to the United States by the Constitution, nor prohibited by it to the States, are reserved to the States respectively, or to the people."

As Franklin Roosevelt's New Deal got under way in the 1930s and as both national and state governments began providing not only a much wider array of services to their citizens but sometimes providing them through concerted, cooperative actions, it became evident that in the American federal system there was no clear, unambiguous division of responsibilities between national and state governments of the type described in dual federalist theory. From the 1930s through the early 1990s there have been numerous attempts to propose new theories of federalism to account for the changes in the actual working relationships between these two levels.

Perhaps the most frequently used term to describe New Deal and post–New Deal national-state relations is *cooperative federalism*. This term emphasizes the large number of governmental programs that are cooperative or joint endeavors of both the national government and the states (as well as local governments). Many of these programs are financed through intergovernmental grants-in-aid, in which programs are created by Congress but administered largely by states and localities. Since national funds partially pay for such programs, the recipient governments must follow federal guidelines, sometimes referred to by critics as "strings," in the administration of the programs. An example of strings is the requirement that states must adopt and enforce a speed limit no greater than 55-miles-per-hour in urban areas in order to receive federal grants for state highway construction. Grants have clearly undermined the descriptive and analytical value of the dual federal model.

In addition to cooperative federalism, modern American federalism has also been described as creative federalism, new federalism, picket-fence federalism, and competitive federalism. *Creative federalism* was used by former President Lyndon Johnson to describe his administration's efforts to combat such domestic problems as slum housing, poverty, and crime. Some of the programs addressing these policy concerns involved the disbursement of federal funds directly to local governments with little or no participation by the states. *New federalism* was a term popular in the administrations of both Richard Nixon and Ronald Reagan. It reflected a desire to return responsibility for some governmental functions from the national government to the states and localities. New federalism had a decentralizing focus, while creative federalism had a centralizing one. *Picket-fence federalism*, a term employed by Senator Terry Sanford of North Carolina, emphasizes the relationships that bureaucrats and programmatic specialists at all levels of government have with one another. It suggests that their ties with each other may be at least as important as those they have with elected policy makers. Finally, *competitive federalism* has been used by political scientist Thomas R. Dye in reference to the competition and rivalry among state and local governments. Dye argues that the national government should encourage this competition because it results in a wider variety and higher quality of services for the public.

Most of the theories of federalism discussed here have both descriptive and prescriptive meanings. That is, they are based both on what the advocate of a particular theory believes about the way the American federal system works and on what he or she believes about how it ought to work.

As the reader will quickly realize, federalism influences all major American governmental institutions as well as the practice of politics in many ways. Therefore, an American unitary political system would be different in important ways from the one to which we are accustomed. But it need not be undemocratic.

By imagining a posited unitary system in the United States, we illuminate the extent to which federalism is enmeshed with the fabric of modern American politics and thus understand it more fully. We are also in a position to make more informed decisions about the directions we would like our government to take in the future.

Truly United States: An American Unitary System

Authors of science fiction have written that they can more effectively communicate with their readers if readers are willing to "suspend" their "disbelief." To encourage readers to do so, authors create elaborate, detailed historical, scientific, or cultural environments in which to tell their stories so that their audiences will accept the "naturalness" of the context of their fiction. No attempt will be made here to create an elaborate historical context from which an American unitary political system might have emerged. However, for those readers who can more easily "suspend" their "disbelief" if a unitary system is placed in a reasonably plausible context, the following is offered.

What If the Constitution of 1787 Had Been Rejected?

The Constitutional Convention of 1787 produced the document that we today know as our Constitution. Before that Constitution became effective, it had to be ratified by state conventions in nine of the original thirteen states. Ratification was by no means a foregone conclusion and opposition to the Constitution was widespread. Failure to ratify the document in one of the larger states could very well have led to its overall defeat.

The battle over ratification was particularly heated at the Virginia state convention. This state was the home of the revered George Washington and of perhaps the most influential of the framers at Philadelphia, James Madison. We will hypothesize that rather than narrowly approving the Constitution, as in fact happened, the Virginia convention rejects it by a narrow margin. Its defeat in this large and important state contributes to its failure in other states also, and thus the Constitution written by the Philadelphia convention fails to be ratified and does not go into effect.

As the states struggle along under the Articles of Confederation for the next several years, they continue to be plagued by the problems that produced the movement for constitutional change in the first place. Barriers to interstate commerce depress trade and economic growth. Outbreaks of popular discontent, similar to Shays' Rebellion (1786–87) that so frightened political and economic elites prior to the Philadelphia convention, are frequent occurrences. These elites become convinced that the nation is in danger of falling into anarchy unless drastic action is taken. Another constitutional convention is held in Boston in 1797. This meeting produces a basic law similar in many respects to the failed proposal that came out of Philadelphia. But such is the fear of mob rule or anarchy that the Boston convention provides for a centralized, or unitary, political system, with a strong national government able to preserve peace and public order. Because of lingering, although weakened, loyalties that many people have to their states, the states are not abolished. But Congress is given the authority, to be exercised through ordinary legislative acts, to determine the states' powers. (There was strong support for a similar provision at the 1787 convention, but it was not included in the document.) Thus the national legislature, at its discretion, may increase or decrease the powers exercised by state governments.

The prevalent climate of fear leads to the ratification of the 1797 Constitution despite widespread opposition by Thomas Jefferson and others who oppose the powers it vests in the national government. Jefferson and the opponents are successful, however, in 1801 in gaining the adoption and ratification of an eight-amendment Bill of Rights designed to protect the civil liberties of Americans from the actions of their new and powerful national government.

This is not the only way or even necessarily the most likely way a unitary system might have been created. It is simply *one* way. Assuming that a unitary system was created in the manner just described, or in any other way that the reader may find more plausible, what might its characteristics be?

The Legislative Branch

Congress under the 1797 Constitution would be *bicameral*—consisting of two chambers, the Senate and the House of Representatives. The members of both chambers would be elected by qualified voters in their individual districts. But the unitary nature of the political system would preclude the granting of equal representation to states in the Senate as the Constitution of 1787 did for the federal system it created. While it is possible to make the case that a *unicameral* (one-house) legislature would have been the more likely product of a convention creating a unitary government, the argument is not especially persuasive. The proponents of a stronger central government at the Philadelphia convention had supported bicameralism. And there were also the precedents of the existing state legislatures and the British Parliament that favored bicameralism. The unicameral Congress under the Articles of Confederation was the exception to the tradition of bicameralism, not the rule. Also the adoption of a unitary political system does not preclude the adoption of a system of separation of powers and checks and balances within the national government. James Madison's preference, as expressed in the *Federalist Papers*, for such restraints on majority rule would quite probably be even more prevalent by 1797, because of the growth in the number of challenges to civil order during the previous decade. A bicameral Congress would be regarded as a prudent check on "unbridled majoritarianism"—on a legislature that was too responsive to popular passions.

Each chamber of Congress would be apportioned in such a way as to reflect the geographical distribution of the population. Each district electing a member of the House would have substantially the same population as every other House district. Senate districts would also have roughly equal populations. With the states occupying no preferred position under the unitary political system, the likelihood is high that House and Senate districts would frequently cross state boundaries and contain land and people from two or more states. The two chambers could, however, differ in size, with the Senate probably being the smaller of the two and its members elected for longer terms, thus presumably less responsive to the momentary whims of public opinion.

The reapportionment of congressional districts in a unitary system would be the responsibility of Congress itself or an administrative body created by Congress for this purpose. Congressional districts would not be redrawn by state legislatures, as is the case today. Also, periodic reapportionment would be necessary in both houses of Congress, and not just in the House of Representatives.

Congress under the unitary Constitution would probably not be a body with *delegated* powers as the 1787 document provided but would be empowered to legislate in all areas not prohibited by the Bill of Rights and other constitutional provisions protecting the civil liberties of the public. The constitutional restraints on Congress would take the form exclusively of provisions protecting individual and collective rights (e.g., freedom of speech, religion, press, and peaceful assembly) rather than those dealing with the division of powers between national and regional governments.

The Executive Branch

The most obvious difference with respect to the executive branch under a unitary system would pertain to the way a chief executive, or president, would be selected. The electoral college, which allots electoral votes to states according to their representation in the House and Senate combined, would not be used. This type of special role for states is compatible with federalism but not with unitary government. While the electoral college has in the vast majority of elections simply affirmed the voting preferences of the public, it has had a considerable impact on the way presidential candidates conduct their campaigns. With electoral votes awarded on a winner-take-all basis to candidates who carry individual states, the incentive for candidates has been to develop strategies to carry states (especially larger ones with more electoral votes) rather than to try to increase their popular votes in states that they are already certain to win or lose. Thus the electoral college forces candidates to campaign with a goal of carrying a sufficient number of states to produce a majority of electoral votes (270), not a majority of the popular vote.

How would the president be selected in a unitary system? One possibility, certainly, would be selection by one or both houses of Congress. This arrangement would be similar to the one found in Great Britain and other parliamentary systems in which the principal executives (the prime minister and cabinet) are responsible to the legislative branch. (See Chapter 5.) But, as has been noted earlier, the creation of a unitary system would not necessarily override the desire of the supporters of a strong central government for a separation of powers and a system of checks and balances within it.

The remaining obvious possible mode of presidential selection is by direct popular vote. Despite the distrust with which many political elites viewed the public in the latter part of the eighteenth century, this seems like a more probable method than selection by Congress. Selection of the president in this manner would dramatically change the way presidential campaigns are conducted. The necessity of considering states as political entities and campaign targets would disappear. One popular vote in a small state like Utah would be as important in determining the outcome of an election as a vote in a larger state such as New York. There would now be definite advantages for candidates to try to increase their support in regions of the country where their chances of winning are small as well as trying to widen their margins in areas already predisposed to support them.

The popular election of the president would not relieve candidates of the need to tailor their campaigns and appeals to make them responsive to particular regional interests and problems. Nor would it completely negate the importance of more heavily populated, metropolitan areas in the electoral process. Candidates would still find it necessary to respond to geographical and other types of constituency interests and to "go where the voters are" in their campaigns, but the structural advantage which the electoral college gives to larger, more populous states would be reduced.

There are other changes in the presidency that are likely to result from the creation of a unitary system. These changes do not relate directly to the constitutional powers of the office but to the president's relations with his political party and with Congress.

As will be discussed later, a unitary government is likely to be accompanied by a more centralized, perhaps more disciplined party system. Presidents have generally been recognized as the unofficial leaders of their parties, but they have not been able to dictate to state and local party organizations or leaders. Even a very skillful party leader like Franklin Roosevelt frequently failed when he tried to convince members of his party to reject incumbent Democratic members of Congress and to nominate Democrats more sympathetic to his policies. More recently, the national Republican party and the Republican party of Louisiana were embarrassed by the election to the state legislature of former Ku Klux Klan member David Duke. A more centralized party system would give the president and other national party leaders greater influence over state and local party decisions pertaining to the nomination of candidates and other party matters. Even without the creation of a parliamentary system and the strict party discipline that goes with it, a unitary government would strengthen the president's role as a party leader.

Stronger party leadership by the nation's chief executive would, in turn, make the president a more effective legislative leader. Post–World War II presidents, with the exceptions of Lyndon Johnson and Ronald Reagan during the early parts of their administrations, have had difficulties obtaining congressional approval of their legislative programs. A presidential candidate who is able to campaign as the head of a reasonably cohesive, unified party ticket, including candidates for Congress, would be in a better position to gain legislative adoption of his policies after an election victory. Presidents in a unitary political system would still not have the legislative clout of prime ministers in parliamentary systems. They would continue, unlike prime ministers, to face situations in which the legislative branch is controlled by an opposition party or parties. But presidents would be in a position to obtain a higher degree of support from legislators of their own parties if the parties were national organizations, with centralized structures, rather than the coalitions of state and local parties that we find today in the United States.

The Judicial Branch

The judiciary of a unitary government would also differ from the one found in our federal system. The United States today has dual systems of courts. The vast majority of both criminal and civil cases are tried in state courts. Our second system of courts, the federal one, consists primarily of the district and appellate courts and the Supreme Court. But in addition to these general jurisdiction federal courts, there are also specialized courts dealing with such matters as taxes, patents, and military appeals.

In a unitary government a single national court system would be probable. Since lawmaking or legislative authority would be concentrated at the national level, most or all judicial bodies with the responsibility for enforcing laws in specific cases would also be national institutions, although all of them except the highest court would still continue to have jurisdictions over geographical areas smaller than the nation as a whole. Thus in a unitary system we can envision a large scale restructuring of the judiciary. The state courts that currently hear most cases would be eliminated, merged into the national judicial system, or retained only to handle the minor legal matters that still arose under whatever limited legislative discretion the national government allowed to its subdivisions. Conversely the national judiciary would have to be vastly enlarged to handle the increased volume of cases that would now arise with a national legislature enacting laws pertaining to matters currently within the province of states and localities.

It would not just be the size of the national judiciary that would be changed. Some types of legal questions that have occupied the attention of federal courts in our federal system would be less likely to trouble seriously the judicial bodies of a unitary government. The American federal system has had to accommodate differences of opinion almost since its inception concerning the proper and constitutional division of powers between the national government and the states. Except in a carefully crafted dual federal system, which the United States has never in practice been, there will be ambiguity about the demarcation of the powers of the two levels of government. In this country the Supreme Court has been the institution most frequently called into service to resolve these disputes.

In a unitary political system, the judiciary would not be burdened with the task of delineating the constitutional powers of the different levels of government. As noted earlier, regional and local governments would possess only those powers the national legislature saw fit to let them have, and if national lawmakers were not satisfied with the manner in which this delegated power was exercised, they could reduce or withdraw it themselves. The involvement of the judicial branch in "boundary disagreements" between levels of government would be almost nonexistent in the long run, although a few Supreme Court decisions might be necessary in the early stages of a unitary system to underscore the constitutionally subordinate relationship of lesser governments to the national government.

While courts would no longer function in this capacity to the extent that they do in a federal system, an American unitary system could perhaps increase the importance of another role of the courts. It needs to be kept in mind that the unitary system posited here is, indeed, an American one. It is an arrangement that retains all of the features of the present American political system that are not fundamentally in conflict with a unitary government. As previously argued, a separation of powers and a system of checks and balances within the unitary government would likely exist. In fact, the absence of the check provided by federalism might have led the framers to create additional and more specific constitutional checks that each of the three branches could use against one another. For example, while judicial review, the power of the federal courts to declare unconstitutional actions of the legislative and executive branches (see Chapter 6) was not explicitly given to the courts in the Constitution of 1787, it is reasonable and consistent to assume that it would have been so provided in 1797. With an extremely strong Congress and weak states, the framers would see judicial review as an important constitutional check on Congress. It would reflect the desire of James Madison as expressed in *Federalist* 51 to make ambition "counteract ambition" and to create "opposite and rival interests."

Political Parties

Constitutions need not articulate the structures and operating procedures of nongovernmental institutions such as political parties and interest groups. Nor do they often have much to say about the conduct of political campaigns or elections. These institutions and processes may be guided by statutory laws or just by custom. Nonetheless, the types of governmental structures established by a nation's constitution are likely to influence extragovernmental institutions and processes.

It has often been noted that the American party system closely parallels in organization and operation our federal system of government. Just as federalism provides for a division of powers among governmental levels, the two major parties permit considerable independence and autonomy to their state and local affiliates. The amount of control that the national Republican and Democratic parties may exercise over their namesakes at the state and local levels is very limited. Political parties in the United States are largely regulated by state laws, not national ones. It is true that in the 1970s Congress enacted laws that had a significant impact on the financing of the presidential campaigns of party candidates. But such major characteristics of political parties as the types of nominating devices they will use; how funds may be raised for local, state, and congressional campaigns; and even the way delegates to national party conventions will be chosen still are largely the product of state laws. It can be argued that modern federalism is actually more clearly seen in our party system than in government.

This decentralization is functional or useful in the sense that it allows parties the flexibility to effectively compete for tens of thousands of state and local offices around the country. Since American parties must compete on such a broad basis and do so in areas with different ethnic and racial mixes, different economies, and different political cultures, it should not be surprising that the Democratic party and its candidates in Texas are different from the Democratic party and its candidates in Michigan. Similar differences are found within the Republican party. To compete and to win elections in a federal system and in a pluralistic society, our parties have found it useful to vary their platforms and appeals to fit the circumstances of their audiences. Although the differences have declined in recent years, Democratic members of Congress from the South tend to be more conservative than their Democratic colleagues from elsewhere in the nation; and the differences between the northeastern or "liberal" wing of the Republican party and their more conservative fellow Republicans in Congress who represent other regions have also been frequently noted.

Such differences within the Republican and Democratic parties would be less functional and would be reduced in a unitary political system. A unitary system would produce political parties organized primarily to participate in contests for national office—the presidency and congressional seats. There would be fewer elective positions to be filled at the state and local levels, and the importance of these offices would be greatly diminished since responsibility for policy making would be vested primarily in Washington.

The national committees and national chairs of the Republican and Democratic parties, although they currently play roles in fund raising, polling, and providing various types of campaign expertise to party candidates, are not in a position to direct the activities of or to issue orders to state and local party organizations or candidates. In a unitary system enhanced roles for national party organizations and leaders are highly probable. To present the electorate with a coherent set of policies and candidates with similar policy orientations, the national parties would at a minimum establish greater controls over sources of campaign finance and over the procedures by which candidates for public office are nominated. The various types of primaries by which most local, state, and congressional candidates are nominated or selected to represent their parties would be replaced by a more uniform national system.

How would parties in a unitary system nominate their candidates? One possibility would be through constituency organizations or conventions. It is possible, for example, to imagine Republican constituency organizations that provide representation to such generally pro-Republican voting interests as business people, anti-abortion groups, gun control opponents, and large farmers. Democratic nominating bodies might be made up disproportionately of representatives of labor unions, ethnic and racial minorities, and environmentalists.

As the above discussion suggests, a unitary government would produce parties that are not so much coalitions of state and local party organizations as federalism has created but rather coalitions of economic, cultural, racial, ethnic, and policy groups. Such parties would also have leadership elites more concerned with public policy and political ideology. Democratic elites would be more uniformly and consistently liberal, and Republican elites would be more conservative.

Elections, Candidates, and Voter Turnout

The conduct of elections in an American unitary system needs to be treated only briefly here. Most of the major points have already been addressed. For reasons previously discussed, the electoral college would probably be replaced by the direct popular election of the president; members of both houses of Congress would be elected from districts that do not take into account state boundary lines; and political campaigns would resemble contests between rival teams of contestants much more than they currently do.

Two additional points deserve some attention: the recruitment of political candidates and voting turnout. Our federal system tends to produce candidates for national office who have had experience in elective offices at the state and local levels. Governors, state legislators, attorneys general, and others are frequent candidates for congressional seats; and governors have not only sought these positions but have represented their parties in several recent presidential elections. Ronald Reagan of California, Jimmy Carter of Georgia, and Michael Dukakis of Massachusetts are examples. But a unitary system would look elsewhere for its political candidates. The reduction in the number and importance of regional and local elected officials would make these positions less attractive ones from which to seek national office.

Where would our new political leaders come from? One good possibility would be that congressional candidates of the two major parties would be taken directly from leadership positions in the party's constituency groups. That is, Republican congressional candidates would often be business and professional leaders. Democratic candidates might be drawn from labor unions and civil rights organizations. Presidential candidates would be selected predominantly from among each party's congressional leadership. Governors, if that office even continued to exist in a unitary system, would no longer enjoy the political influence or status to make them viable presidential candidates.

It is difficult to speculate with much confidence about the level of voter turnout in a unitary system. It seems reasonably safe, however, to say that it would not be lower than what the United States has experienced in recent elections. Only approximately one-half of the voting-age population actually votes in presidential contests, and the turnout is normally even lower for congressional races and state and local contests. While it is by no means certain that a unitary system would significantly increase the level of voter participation, it is worth keeping in mind that the system posited here possesses characteristics that some commentators believe contribute to higher rates of turnout: more centralized, ideological, and programmatic parties, and closer relationships between politicians in the executive and legislative branches. A unitary government would probably produce uniform, national systems of voting qualifications and registration. At present, some states establish difficult residency requirements for registering and voting and also make the process of engaging in these civic responsibilities cumbersome and complicated. A national system would be uniform and less complicated—features that could also serve to increase turnout. But the level of voter turnout in a unitary system, like turnout in a federal one, can be influenced more by factors relating to political culture and public opinion that develop over a long period of time and about which it is difficult to speculate in any intelligent way.

Interest Groups

In addition to parties, another type of nongovernmental organization that would find its role considerably changed in a unitary political system is the interest group. *Interest groups* are organizations of individuals who share common goals and who seek to influence government officials and policies. The American federal system provides interest groups with literally tens of thousands of points of access to government. Groups attempt to influence not only the actions of the president and members of Congress but also of governors, state legislators, mayors, city councilors, county board members, and many other types of elected state and local officials. They also lobby to influence the decisions of appointive and civil service administrators who work in the bureaucracies of governments at all levels. An interest group that is unable to get what it wants from one governmental level, institution, or official in a federal system can often find another point of access where it will be successful. If a civil rights group fails in its efforts to get a state legislature to end practices that are racially discriminatory in the employment of state workers, it can attempt to persuade Congress to correct the problem through a national law or file suit in federal court and seek a judicial decision in its favor. Conversely, an environmental group unable to persuade Congress to pass a law restricting automobile exhaust emissions because many members represent states and localities where the problem may not be considered important or where automobile manufacturers have considerable power could be successful in gaining the passage of similar legislation by state legislatures in such highly urban states as California and New York. Here citizens and legislators may be more sensitive to the need to reduce air pollution and less sensitive to pressures from automobile manufacturers.

Unitary government would clearly reduce the number of access points into the political system through which interest groups attempt to influence governmental policy. With the number of state and local elected officials dramatically reduced and with the responsibility for policy making vested primarily in the national government and its leaders, there would be less interest group activity at the state and local levels. Groups would focus their lobbying efforts on the smaller number of officials and institutions in positions to make decisions affecting them: presidents, members of Congress, and national bureaucrats. Thus, these officials would find themselves the targets of even more intensive efforts to influence their actions than they are today.

It is also probable, however, that national elected officials would be in a somewhat better position to resist pressures to support policies they disagree with or believe contrary to the public interest. The more centralized party structures and the somewhat more disciplined political parties would, as noted earlier, produce members of Congress more loyal to their party leadership. Members would be more concerned about how their votes would affect the ability of their party to win the next election and less concerned about the impact of their decisions on particular groups.

With rank-and-file members of Congress at least to some degree less susceptible to their influence, one would expect interest groups to focus their lobbying efforts more strongly on party leaders in Congress and on the president. Presidents, Speakers of the House, and the majority and minority leaders in each chamber would receive more attention because of their increased ability to influence the votes of individual senators and representatives.

People in positions of power in the national bureaucracy would also be primary targets for interest groups. The vast majority of domestic governmental programs today are actually delivered by state and local administrative agencies, although they are often subject to federal supervision. In a unitary government the national bureaucracy would assume a larger, more direct, and perhaps even an exclusive role in program delivery. Interest groups in a federal system are at least as active in their efforts to influence the decisions of state insurance commissions, state environmental agencies, and other state agencies as they are the federal bureaucracy. But in a unitary system, since the discretionary decision making authority of administrative agencies would be limited largely to the national level, interest groups would shift their lobbying efforts there.

With interest group activity directed toward national governmental institutions and officials, what types of groups would be stronger and what types weaker? Interest groups with memberships concentrated in relatively small geographical areas would see a decline in their influence. In a federal system such groups suffer in competition with other groups in national politics, but their concentrated memberships enhance their abilities to influence government at the state and local levels. But in a unitary political system these groups would have little clout. Among the groups that would experience such declines are those representing farmers growing crops restricted to a few scattered localities, such as sugarcane and apples. Interest groups with large and geographically dispersed memberships would be in a better position to continue playing effective roles in politics, especially those with the financial resources to maintain full-time headquarters and lobbyists in the nation's capital.

As was suggested in the discussion on political parties, a unitary system might create a situation in which some population segments, and the interest groups that represent them, almost become component parts of the national parties themselves. Many labor unions in Great Britain are so closely tied to the Labour party that it is difficult to discuss them as separate entities. Unions there sometimes act as constituency or local units of the Labour party. In the United States more centralized, disciplined political parties might also seek to tie themselves very closely with large, well-financed interest groups that share their political views. As was previously noted, a Republican party closely tied to groups representing business and professional interests, such as the Chamber of Commerce and the American Medical Association, can be easily imagined. So can a Democratic party that contains within its organizational structure groups like the American Federation of Labor–Congress of Industrial Organizations and the National Association for the Advancement of Colored People.

Intergovernmental Relations, Public Policy, and Service Delivery

Some of the terms presented in the introductory portion of this chapter describing twentieth century relationships between the levels of government in the United States, such as cooperative and picket-fence federalism, emphasize the fact that all levels of government are involved to some extent in the provision of most government services. Even national defense, which is generally thought of as exclusively a function of the national government, is a policy area in which states play a role through national guard units subject to the limited control of governors.

A unitary system would greatly simplify the situation. Ultimate responsibility for the delivery of governmental services would be vested in the national government. Unlike our federal system in which the relations between governments are determined by a complicated fabric of Constitutional provisions, laws, and considerations of practical politics, a unitary system would clearly place responsibility at the national level. It would be up to national political leaders to determine if the administration of some governmental programs and the actual provision of some services could be handled by state or local governments or whether all these tasks would be given to national agencies. Even if national politicians decided to retain the lesser governments and allow them to provide some services to the public—law enforcement and fire protection for example—these governments would merely be administering policies established at the national level. Moreover, the national government, whenever it chose, could reorganize the structures, change the powers, or even abolish lower-level governments. Political considerations might keep national politicians from exercising this power to the fullest, but the relationship between the national government and lesser governments would in all respects be one of a legal and political superior to legal and political inferiors.

How would this situation affect the nature of the services that the American public receives from its governments? There would be considerably more uniformity in the quantity and quality of governmental services nationwide. Such governmental programs as elementary and secondary education, land use controls, and fire protection now vary tremendously from state to state and even from locality to locality within the same state. These differences would be greatly reduced. The greater uniformity would result in more and better services for Americans in economically depressed areas with inadequate tax bases, but, at the same time, services in wealthier areas would decline. Uniformity would also eliminate the advantage that is sometimes said to accrue to federalism of permitting state and local governments to function as "laboratories" and to conduct "experiments" in new ways to provide and deliver governmental services. In this regard, some state governments adopted child-labor laws, welfare programs, and environmental-protection standards before the national government enacted similar legislation. It is true that a national government in a unitary system could still institute unique pilot projects in a few areas to determine their viability before undertaking them on a national basis; nonetheless, the adoption of a unitary government would probably result in a loss of some flexibility in the development of new approaches to deal with policy problems and new ways of service delivery.

Summary and Conclusion

The foregoing discussion illustrates the tremendous impact federalism has on politics in the United States by suggesting how different our political institutions and processes would be in a unitary system. The unitary system that is described here is as distinctively American as I can devise. That is, it retains all of the institutions and processes of the American political system that are not closely linked to federalism. But at the same time it demonstrates that "you can't change just one thing." By hypothesizing the replacement of federalism by a unitary system, we see that numerous other aspects of politics and government in the United States would also have to change.

A separation of powers and a system of checks and balances among the three branches of government could be retained. But the legislative, executive, and judicial branches would be considerably different from the ones we currently have. A two-chamber Congress would be kept, but its members would no longer be elected from states, as is the case in the Senate, nor would the members of the other house necessarily be chosen from districts encompassed within the boundaries of individual states. The voting districts from which members of both houses are elected would probably cross state boundary lines. It would no longer be possible to talk about a state's representation in Congress. There would no longer be a California congressional delegation or a New Hampshire one.

The head of the executive branch, the president, would no longer be chosen by the electoral college, which gives a distinct role to states in the electoral process. Instead the president would be chosen directly by popular vote in a national election. And this election system would change the way presidential candidates conduct their campaigns and could possibly weaken the influence of some states in the selection of the president. However, the stronger, more centralized political parties that would accompany a unitary governmental system could produce presidents more effective in gaining the approval of their legislative proposals in Congress.

A single national court system, rather than a dual system of state and federal courts, is another likely product of a constitution creating a unitary form of government. These courts, particularly the Supreme Court, would not have to spend much time arbitrating disputes between the national government and the states. In a unitary government, if states continued to exist at all as distinct governmental entities, their constitutional and political subordination to the national government would be beyond dispute. Instead, the courts would focus more on maintaining the system of checks and balances among the three governmental branches.

Political parties and interest groups would also be greatly altered. The more centralized parties would be organized primarily to conduct campaigns for national office rather than for state and local office. They would be more ideologically and policy oriented than are the Democratic and Republican parties we now have, and they would have more internal cohesion or unity in Congress. However, the separation of powers that remains a part of American government would militate against the development of parties as unified as those in parliamentary governments like Great Britain. Candidates representing the parties in congressional races would be less likely to be recruited from state and local offices and more likely to be people in positions of influence in the private constituency groups that make up each party's voting coalition. Interest groups, like parties, would function differently. Their efforts to influence governmental decisions would focus primarily on the national level of government, particularly on the leaders of each party in Congress, on the president, and on national bureaucrats.

Rather than the complicated maze of local, state, and national governments that currently provide governmental services, in a unitary system services would be provided principally by the national government. This arrangement would produce a more uniform level and quality of services with little variation among different sections of the country. But it might also reduce the flexibility of government to tailor programs to meet the different needs of people in different circumstances.

How well would a unitary system meet the needs and expectations of the American public? Since it is not possible to create such a system in a laboratory and study its operation to determine if we would prefer it over our federal system, that is a question that each person will have to decide on the basis of incomplete information. But it is hoped that this discussion has at least contributed to a greater understanding of the ways in which governmental powers are distributed in both federal and unitary systems and the types of political institutions and processes associated with each.

Sources and Suggested Readings

One of the foremost scholars of federalism is Daniel J. Elazar. His *Exploring Federalism* (Tuscaloosa, Ala.: University of Alabama Press, 1987) examines federalism from comparative and theoretical perspectives. Another good general work, with a strong historical perspective, is *Toward a Functioning Federalism* by David B. Walker (Chicago: Scott Foresman, 1981).

A number of excellent works published in recent years focus on the actual working relationships among national, state, and local governments—that is, on intergovernmental relations. Among the best are Deil S. Wright, *Understanding Intergovernmental Relations*, 3d ed. (Pacific Grove, Calif.: Brooks/Cole Publishing Company, 1988); David C. Nice, *Federalism: The Politics of Intergovernmental Relations* (New York: St. Martin's Press, 1987); and a volume edited by Laurence J. O'Toole, Jr. entitled *American Intergovernmental Relations: Foundations, Perspectives, and Issues* (Washington, D.C.: Congressional Quarterly, 1985). Studies of intergovernmental relations that give particular attention to developments of the last twenty years include the Advisory Commission on Intergovernmental Relations, ed., *Readings in Federalism: Perspectives on a Decade of Change* (Washington, D.C.: Advisory Commission on Intergovernmental Relations, 1989); and Timothy Conlan, *New Federalism: Intergovernmental Reform from Nixon to Reagan* (Washington, D.C.: Brookings Institution, 1988).

Also worthy of attention are Janice C. Griffith, ed., *Federalism: The Shifting Balance* (Chicago: American Bar Association, 1989), which contains five essays on legal and constitutional issues related to federalism; Thomas R. Dye's stimulating defense of competitive federalism in *American Federalism: Competition among Governments* (Lexington, Mass.: Lexington Books, 1990); and Paul E. Peterson, Barry G. Rabe, and Kenneth K. Wong, *When Federalism Works* (Washington, D.C.: Brookings Institution, 1986), which examines a number of grant-in-aid programs and argues that when certain characteristics are present they can work.

JOHN J. PITNEY, JR.

3 | What If There Were Three Major Parties?

Americans tend to think of the two-party system as a defining characteristic of our government, like federalism and the separation of powers. But the Constitution does not mention parties at all. In principle, a
free country need not limit itself to just two parties. Democracies such
as Italy get along with multiple parties in their national legislatures.
Canada has a third party that has controlled provincial governments
and consistently won a significant share of seats in the national parliament.

In the United States, by contrast, two-party politics has generally
prevailed since Thomas Jefferson's day. Through the first half of the
nineteenth century, the system took various forms with the rise and fall
of Federalists and Whigs and the evolution of Jeffersonian Demo-
cratic-Republicans into Jacksonian Democrats. During the 1850s, the
Republicans began as a third-party effort but quickly replaced the
Whigs as the second major party. Ever since, our two-party system has
consisted of the Democratic and Republican parties that we know
today.

On the presidential level, this two-party monopoly has faced serious
challenges from third-party candidates, including:

1892: James B. Weaver, Populist

1912: Theodore Roosevelt, Progressive "Bull Moose"; Eugene V.
Debs, Socialist

1924: Robert La Follette, Progressive

1948: Henry Wallace, Progressive (different party from that which
nominated Roosevelt and La Follette); Strom Thurmond, States'
Rights Democratic ("Dixiecrat")

1968: George Wallace, American Independent

1980: John Anderson, Unity

Several of these parties did prompt changes in the major parties, but none succeeded in electing a president. Recent third-party efforts have been "one-man bands" focused only at presidential elections. Earlier third parties had significant strength at the grass roots. In the early 1900s, for example, the Socialist party elected more than a thousand local officials, but then it fizzled during World War I. Various socialist parties have kept running candidates to this day, with little impact. Other minor parties, most notably the Libertarians, have perennially found places on state and local ballots. They, too, have failed to break the two-party grip.

What accounts for this pattern? Could a third party ever make its way to major-party status? What would happen if it established a powerful long-term presence in American government? With three major parties instead of two, would our constitutional structure work the same?

Answering these questions will tell us a great deal about the architecture of American government and the place of parties in our politics. Before we contemplate a three-party system, we should take a brief look at how the two-party system works today.

Political Parties in America

Many people believe that the Democratic and Republican parties have a military-style chain of command. According to this image, the national party leaders tell the state and local leaders which candidates to run for office and supposedly demand that elected officials make policy according to the party platform, just as soldiers should follow military field manuals.

This image strays far from the truth. A more accurate picture is suggested by the title of a major study of the national party committees: *Politics Without Power*.[1] While these organizations provide political services to party operatives and elected officials, their leaders have no command authority over anyone other than their own staffs.

It is a mistake to think of the Democratic or Republican party as a pyramid topped by its national committee. Instead, consider each as a mosaic consisting of these interconnected parts:

First is the party in the electorate: voters who think of themselves as

Republicans or Democrats. Although *ticket-splitting* (voting for candidates of different parties for different offices) has been increasing in the past few decades, the best way to learn how people might vote is to ask them which party they identify with. In the 1988 election, at least 83 percent of those who considered themselves Democrats voted for Michael Dukakis, while at least 91 percent of Republican identifiers voted for George Bush.[2]

In many states, voters can formally register as Republicans or Democrats, thereby qualifying to vote in primary elections to pick their party's candidates. (States have a variety of rules as to who can vote in primaries.) Party registration differs from party identification. In a community where one party is unpopular, people who privately identify with that party may publicly register in the other—while continuing to express their real preference in the secrecy of the voting booth.

Elected officials make up the second component of a political party. When we think of party leaders, we often think of the president, members of Congress, state lawmakers and local officeholders (although many localities have nonpartisan elections). Again, lay aside any notions of a single "chain of command." The Constitution empowers each layer of officials to work more or less independently of the others. Under the separation of powers, the president does not necessarily control members of Congress belonging to the same party. In 1990, when House Republicans split with President George Bush's stand on tax increases, one of their leaders explained, "We admire the president, we support the president, but we don't work for the president." Under bicameralism, a party's House members may sometimes clash with its senators. Senate Republican leader Robert Dole once reportedly told his counterpart in the House, "We all know that you all think we are jerks." And under federalism, governors and state legislators do not answer to federal officials. In the 1930s, many Democrats in Congress were fighting for labor legislation while Jersey City's Democratic mayor was having police, prosecutors, and judges harass union representatives.[3]

National, state, and local party committees constitute the third component. While the national committee may encourage people to run for office, it does not put them on the ballot. State and local committees generally can endorse candidates for nomination to various offices; but in most places, the party's primary-election voters are free to choose somebody else. Party organizations at all levels supply their nominees with advice and assistance; but candidates may make their own decisions about issue positions and campaign strategies.

This system mystifies people from countries where parties are more unified and centralized. These people are also bemused by the absence of clear-cut party ideologies: some Democratic officials sound like Republicans and vice versa. In part, the blurring of party lines stems from the fragmented structure that we have just sketched. President Bush lacked the authority to impose his views on members of his party in Congress: on average, 27 percent of House Republicans voted against his position in 1989 roll-call votes.[4]

A three-party system might clarify distinctions among the parties. As things stand today, the Republicans and Democrats each include a broad coalition of people, interests, and philosophies. With three parties instead of two, each party's base of support would be narrower, so its identity and philosophy might take on a sharper edge. This observation points to a puzzle. In a country as vast and diverse as the United States, where consumers demand dozens of brands of beer, why can voters usually only choose among two major parties? Understanding the reasons for the two-party monopoly will help us imagine a set of conditions that could have changed it.

Constraints on Third Parties

Most American elections operate on the *single-member district plurality system*, under which we have a separate race for each office, which goes to the candidate who gets the most votes.[5] Many Americans might think of the plurality system as the only possible way to hold elections, but some countries use a different method, called *proportional representation*. This system allots legislative seats according to the total number of votes that each party gets; this way, a party could win only a small fraction of the vote and still take some seats. Under our plurality system, a party's candidates could win 20 percent of the vote in every congressional district without winning a single House seat. While proportional representation opens the door to third parties, our own system discourages them because people do not want to waste their votes on a party that will not win any offices.

The plurality system has hindered third parties on the presidential level as well. We elect presidents through an electoral college, not by direct popular vote. The Constitution authorizes each state government to choose its own electors but says nothing as to how the states should allocate electors among candidates. All except Maine currently use the winner-take-all system, whereby the presidential candidate who wins the most popular votes gets *all* of the state's electors. (In Maine, presidential candidates get one elector for each congressional district they carry, and the candidate who leads statewide gets two additional electors.)[6] In 1980, John Anderson got 5.7 million popular votes—6.6 percent of the total—yet failed to capture a single electoral vote because he did not achieve a plurality in any state.

There is a way for third parties to deal with this hurdle: winning concentrated support in one or more geographical regions. In 1948, Strom Thurmond got only 2.4 percent of the popular vote—less than half of Anderson's level—but won thirty-nine electoral votes because he achieved pluralities in a few southern states. In 1968, George Wallace won five southern states with forty-six electoral votes, and he would have denied the winner, Richard Nixon, an electoral college majority if he had switched 129,000 Nixon voters to his side in Missouri, Tennessee, and the Carolinas.[7]

Ballot access constitutes a second obstacle. In most places, candidates seeking a Republican or Democratic nomination must gather petition signatures to get on the primary ballot, but the party's eventual nominee appears on the November ballot automatically. For third parties, however, the fifty states and the District of Columbia have a wide and confusing variety of rules governing ballot access. All require third parties to gather a certain number of petition signatures. California's requirement exceeds 100,000 names. State legislatures, which write the ballot access laws, are dominated by the two major parties. Third-party candidates have often claimed that the legislatures have rigged the rules so as to preserve the two-party monopoly.[8]

Third parties have either had to meet the requirements or fight them in court. Such efforts have drained precious resources from the campaign itself—which brings us to a third obstacle: shortages of money and manpower. Third parties are born in rags because they generally grow out of challenges to the existing social order. Almost by definition, such movements consist of people without wealth and other political resources. In 1968, George Wallace played on the passions of working-class whites who resented the social and civil rights policies pushed by "pointy-headed intellectuals." During that campaign, Nixon's officially reported expenditures were three times greater than

Wallace's. (Because of the rickety campaign finance laws of the time, Nixon probably spent much more than reported.)

Moreover, third parties face a vicious circle: they need these resources *before* they can have a chance of winning, but people will balk at giving them their time and money *until* they have a chance of winning.

If a third party could tap resources outside its mass political base, then it might have a chance. This effort would require a leader with great leverage over wealthy interests—that is, the power to grant or deny them something they crave. Third-party leaders have fallen short on this point. Even when they have enjoyed national prestige, they have lacked immediate political power. In 1948, former Vice-President Henry Wallace's fame was matched by his inability to influence policy. (*Henry* Wallace, a left-wing candidate, was no kin of *George* Wallace, who ran in 1968 as a right-winger.)

Co-optation—the effort of major parties to take away the third party's issues—has been another obstacle. Time and again, leaders of the major parties have changed positions so as to hold onto voters who might otherwise go with third parties. In the early 1930s, the Great Depression seemed to enhance the prospects of a third party committed to the redistribution of wealth. Franklin Roosevelt prevented this development. By offering hope to the poor and fearful, his New Deal policies brought them into the Democratic fold and kept them from forming the base for another party.

A Third-Party Breakthrough

For most of American history, these barriers have foiled clever and resourceful politicians trying to launch a major third party. Can we think of a plausible set of circumstances that would have led to a third-party breakthrough? Suppose, for instance, that the United States had stayed out of the First World War. The Socialists might have been able to focus Americans' attention on economic issues instead of foreign conflict; and they probably would have avoided the political persecution they suffered during the war. Thus the Socialists could have emerged as a major national party. Or suppose that George Wallace had converted the requisite number of Nixon voters in key states during the 1968 election. By playing kingmaker, he could have positioned himself to lead a more permanent third-party movement.

Perhaps an even greater opportunity would have occurred for another Southerner three decades earlier—if only two bullets had landed differently.

A Two-Bullet Theory

At 9:30 in the morning of February 15, 1933,[9] President-elect Franklin Roosevelt had just finished making a speech in Miami when a jobless bricklayer named Giuseppe Zangara pointed an eight-dollar revolver at him. A spectator in the crowd, Mrs. Lillian Cross, disrupted Zangara's aim by grabbing his shooting arm. Zangara fired five shots, missing Roosevelt but fatally wounding Chicago Mayor Anton Cermak, who had come to Miami to visit the president-elect.[10]

Suppose Mrs. Cross had failed to stop Zangara from killing Roosevelt.[11] Vice-President–elect John Nance Garner would have taken FDR's place at the inauguration three weeks later. Garner was no Franklin Roosevelt. As vice-president, Garner made it clear that he disliked much of the New Deal, and in 1940 he fought Roosevelt's bid for a third term. If Garner had led the nation from 1933 to 1937, he probably would have continued Herbert Hoover's policies, which many people at the time blamed for deepening the Great Depression. Whatever the economic effects, voters would have seen such an approach as callous and disastrous. Conditions would have been ripe for a third party.

Huey Long of Louisiana would have been just the man to lead it. Elected governor in 1928, Long revolutionized his state's public works and social services while establishing near-dictatorial control of Louisiana politics. In 1930, he won a seat in the U.S. Senate but continued to rule the state government by proxy. As senator, he started a national Share Our Wealth movement that gained nearly 5 million members and appeared to be the nucleus for a third party. Long was a spellbinding speaker and brilliant political strategist, so Democratic officials feared that a Long party could grow strong enough to hold the balance of power in the 1936 election.[12]

Long did not live to run. On September 8, 1935, he was standing in a corridor of the Louisiana State Capitol when a young physician named Carl Weiss pulled out a pistol. A state judge standing nearby struck at Weiss's arm, but too late to keep him from shooting Long, who died two days later.

Suppose the judge had saved Long by acting just a moment sooner. Now we have a scenario in which FDR had died and Long had lived. Long might then have gone ahead with the third-party effort—provided that another assassin did not strike and that Long's enemies did not successfully prosecute him for income-tax evasion, as they wanted to. Assume that the 1936 Democratic convention would have nominated Garner for a second term. (If this sounds self-destructive, remember that the Republicans renominated Hoover in 1932.) Also assume that the Republicans would have nominated Kansas governor Alf Landon, as they actually did. In this scenario, Long could then have broken the traditional barriers to a third-party victory by taking advantage of a unique set of circumstances:

First, Long espoused a philosophy called *populism*. Though the term has taken on various meanings, populists tend to oppose big business and support economic policies that favor "the little guy." Populists seek to use government power to protect traditional values of rural American life but generally balk at using it to further "liberal values" such as civil rights. Such a philosophy would have had powerful appeal during the depression. More important, it would have enabled Long to overcome the plurality hurdle by building a strong base in his native South. Although today we think of the South as uniformly conservative, southerners in the 1930s were more likely than northerners to support old-age insurance and tighter government regulation of business.[13] At the same time, they showed less favor toward civil rights laws.

Long could also have taken states in the West and rural Midwest, whose economies had been gashed by the depression. During the farm crisis of 1892, the Populist party—whose policies resembled Long's in several respects—had done especially well in these states.

Second, Long would have had the resources necessary to get on every state ballot and to campaign throughout the country. By 1935, his political machine had amassed a huge war chest by demanding kickbacks from Louisiana government employees and firms doing business with the state.[14] In a presidential race, he could have squeezed them all that much harder. And the bigger his treasury, the better his chances, and the more likely that other interests would have contributed—in hopes that he might return the favor by making some exceptions to the Share Our Wealth policy.

Third, the major parties would not have co-opted him. In the real

1935, FDR had already cut deep into Long's base by getting Congress to pass the Social Security Act; but in our alternate scenario, Garner would never have tried any such thing. Likewise, Republican Alf Landon would still have limited his appeal largely to small-town business interests. Long would have had the poor and the fearful all to himself.

Long might well have won the White House. Once he assumed office, the structure of a permanent third party would have started to take shape. His popularity and command of patronage might well have induced a number of senators and House members to switch to his party. On the state and local level, politicians in many places would have seen political profit in running under Long's banner. People who had felt "locked out" of the two-party system would now start to enter politics through the new party.

Provided that Long wanted to build a movement larger than himself (this assumption requires a leap of faith), Long's supporters would then have set up party committees from coast to coast and fielded candidates for every office from sheriff on up. Over time, his party would have controlled a large share of state governments, which would have changed election laws to ensure the party a permanent place on the ballot.

Thus the United States would have had a three-party system, consisting of:

• *Long's party*, supporting liberal economic policies such as wealth redistribution, social insurance, tight government control of business; but opposing liberal policies on civil rights and other social issues. We shall refer to Long's party as the *Populists*.

• *The Democratic party*, supporting liberal policies across the board, although not nearly as radical as Long's party on economic issues. Long would have had particular appeal to many Democrats, particularly in the South, so much of the party's base would have disintegrated. But a large number would still have spurned Long. His acceptance of segregation would have alienated blacks and northern liberals, while urban machines and trade unions would have persisted in their general distrust of southern politicians. In the actual world, the need to hold the South delayed national Democrats from fully embracing civil rights. In 1956, Democratic presidential candidate Adlai Stevenson opposed civil rights legislation and the use of federal troops to enforce school desegregation orders by federal courts.[15] Under this three-party system, the national Democrats would have largely conceded white southerners to the Populists and so would have taken a strong stand on civil rights much earlier.

• *The Republican party*, supporting free-enterprise economics and go-slow social policies, much as it has throughout the century. From the 1930s through the 1970s, Republicans were the minority party nationwide. But in the three-party system, the split competition would have enabled the Republicans to win more elections.

If this system had taken root, either in our hypothetical scenario or some other, how would American politics work? We now explore this question, and we start from the assumption that each party's strength would vary from election to election and from state to state, but that all would have roughly equal national support over the long run. Public opinion polls support this assumption: people whose opinions fall in the populist category make up anywhere from one-fourth to one-third of the electorate.[16]

We also assume that all the structures and procedures of today's government would still be in place. This is particularly important. Extraordinary results would come from adding a three-party system to the familiar mix of separated powers, bicameralism, and federalism.

Presidential Elections

No other major democracy chooses its head of government in the same way the United States does. Our method of electing the president has many peculiar features and can lead to bizarre outcomes. It is easy to forget this because every election between 1892 and 1988 went to the winner of the popular vote. Under a three-party system, by contrast, presidential elections would take odd turns because long-dormant procedures would frequently come into play.

The electoral vote, not the popular vote, ultimately decides who gets the presidency. In the two-party system, the same candidate tends to win both the popular and electoral vote. There were some exceptions during the nineteenth century, and as late as 1976, a switch of fewer than fifteen thousand votes in Ohio and Mississippi would have tipped the electoral college to Gerald Ford even though Jimmy Carter would still have led the popular vote tally.

In our three-party system, popular vote losers could be much more likely to win in the electoral college. Say that a Populist candidate sweeps the South, but with a low voter turnout. (The South traditionally lags in registration and voting.) The Populist also wins most western and rural midwestern states in narrow three-way races and runs poorly elsewhere. The Democrat and the Republican split the eastern and Great Lakes states. If the 1988 election had happened this way, the Populist could have won a majority in the electoral college while finishing *third* in the popular vote:

	Popular Vote	Electoral Vote
Democrat	35%	123
Republican	34%	123
Populist	31%	292

This outcome would hinge on a very specific vote distribution. More likely, a race among three candidates of comparable strength would end with none having a majority in the electoral college. You might be thinking that such an election automatically goes to the House of Representatives, right? Wrong—it is not quite that simple.

Remember how the electoral college works. Each state gets a number of electors equal to its number of House members plus two senators. When you vote in a presidential election, you are technically voting not for the presidential candidate but for a slate of would-be electors who will presumably vote for that candidate in the electoral college. When a presidential candidate wins a plurality in a state, his entire slate is chosen for the electoral college—except in Maine, as explained earlier. On the first Monday after the second Wednesday in December, each state's electors meet within the state to vote for president and vice-president. So far, the process seems straightforward. But nowhere does the Constitution say that these electors must support the popular vote winner in their state. Though some states do have laws requiring their presidential electors to vote for the candidate under whose banner they were elected, the Supreme Court has not addressed the constitutionality of such pledges. The framers expected that electors would be free agents, so the Court might conclude that these laws run afoul of constitutional intent.

Electors could switch. Therefore, if one of the three presidential candidates saw no chance of winning in the House of Representatives, he could then try to make a deal with one of the other two: "I shall elect you president by telling my electors to vote for you instead. In return, you adopt certain policies and name certain people to office." In

1968, George Wallace hoped to win enough electors to force Richard Nixon into a number of concessions, including the abandonment of civil rights laws and antipoverty programs.[17] If Wallace had achieved the necessary strength, he would have learned how difficult it would be to make such an arrangement. As all sides would realize, the president could simply bust the deal once in office, leaving the other candidate with no legal recourse. Although public opinion and a sense of honor might restrain such welshing, presidents have been known to break their promises from time to time.

Furthermore, no one can say whether candidates could "deliver" electoral votes to one another. Although Wallace had his electors sign pledges that they would vote as he instructed, courts have not directly ruled whether such pledges are legally binding. Electors might still vote for the candidate for whom they were elected, even if he told them to support one of the two other rivals. They might even vote for someone who had not run in November, a possibility that we will explore shortly.

If candidates could not carry out a deal in the electoral college, then the election would indeed go to the House of Representatives. In the normal course of House floor business, each representative has one vote; but the Twelfth Amendment sets out a different procedure for the selection of a president: "The votes shall be taken by states, the representation *from each state* having one vote" (emphasis added). In other words, Wyoming's one House member would have the same weight as California's huge delegation. According to the precedent set when the House last chose a president (1825), a candidate must get a majority of the state's whole delegation in order for that state to cast its vote. If no candidate gets a majority, the state is recorded as divided and its vote does not count.[18]

State delegations range in size from one to more than fifty, so a party can control a majority of seats without controlling a majority of state delegations, and vice versa. Under the 1990 apportionment, twenty-eight states had six or fewer House members. A party could thus elect its presidential candidate by controlling twenty-six of these twenty-seven delegations, which it could accomplish with as few as fifty-eight seats. Conversely, it is mathematically possible for a party to hold a majority of seats while controlling as few as nine or ten delegations (i.e., by winning all the seats in the largest states). This arrangement would benefit our Populists, since they would draw most of their strength from small states; and it would hurt the Democrats, who would be based mainly in large states.

Quite often, though, no party would control a majority of delegations, and the House would deadlock. After the 1824 election, a House impasse ended when Henry Clay threw his votes to John Quincy Adams—who then named Clay secretary of state. Other stalemates might not break so neatly. The separation of powers means that House members do not answer to their parties' presidential candidates, so vote trading would be even tougher in the House than in the electoral college. Say that the first ballot results in twenty states for the Populist and fifteen each for the Republican and the Democrat. The Populist could then try to dicker for the fifteen Democratic states. The bargain would fail if some Democratic members disliked the terms and refuse to vote for the Populist. As few as ten members could scuttle the deal.

Vice-Presidential Deadlock

The Constitution provides that as a deadlocked presidential election goes to the House, the selection of the vice-president must go to the Senate. The House and Senate might have different party makeups, so the House could choose a Populist president while the Senate chooses a Republican vice-president.

If the House fails to choose a president, the vice-president becomes acting president. Constitutional scholars disagree about what would happen next. Some claim that the Twelfth Amendment sets a March 4 deadline: if the House cannot decide by that date, the vice-president stays as acting president for the rest of the term.

Others claim that the March 4 deadline was superseded by the Twentieth Amendment. According to Laurence H. Tribe and Thomas M. Rollins, "The House could go on voting, with interruptions for other business and indeed with an infusion of new members in mid-term, for four full years."[19]

Unlike the House, the Senate can only choose from the top *two* candidates, so an impasse is less likely in the selection of a vice-president. But it is possible. The Twelfth Amendment forbids the Senate to vote on the vice-presidency without a quorum of two-thirds of its members. Thirty-four senators could block a quorum by staying away from the chamber; with this minimum level of strength, members of one party could keep the others from combining to elect a vice-president.

The Twentieth Amendment says that "Congress may by law provide for the case wherein neither a President-elect nor a Vice-President–elect shall have qualified, declaring who shall then act as President, or the manner in which one who is to act shall be selected, and such person shall act accordingly until a President or Vice-President shall have qualified." The Presidential Succession Act (1949), which carries out this provision, puts the Speaker of the House next in line after the vice-president. After the Speaker comes the president pro tempore of the Senate, a largely honorary post that generally goes to the majority party's senior senator.

As we shall discuss below, with no party having a majority in either chamber, the House and Senate might also deadlock in the selection of their own officers. If that were the case, then the process would move on to members of the cabinet, starting with the secretary of state. A cabinet member serving as acting president would remain in position until the House chose a speaker. At that point, the speaker would resign from the House to become acting president and the cabinet member would resume his or her normal duties.

Consequences

Does the system sound complicated? It is. This intricate chain of steps—from the electoral college to the law of presidential succession—could lead to a dizzying variety of outcomes, which would weigh on politicians' minds as they made their calculations and crafted their campaign strategies. Some examples:

• In the middle of the presidential campaign, polls show that no party will come close to a majority in the electoral college. Knowing that the election will probably go to the House, all three parties divert much of their attention from the presidential race to campaigns for the House. And they concentrate their effort on small states, where the turnover of a single seat could switch control of the delegation from one party to another. On election night, the television network anchors report from the center of the action: the headquarters not of the presidential candidates but of House contenders in Butte, Montana, and Burlington, Vermont.

• As the party convention draws near, stalemate seems likely in both the electoral college and the House. The Republican party has a majority in the Senate. But of the thirty-three Senate seats that are up for election this year, most are held by Democrats and Populists, so the Republicans have little fear of sustaining a net loss. Whoever gets the Republican vice-presidential nomination will probably be selected for the office by the Senate. And the vice-president will become acting president while the party's presidential nominee lingers in constitutional limbo. Therefore, the vice-presidential nomination becomes more desirable than the presidential nomination. Some candidates drop their presidential bids to fight for the *second* spot on the ticket.

• After the November election, the preliminary electoral vote count is: Populist, 200; Republican 268; Democratic, 70. Nobody has a majority. After prolonged bargaining, the Democrat and Populist make a deal: the Democrat will throw his electoral votes to the Populist, who will then nominate the Democrat's choice to the next opening on the Supreme Court. On December 17, the electors vote in their respective states. As of late afternoon, Eastern Standard Time, informal reports indicate that all the Democratic electors are abiding by the agreement. Hawaii, being several time zones behind the East, is last to vote. Its four Democratic electoral votes are supposed to switch to the Populist, giving him the absolute minimum of 270 needed to win. Shortly before the Hawaii electors meet, one of them tells Cable News Network that he is having second thoughts about the deal. From Washington, the Populist candidate makes a frenzied telephone call to Honolulu. It then turns out that all four electors vote for him. A few months later, the Populist president quietly nominates a new chief of protocol at the State Department: the reluctant elector from Hawaii.

• The electoral college has deadlocked. The House cannot muster a majority of states for any candidate. The Senate does pick a Republican vice-president, who becomes acting president. The Supreme Court rules that there is no deadline for presidential selection by the House, so the chamber keeps voting. Several House Republicans realize that they have enormous leverage over the acting president: by switching their votes to the Populist candidate, they can make him president and turn the acting president back into a mere vice-president again. This group then dictates executive policy—until the midterm congressional elections, when a vote for each party's House candidates also becomes a vote for its presidential candidate.[20] This way, the deadlock would break—or drag on.

Congress and the Balance of Power

Under the two-party system, each chamber of Congress has organized itself in a fairly straightforward manner. After every election, the majority party runs the chamber's business and gets all the committee chairs. Currently, the chamber can be controlled only by one of the two parties. Under our hypothetical three-party system, the Democrats, Republicans, and Populists might each have an absolute majority and do business in today's manner. But congressional elections could result in deadlocked chambers. The last time the House lacked a partisan majority came in the Thirty-sixth Congress (1859–61), when the chamber's 113 Republicans, 101 Democrats, and 23 minor-party members took two months to settle on a Republican as Speaker.

In such a circumstance, two of the parties would have to form a coalition to organize the chamber, with both getting a certain share of chairs and other official resources. Coalitions could take one of three forms: Democratic-Populist, Republican-Populist and Democratic-Republican.

Each coalition would work in a different way. The Democrats and Populists would tend to agree on broad economic policy, so they would probably find it reasonably easy to settle on the chairs of the money committees: Appropriations, Ways and Means, and Budget. (These examples are from the House.) But the two parties would clash on social issues, so they would have difficulty agreeing on chairs for Judiciary and Education and Labor. A Republican-Populist coalition would work in just the opposite way, with harmony over social issues and discord over the economic ones. And a Republican-Democratic coalition would prove most difficult of all, since members of the two parties would tend to disagree across the entire range of issues. But they might be driven into such an uneasy arrangement if the Populists refused to compromise with either.

Inherently unstable, any of these coalitions might break down during a congressional session. If the Democrats and Populists split over a civil rights bill, for instance, a House member could move to declare a vacancy in the speakership. If the motion passed, the House would have to reorganize and the tortuous bargaining process would have to start all over again.

Relations between the House and the Senate could sour. To prevent legislative tyranny, the framers aimed to induce friction between the two chambers, or as James Madison said, "to render them, by different modes of election and different principles of action, as little connected with each other as the nature of their common functions and their common dependence on the society will permit."[21] Under our three-party system, the potential for friction would increase. Each chamber could be organized in any of six different ways: that is, through majority control by one of the three parties, or by one of the three possible coalitions. Thus there would be six times six, or *thirty-six* different possible combinations of House and Senate control (i.e., Republican Senate with Democratic House, Populist Senate with Democratic-Populist House, Republican-Democratic Senate with Populist House, and so on). Under the current party system, some scholars argue, split control of Congress makes little difference in policy because both parties tend to compromise. Under our three-party system, however, members of each party would tend to take stronger ideological positions, which would make conflict more likely than compromise.

To become law, a bill must pass both chambers in exactly the same form and then obtain the president's signature (except in the case of an overridden veto). This procedure adds a further layer of complication. Since the president could belong to any of the three parties, the number of possible combinations of White House–Senate–House control would be three times thirty-six, or *108*. (A two-party system, by comparison, yields only eight possible combinations, i.e., two times two times two.) All other things being equal, each party would have only a tiny chance of enjoying exclusive control over all three institutions at a time.

It would take a thick volume to explore all of the possibilities raised in the preceding paragraphs. A few examples, though, will suggest the variety of courses that institutional politics could take.

• The president wins both the popular and electoral vote. No party wins a majority in either the House or Senate. Coalitions rise and fall in each chamber, leaving its committees unable to accomplish much. As soon as they start work, the existing coalition comes apart and a new coalition arises to name a new set of committee chairs. With Congress largely paralyzed, the president scours the Constitution for additional powers. Instead of seeking to pass legislation, he makes policy by executive order. While members of Congress grumble about "executive tyranny," they are unable to organize an investigation.

• The electoral college, the House, and the Senate are all stalemated.

According to the line of succession, the previous administration's secretary of state becomes acting president. Not only has he not been elected, his party ranked third in the popular and electoral vote, so the acting president can hardly claim a mandate to govern. Since neither chamber can organize itself, Congress can pass little legislation. The government comes to a standstill.

• The electoral college deadlocks. A fragile Democratic-Populist coalition in the House selects the Democratic candidate as president. In the Senate, an equally fragile Republican-Populist coalition chooses a Republican as vice-president. Once in office, the Democratic candidate makes a political blunder by vetoing a bill for mandatory school prayer, a proposal vital to the Populists. In the House, Populists turn against the president they had helped to elect and launch impeachment proceedings. When asked if impeachment is an appropriate way to handle a policy disagreement, a leading House Populist replies, "An impeachable offense is whatever the House says is an impeachable offense." The impeachment passes the House by the necessary majority vote. A two-thirds vote in the Senate convicts the president. The Republican vice-president then becomes president. Congress then passes a new version of the Mandatory School Prayer Act, which the new president is happy to sign. A few months later, however, Congress presents him with the Wealth Redistribution Act. As a Republican, he is philosophically opposed to the bill. But just before he is about to sign a veto message, he thinks to himself, "Uh, oh. If I veto this, the Populists and Democrats in the House will try to impeach me."

Politics in the States

In states where the three parties had equal strength, legislatures might often stalemate in the selection of their leaders, just as Congress would. In other instances, control of the governorship and the two houses of the legislature might be split among the three parties. Yet there are two reasons why state governments would be less likely to come to a complete halt in such situations.

First, governors tend to have stronger constitutional positions than presidents. Governors are elected by popular vote, not by electoral colleges, so even when a state's legislature could not organize itself, the state would at least be assured of having a chief executive. Just as important, a majority of governors have a power that the president lacks: the ability to veto line items of appropriations bills. This power gives these governors great control over fiscal policy and a significant leverage over individual lawmakers. Regardless of whether they belong to the governor's party, they must heed the governor's preferences, since he or she could item-veto their pet projects. Some governors, however, have relatively weak constitutional authority. The most extreme case is perhaps North Carolina, whose governor has no veto power at all. In that state a deadlocked legislature probably would stymie governmental operations.

Second, a number of states provide for direct *initiatives,* a process in which proposed state laws can be put on the ballot by citizen petition and then passed or defeated by the voters. If the governor and legislature could not make a collective decision on legislation, the voters could do it for them. Even with just two major parties, California in the 1980s endured prolonged policy stalemates between the governor and legislature. As a result, California voters sponsored twice as many initiatives as in the 1970s.[22]

Keep in mind our assumption that party strength would vary from region to region. Each party would enjoy disproportionate voter support in certain states, where it could usually expect to control the governorship and both chambers of the legislature. With such power, the party's elected state officials could make the state a showcase of its public philosophy. In Louisiana, our Populists would continue in Long's tradition and carry on with massive programs in education and public employment. In Rhode Island, Democrats would enact landmark civil rights legislation. And in New Hampshire, Republicans would keep government to a minimum, with the aim of showing how conservative economic policies create jobs and lead to overall prosperity. To a large extent, of course, states already perform a "showcase" function; one author calls them "laboratories of democracy."[23] In a three-party system, the parties would be more distinct from one another, so they would try to make their policy models even bolder.

Even under the three-party system, however, state policy innovation would face a major constraint: the ability of individuals and businesses to move away. If Louisiana passed a law to confiscate wealth, rich Louisianians could move to low-tax New Hampshire. Similarly, if New Hampshire abolished public éducation, parents of school-age children might relocate a few miles south, to education-oriented Massachusetts.

States have jurisdiction over much of the election process, so if a party controlled a state government for a long period of time, it would probably seek to "adjust" the rules so as to disadvantage the other two. If Republicans saw the Populists as their main competition in a state, they might try to raise petition requirements so as to hinder Populists from getting on the ballot. By the same token, if they thought that the Populists were winning votes that would otherwise go to *Democrats*, they would try to make it *easier* for Populists to get on the ballot.

In most states, the legislature draws the boundaries for congressional and state legislative districts. Since the earliest days of the Republic, state legislative majorities have used the redistricting process for partisan advantage, a practice called *gerrymandering.* The party controlling the legislature can try to ensure its continued dominance by packing the opposition's voters into a small number of districts, where lopsided elections waste its voting strength, and by fragmenting the opposition's remaining strength to create districts where the controlling party can always win. With a three-party system, the controlling party's candidates would need only pluralities, not absolute majorities. Thus it could try to turn a minority of the total vote into a large majority of seats by drawing a number of districts where its candidates would just edge out those of the other two parties.

This tactic could backfire badly if the losing parties decided to cooperate with each other. Say a Republican legislature drew a number of districts each with 40 percent Republican voters, 30 percent Populist, and 30 percent Democratic. If all these districts were contested by all three parties, the Republicans would probably win every one. But the Democrats and Populists could then make a deal in which the Democratic party would endorse Populist candidates in half of the districts and the Populist party would endorse Democratic candidates in the other half. That way, the Democrats and Populists would each win half of the districts and the Republicans would win none!

Turnout and Participation

A century ago, more than 80 percent of eligible adults voted in presidential elections, and more than 65 percent voted in congressional elections. Nowadays, those figures are about 30 points lower.[24] The decline in turnout has stemmed from several causes—all of which would be reversed by a three-party system.

Many people stay home on election day because they see no distinctions between the parties. If it makes no difference whether the Republican or the Democrat gets in, why take the time and trouble to go to the polls? In our three-party system, the differences would be clearer, so the voters would see that they had more of a stake in the outcome. To take one example, members of racial and ethnic minorities would probably not want to see the Populists get into positions of power.

Declining competition has been another cause of declining turnout. Even if a voter considers an election fairly important, he or she is less likely to cast a ballot if the outcome seems a foregone conclusion. Amid a landslide, after all, what difference could that one vote possibly make? In recent years, the advantages of incumbency—the free mail and other tax-financed benefits that help lawmakers curry favor— have reduced competition in races for the House of Representatives and many state legislatures.[25] More House members left the 100th Congress (1987–1988) through death (seven) than through defeat in a general election (six). If this chapter has shown anything, it is that three-party politics in the United States would be unpredictable. With election outcomes more in doubt, each voter would be more likely to think that his or her ballot would count.

The turnout gap between presidential and congressional elections might narrow considerably. Voters tend to see presidential campaigns as more dramatic and important than congressional races. But in a system in which electoral college deadlocks would occur frequently, people would know that a vote for Congress would often *become* a vote for president. Under certain circumstances, as suggested before, politicians might regard the congressional outcome as the decisive factor in a presidential election.

Party and Policy

If the United States had a three-party system, how would public policy and party composition be different?

For one thing, Americans would have a more diverse menu of issues and policy alternatives. Critics of the two-party system say that it amounts to a conspiracy to keep many issues off the national agenda.[26] In the late twentieth century, national Republicans agreed with Democrats in accepting the core of the American welfare state; party differences mainly involved marginal changes in certain programs. Similarly, the interparty debate over the "war on drugs" focused on who wanted to spend more on which elements of a control strategy. The Libertarian party, by contrast, sought to scrap the welfare state and legalize drugs. Had the Libertarians achieved major national status, the debate on these issues would have been about fundamentals instead of margins.

Our hypothetical Populist party would also have radically changed the national agenda. Whereas Franklin Roosevelt's social policies made only moderate reforms in the American capitalist system, Huey Long sought fundamental redistribution of wealth and power. He proposed taxes that would keep a family from earning more than $1 million a year or owning a fortune of more than $5 million in all. He claimed that the revenue from these taxes would enable the government to give every American family a $5,000 "homestead," or "enough for a home, an automobile, a radio, and the ordinary conveniences." Long would also have guaranteed every family an annual income of up to $3,000; financed the college education of qualified young people, and paid large bonuses to veterans. Finally he would have had the federal government regulate the economy more strenuously, limiting the hours of labor to thirty hours a week and eleven months a year.[27]

Thirty-nine years later, a real-life self-described populist from Oklahoma named Fred Harris favorably quoted Long and updated his agenda (Harris, however, favored strong civil rights policies). To limit the power of interstate corporations, Harris proposed federal chartering, including a workers' bill of rights that would guarantee employees a share of ownership and control. Referring to the concentrated ownership of land as a "New Feudalism," he called for breaking up huge landholdings by railroads and parceling them out on easy terms to people who would live and work on the land. He spoke of a "social contract" that would "depend on a better distribution of wealth and income and economic power. Absolute equality is not required. But the imbalances must not be so great as to produce political inequality."[28] (Harris twice sought the Democratic presidential nomination, but did not get far. With a separate third party in place, his candidacy might have met a different fate.)

A Populist party might not have been able to enact such proposals, but it would have ensured them more public attention than they ever received. That way, it might have tugged at least one of the other parties in its direction. In the early 1960s, the Democratic administration of John Kennedy put as much emphasis on cutting taxes as on enacting medicare for the elderly. Voters who favored more redistribution of wealth were impatient with Kennedy, but where could they turn—to the party of Richard Nixon and Barry Goldwater? If they had had a Populist alternative, Kennedy would have been forced to move leftward on economic policy to hold their support.

President Kennedy's example also shows how the Democratic party would have been different under a three-party system. Though more sympathetic to civil rights than Adlai Stevenson, Kennedy hesitated to push for strong legislation. He saw civil rights as the one issue that could rend the Democrats' electoral majority. Polls showed him far ahead of potential opponents for reelection, but without white southerners, who had helped put him over the top in 1960, his chances would have been in great jeopardy.[29] Kennedy eventually embraced civil rights, and he probably would have done so much sooner if the white southerners had not been in his corner to begin with.

The Republicans would have been different, too. Until Ronald Reagan became president, the party's liberal-to-moderate wing tended to have a fair degree of influence in presidential politics. Dwight Eisenhower was a product of this wing; Richard Nixon mollified it with moderate domestic policies; and Gerald Ford confirmed its clout by giving the vice-presidency to its leader, Nelson Rockefeller. In appealing to voters in Republican primaries, this faction played on their desire to nominate candidates who could win the general election. The liberal Republicans argued that a strong conservative could never do this; and conservative Barry Goldwater seemed to confirm that argument in 1964, when he won only 38 percent of the popular vote. In a three-party system, that percentage could have been more than enough to ensure victory, so conservative Republican primary voters would have had no reason to trim their sails. The Republicans probably never would have nominated Eisenhower; instead they would have turned to his conservative rival, Senator Robert Taft. Reagan might have won the nomination twelve years earlier than he actually did. And once in office, his policies would have tacked even harder to the right. The Reagan of the 1960s opposed medicare and favored making social security voluntary. The Reagan of the 1980s signed a bill expanding medicare and proposed only marginal reforms in social security.

To paraphrase Goldwater's 1964 motto, a three-party system would have given the voters a choice, not an echo.

Alternative Views

This chapter has made a number of assumptions that could be subject to dispute. It is appropriate to conclude by questioning these assumptions and sketching some alternative viewpoints.

Would the three parties have such sharp ideological distinctions? Some argue that because the United States lacks a class system on the European model, it offers no basis for sharp ideological divisions. According to this point of view, Americans generally tend to agree about the basic structure of politics and society and would reject any radical alternative. Once in office, then, our hypothetical Populists would soften their policies; the other parties would likewise move closer to the center. Without clear-cut philosophies to unite them, the three parties would be subject to the same kinds of regional and factional conflicts that help fragment the two American parties today.

Would the Populist party have survived, or would it have merged with one of the other parties? In his definitive study, *Dynamics of the Party System*, James Sundquist argues that would-be leaders of a third party might find it easier instead to capture one of the existing parties, since it offers the prize of a large body of traditional adherents while a new party must start from scratch.[30] If this were always so, then Huey Long might have abandoned his third party after winning the presidency and set about taking over the Democratic party.

Would the confusion and turmoil resulting from three-party politics have led to demands for a new structure of politics? Remember the confusing results that a single presidential election could produce:

• The Populist could win a plurality of the popular vote.

• The Democrat could win a plurality of the electoral vote but not a majority.

• The Republican party could win a plurality of House seats, but the Democratic party could win a plurality of House delegations—without winning the required majority.

• The Populist party could win an absolute majority of Senate seats but could not elect a vice-president because it could not muster the two-thirds quorum.

• Neither chamber could choose its leader.

• And so an unelected cabinet member could become acting president.

If even one election turned out this way, people might want to change the system. They might blame one of the parties for being the "spoiler" and create pressure for its merger into one of the other parties. Or support might arise for a parliamentary system, in which the leader of the legislative branch becomes the head of government. In Canada's parliamentary system, the party with the most seats in the House of Commons can form a government even if it lacks a majority. If the United States followed the Canadian example, many of the complications described in this chapter would not be possible.

Yet another reform would be to abolish the party system altogether. Although no major democracy functions without political parties, a number of major American communities do. For instance, elections for public office in the City and County of Los Angeles are conducted on a nonpartisan basis—and both entities have larger populations than some *countries*.

Finally, would a three-party system enhance turnout and participation? If the winner of the popular vote were often to lose the battle in the electoral college and the House, people might question the value of voting in presidential elections. People also go to the polls because they think that their ballots might have some impact on public policy. But if Congress and the state legislatures were constantly snarled in three-way partisan stalemates, elections might not make much difference after all.

Since the Civil War, the two-party system has "worked" to the extent that it has usually filled executive and legislative posts with a minimum of postelection turmoil. Given our country's constitutional structure, a permanent three-party system would do that job rather poorly. Such a system will probably remain little more than a useful thought experiment. On the other hand, the current conditions of low voter turnout and high voter cynicism scarcely allow us to conclude that the existing two-party system is the picture of health. Many people think the parties are offering the solutions of the 1930s to the problems of the 1990s. The Democrats and Republicans need a jolt. Perhaps a short burst of significant third-party activity would do them some good.

Notes

1. Cornelius P. Cotter and Bernard C. Hennessy, *Politics without Power: The National Party Committee* (New York: Atherton, 1964).

2. Network exit polls, cited in Gary Maloney, ed., *The Almanac of 1988 Presidential Politics* (Falls Church, Va.: American Political Network, 1989), p. 35.

3. Rep. Mickey Edwards, quoted in John Yang and Tom Kenworthy, "House GOP Takes Stand Against Any Tax Increase," *Washington Post*, July 19, 1990, p. A7; Robert Dole, quoted in David Sherman and David Rogers, "Relationship Is Tense Between Republicans in House and Senate," *Wall Street Journal*, May 1, 1985, p. 1; David Mayhew, *Placing Parties in American Politics: Organizations, Electoral Settings, and Government Activity in the Twentieth Century* (Princeton, N.J.: Princeton University Press, 1986), p. 322.

4. Janet Hook, "Bush Inspired Frail Support for First-Year President," *Congressional Quarterly Weekly Report*, December 30, 1989, p. 3542.

5. Steven J. Rosenstone, Roy L. Behr, and Edward H. Lazarus, *Third Parties in America: Citizen Response to Major Party Failure* (Princeton, N.J.: Princeton University Press, 1984), p. 17.

6. As of 1991, Nebraska had adopted the district system and several other states were considering it.

7. The Wallace switch would have tipped Missouri to Hubert Humphrey, with Wallace winning the other three states. All popular and electoral vote data are from Carolyn Goldinger, ed., *Presidential Elections since 1789*, 4th ed. (Washington, D.C.: Congressional Quarterly, 1987).

8. Frank Smallwood, *The Other Candidates: Third Parties in Presidential Elections* (Hanover, N.H.: Dartmouth University Press, 1983), pp. 254–55.

9. Under provisions of the Constitution then in effect, Roosevelt would not take office until March 4. The Twentieth Amendment, ratified in 1933, changed the date for subsequent inaugurations to January 20.

10. Kenneth S. Davis, *FDR: The New York Years, 1928–1933* (New York: Random House, 1985), pp. 428–35.

11. I borrow this premise from a science fiction novel by the late Philip K. Dick: *The Man in the High Castle* (1962; reprint, New York: Ace, 1988).

12. Rosenstone, Behr, and Lazarus, *Third Parties*, p. 99.

13. William S. Maddox and Stuart A. Lilie, *Beyond Liberal and Conservative: Reassessing the Political Spectrum* (Washington, D.C.: Cato Institute, 1984), pp. 18–20; Everett Carll Ladd, Jr., and Charles D. Hadley, *Transformations of the American Party System*, 2d ed. (New York: Norton, 1978), pp. 131–32.

14. T. Harry Williams, *Huey Long* (New York: Vintage, 1981), pp. 756–57.

15. Michael Barone, *Our Country: The Shaping of America from Roosevelt to Reagan* (New York: Free Press, 1990), p. 288.

16. Maddox and Lilie, *Beyond Liberal and Conservative*, p. 68.

17. Daniel A. Mazmanian, *Third Parties in Presidential Elections* (Washington, D.C.: Brookings Institution, 1974), p. 14.

18. Walter Berns, ed., *After the People Vote: Steps in Choosing the President* (Washington, D.C.: American Enterprise Institute, 1983), p. 14.

19. Allan P. Sindler, "Presidential Selection and Succession in Special Situations," in *Presidential Selection*, ed. Alexander Heard and Michael Nelson (Durham, N.C.: Duke University Press, 1987), p. 355; Laurence H. Tribe and Thomas M. Rollins, "Deadlock: What Happens If Nobody Wins," *Atlantic Monthly*, October 1980, pp. 60–61.

20. Tribe and Rollins, "Deadlock," p. 61.

21. James Madison, *Federalist*, 1788, in Alexander Hamilton, James Madison, and John Jay, *The Federalist Papers*, ed. Clinton Rossiter (New York: Mentor/New American Libary, 1961), p. 322.

22. John Balzar, "Initiative: Time for Reform?" *Los Angeles Times*, March 27, 1990, p. A23.

23. David Osborne, *Laboratories of Democracy: A New Breed of Governor Creates Models for National Growth* (Boston: Harvard Business School Press, 1990).

24. Walter Dean Burnham, "The Turnout Problem," in *Elections American Style*, ed. A. James Reichley (Washington, D.C.: Brookings Institution, 1987), pp. 113–14.

25. Karen Hansen, "1988: An Election without Change," *State Legislatures*, November/December 1988, pp. 12–16, 25.

26. Matthew Rothschild, "Third Party Time?" *Progressive*, October 1989, pp. 20–25.

27. Williams, *Huey Long*, p. 693.

28. Fred Harris, *The New Populism* (Berkeley, Calif.: Thorp Springs Press, 1973), p. 181.

29. Barone, *Our Country*, p. 350.

30. James L. Sundquist, *Dynamics of the Party System*, rev. ed. (Washington, D.C.: Brookings Institution, 1983), p. 66.

Sources and Suggested Readings

The two standard works on the "major" minor parties are Daniel A. Mazmanian, *Third Parties in Presidential Elections* (Washington, D.C.: Brookings Institution, 1974); and Steven J. Rosenstone, Roy L. Behr, and Edward H. Lazarus, *Third Parties in America: Citizen Response to Major Party Failure* (Princeton, N.J.: Princeton University Press, 1984). In *The Other Candidates: Third Parties in Presidential Elections* (Hanover, N.H.: Dartmouth University Press, 1983), Frank Smallwood surveys the Libertarians and other recent third parties.

The essential reference on the intricacies of presidential selection is Walter Berns, ed., *After the People Vote: Steps in Choosing the President* (Washington, D.C.: American Enterprise Institute, 1983). Allan P. Sindler supplies further detail in: "Presidential Selection and Succession in Special Situations," in *Presidential Selection*, ed. Alexander Heard and Michael Nelson (Durham, N.C.: Duke University Press, 1987).

Any student with a serious interest in American party history must read James L. Sundquist's magisterial *Dynamics of the Party System*, rev. ed. (Washington, D.C.: Brookings Institution, 1983). Everett Carll Ladd, Jr., and Charles D. Hadley use a wealth of survey data to add to this history in: *Transformations of the American Party System*, 2d ed. (New York: Norton, 1978). David Mayhew, in *Placing Parties in American Politics: Organizations, Electoral Settings, and Government Activity in the Twentieth Century* (Princeton, N.J.: Princeton University Press, 1986), shows that each state's party system has a peculiar character.

To understand populism in its contemporary context, read William S. Maddox and Stuart A. Lilie, *Beyond Liberal and Conservative: Reassessing the Political Spectrum* (Washington, D.C.: Cato Institute, 1984). And for a favorable view of a multiparty system, see Theodore J. Lowi, *The Personal President* (Ithaca, N.Y.: Cornell University Press, 1985).

HERBERT M. LEVINE

4 | What If There Were No Television?

Idiot box ... boob tube ... vast wasteland: these are just a few of the names television has been called. Yet television has become such an important feature of American life that a person without at least one set is regarded as either abjectly poor or hopelessly eccentric. Television is a subject of wonder and fascination—at its worst a harmful addiction that undermines traditional values and addles the brains of its viewers and at its best a source of both education that enlightens the mind and entertainment that lifts the spirit.

Television has become pervasive in American life in a short period of time. In 1948, 172,000 homes had television sets. By 1958, that number had reached 42 million, representing nearly 90 percent of American households. Today, nearly every home has one television set, and many homes have more than one.

American adults spend at least half their leisure time looking at television, and American children devote more time to watching television than to attending school. The typical American family has its television set on more than six hours a day.

About two-thirds of the American people say that they get their news mainly from television. Nearly all of the great news stories since the 1950s have been covered extensively on television. Among the most memorable were the Army-McCarthy hearings of 1954 in which Senator Joseph McCarthy of Wisconsin charged that the U.S. Army was coddling communists, the 1960 John F. Kennedy–Richard M. Nixon presidential debates, Kennedy's funeral three years later, the civil rights marches in the 1950s and 1960s, the war in Vietnam in the 1960s and 1970s (actual combat scenes abroad and the protest movement at home), the Watergate scandal that concluded with Nixon's resignation as president, assassination attempts against presidents Gerald R. Ford and Ronald Reagan, the Iran-Contra hearings investigating an illegal arms-for-hostages deal, and the adventures in space—successful ones, like the landing of the first Apollo astronauts on the moon, and failures, like the explosion of the spacecraft *Challenger* and the death of its crew.

In addition to covering major events, television has anointed celebrity status to political leaders and entertainment stars. Television personalities are often taken more seriously than national leaders. In a 1989 poll, for example, more Americans recognized the name of Judge Joseph Wapner than the name of William Rehnquist. Wapner is the judge on a syndicated television series, "The People's Court," in which ordinary citizens bring minor disputes before the judge. Rehnquist is merely the chief justice of the U.S. Supreme Court, an institution that has had an extraordinary impact on American life.

What is true of Judge Wapner is equally applicable to television news broadcasters, who often have more fame and credibility than the people they describe. Television news celebrities Connie Chung, Sam Donaldson, Mike Wallace, and Barbara Walters, for example, have more name and face recognition than most members of Congress. For years, public opinion surveys in the United States revealed that CBS Television news anchor Walter Cronkite was the most trusted man in America.

Because of television's pervasiveness, a cottage industry of critics warns of its perils to people, home, and country. Religious leaders complain about its preoccupation with sex and violence. Feminists criticize the demeaning way it depicts women. Educators condemn its seduction of young minds from reading and writing. And social commentators denounce the mass culture that it produces.

Television has also been condemned because of its influence on the political life of Americans. Conservatives argue that television news is dominated by liberals who slant their reports in support of their biases, most notably regarding the evils of capitalism, the need for environmental protection, and the irrationality and waste of U.S. military power. Neoconservatives contend that the news media—and television news in particular—constitute an adversary press in which the television journalists are actively hostile to existing political and economic institutions in the United States. In contrast, Marxists say that television newscasts are instruments of the capitalist ruling class used to suppress the exploited classes through cultural domination. Other critics, not easily pigeonholed by political label, say television has contributed to the superficial, irrelevant nature of the nation's editorial dialogue.

Television as a political phenomenon is the subject of this chapter. We will try to imagine what our political system and political life would be like if television had never been invented. In this way we can evaluate how much of the character of American politics today derives from television and how much from features that have nothing to do with that particular medium.

Political Behavior

Television has had a profound effect on political parties and elections. Without it, they would be very different, with consequences for campaigns, candidates, and voter turnout. Popular participation in politics would also take a somewhat different form.

Campaigns and Candidates

Without television, candidates would seek the attention of newspapers, magazines, and radio. Consequently, the cost of political campaigns would be much less than it is—maybe more than 50 percent less—since today most campaign expenses are devoted to paying for television ads.

In the pretelevision age, political parties raised the funds necessary to conduct campaigns, but today that role has been taken over by the candidates themselves, who form their own campaign finance organizations. Parties lost their ability to raise money because they no longer had a monopoly over the selection of candidates. Primaries and the direct appeals to the public by candidates in those primaries have meant that one does not necessarily need the approval of party leaders to secure a nomination. Reforms in the nominating process at party conventions have further undermined the ability of party leaders to choose party candidates.

Candidates now rely principally on *political action committees* (PACs)—private groups established to support and finance political candidates. PACs are business, labor, and professional groups that financially support candidates who are aligned with them in outlook and interests.

Although legal limitations have been placed on the amount of money that a PAC can spend for each candidate, some PACs circumvent this restriction by forming multiple PACs, allying with other PACs, or contributing "soft money" to political parties. Soft money consists of funds that are not used for direct electioneering but can be used to pay for land, buildings, equipment, and other items. By law, soft money need not be reported to the Federal Election Commission. Candidates need PAC money to finance their campaigns, which are expensive particularly because of the high cost of television advertising. Without television, then, PACs would not be as influential as they have become; instead, the political party would be stronger in financing campaigns and, consequently, in selecting candidates to carry the party banner.

Some features of political campaigns would also be different. Campaigning today is largely a quest for media attention through the best pictures and most memorable sound bites. *Sound bites* are short, pithy comments made by candidates that are likely to get on the television newscasts.

Today, candidates frequently travel from city to city not to speak to different groups and meet leading political figures, as they did in the first half of the twentieth century, but to get coverage from local television stations. A presidential or vice-presidential candidate can reach larger local audiences by making studio visits than by addressing crowds.

The importance of media coverage—and especially television coverage—has put media consultants on top of campaign organizations. In the nineteenth century, political party officials and officeholders ran campaigns. Since the 1960s, however, every important candidate for a major office is advised by an expert in media coverage and public opinion polling—sometimes called a handler—who shapes the candidate's image to appeal to the public.

Television debates have become a feature of campaigns, particularly for primary and interparty contests for the presidency. But political debates without television were held before television, and today's debates are on radio, too. Debates have a long tradition, with those between Abraham Lincoln and Stephen A. Douglas among the most memorable. Debates have long been common within legislative chambers at every level of government. So television has not introduced campaign debates, but it has shaped their character.

Televised presidential debates have been criticized for not permitting serious discussion of the issues. A rigid format of question, response, comment by the opponent, and rebuttal is adhered to, and the debaters more often make set speeches than speak to the issues. Candidates try for one-line "zingers" that will play well on television.

Television has, in fact, been blamed for the triumph of personality over issues in American campaigns. The format of televised debates as well as the emphasis on *spots* (thirty- or sixty-second commercials), photo opportunities, and sound bites are held responsible for both issueless and *negative campaigns*—contests that feature personal attacks and misrepresentation. These, it is said, undermine democracy. According to some theorists, democracy requires a discussion of values and policies in which the people decide which values and policies will prevail.

Without television, would values and policies be more influential in determining the outcome of elections? And is there something about television's emphasis on visual appeal that makes serious discussion impossible? The answer to both questions is no.

First, even in the pretelevision era, much attention was given to slogans and images at the expense of issues. Successful campaign slogans were vivid and were easy to remember. William McKinley's presidential campaign of 1896 used posters, cartoons, and envelope stickers with messages such as "The Advance Agent of Prosperity," "Full Dinner Pail," and "Poverty or Prosperity." Foreshadowing what critics today say about political consultants, Theodore Roosevelt (also a Republican and McKinley's running mate in 1900) said that Mark Hanna, McKinley's political boss, "has advertised McKinley as if he were a patent medicine!" Woodrow Wilson campaigned in 1916 under the slogan, "He kept us out of war." This simple and clear message— comparable to a sound bite—had a powerful appeal to Americans who hoped to stay out of the war in Europe.

Moreover, successful sound bites often carry messages about important issues. Ronald Reagan, whose career as a Hollywood actor contributed to his effectiveness in political communication, rose to prominence only in part because of his skills. He also stood for conservative principles that were brilliantly presented in his sound bites during the 1980 campaign. He made pithy statements with clear-cut messages about reducing government spending on social programs, improving the economy by decreasing inflation and raising employment levels, strengthening U.S. military power, and initiating a tough

foreign policy toward the Soviet Union. Reagan's campaign used television masterfully, and he offered a message that voters found compelling. In this instance, at least, the use of television helped to highlight
issues as democratic theorists favor.

In a democracy the people generally vote out a government when
the economy is grim. No amount of media manipulation can convince
voters that life is good when they are unemployed and have exhausted
their savings. Although Reagan remained a popular president for most
of his two terms in office and left the presidency in January 1989 with
the highest popularity rating of any president who completed a term in
the twentieth century, his ratings plummeted when the nation was
gripped by the recession of 1982. At that time two-thirds of the public
disapproved Reagan's presidency—and confirmed that factors other
than television had played an important role in his popularity ratings.
In the past as in the present, issues are important in political campaigns, and they have to be clear and brief to gain popular support.
Television has not changed that political fact.

But is television responsible for negative advertising? In the 1988
presidential campaign, Republicans made a horrifying legend of Willie
Horton, a convicted murderer with no chance of parole who had been
allowed furloughs (as state law provided) by Massachusetts governor
Michael Dukakis, the Democratic presidential standard-bearer. On one
such furlough, Horton abused a Maryland couple. The fact that Horton
was black and the victims were white was perceived as a way to
introduce racism into the campaign as well as to associate Dukakis
with a foolish innocence about the dangers hardened criminals present
to other people. Bush campaign commercials also called Dukakis's
patriotism into question by focusing on his veto of a Massachusetts bill
to make recitation of the Pledge of Allegiance compulsory in Massachusetts public schools. In fact, Dukakis had been advised by his attorney general that the bill was unconstitutional.

A classic example of negative campaigning was the so-called Daisy
spot in the 1964 presidential campaign. It associated a child counting
the petals of a daisy with a countdown to a nuclear explosion, suggesting that if the Republican candidate Barry Goldwater were elected, the
child and the rest of the world would be destroyed in a nuclear war.
The ad was so controversial that Lyndon Johnson's campaign withdrew it after only one showing on television.

But television did not invent negative campaigning. In the late eighteenth century supporters of Thomas Jefferson distributed handbills accusing John Adams of being a monarchist and an aristocrat. Followers of John Adams labeled Jefferson a free-thinker and an enemy of the Constitution. In a campaign pitting John Quincy Adams against Andrew Jackson, the latter was charged with ordering executions of his own soldiers and stabbing a man in the back. In the presidential campaign of 1884, supporters of James Blaine, the Republican candidate, accused Grover Cleveland, the Democratic candidate, of siring an illegitimate child—a charge he admitted to.

The stakes in electoral politics are high and include not only personal glory, but a chance to shape public policy and affect the well-being of the American people. It is tempting for candidates and their supporters—who may have their eyes on job opportunities—to use any technique that works. If negative campaigning works, then it will be used. The spirit that marks political campaigns is not unlike that in a different kind of contest. As Vince Lombardi, the legendary football coach of the Green Bay Packers, once remarked, "Winning isn't everything; it's the only thing."

Political Parties

Television has not only changed the nature of financing and conducting political campaigns; it has also contributed to the decline of political parties. But it is wrong to conclude that political parties would have remained strong even without television. Were there no television, political parties would have been in decline anyway, but the decline would not have been so precipitous.

A *political party* is an organization formed to contest elections. Political parties traditionally have been vital to democracy. Although national political parties did not exist at the time of the adoption of the Constitution, they emerged by the 1790s when Thomas Jefferson formed the Democrat-Republican party to combat the ruling Federalists. Ever after American politics has been dominated by two opposing parties. In a democracy political parties aggregate interests so that different economic, social, religious, and racial groups find common ground for political unity. The parties also formulate and present a governmental program for consideration by the general public, nominate candidates for government offices, run the government when elected to office, and serve as a link between government and people.

Because of television and other factors, political parties are less able—and at times are unable—to perform these functions.

Political parties began to decline in the early twentieth century through the deliberate attempt of Progressive reformers to weaken them. The reformers believed that the political parties were corrupt and that American democracy would be strengthened by more direct popular participation in government. Hence, they advocated measures such as the *direct primary*, in which voters directly choose their party's candidates. Throughout the nineteenth century party leaders had met in *caucuses* and *state conventions* to select candidates acceptable to party supporters. State party leaders formed alliances at *national conventions*, which were truly decision-making gatherings. But party politics began to be bypassed with the introduction of primaries. The first one was held in 1904.

In spite of direct primaries, political parties remained relatively strong—at least by American standards. To be sure, American political parties were always weaker as national institutions than British political parties, because the United States has a federal system of government (see Chapter 2) in which party organization is largely decen- tralized. Yet state party organizations remained the dominant institution for selecting candidates for national offices. As late as 1968, Hubert Humphrey won the Democratic nomination for the presidency without entering a single primary, relying instead on the support of powerful party leaders. At that convention, however, the Democrats adopted reforms that made primaries the chief means by which candidates are selected. Later, the Republicans made similar changes.

Today, a candidate is usually not beholden to his or her party for a nomination to public office, as primary victories depend on the direct appeal of candidates to voters. Here television plays a powerful role. With the rise of television, the importance of national conventions declined. Today a party's candidate for the presidency usually wins the nomination well before the convention is held. The last time more than one ballot was needed to decide a presidential nominee was in 1952, when the Republicans selected Dwight D. Eisenhower.

Since primaries are now the means of selecting presidential candidates, the focus of political activity has moved to them. Because of the new importance of primaries, there is less need to reconcile the different groups within the party to obtain the party's nomination than was the case before the development of these contests.

Television is a business—a commercial activity that demands profits for its survival. To obtain profits, it must attract viewers. The more viewers, the higher the advertising rates, which are the source of profits. Consequently, television news programs look for the dramatic in an effort to hold interest and obtain high ratings. In reporting on campaigns, they emphasize who is ahead and who is behind—the "horse race" aspect of politics. By deciding who is and who is not a front-runner, what success is unexpected and what failure a surprise, they have become major players in actually determining who will win and who will lose. When the television newscasters render such judgments, they generate so much attention that money pours into the coffers of the media-declared winners while funds dry up for the media-declared losers.

In the past, the party emblem came to represent a label that many voters could recognize as signifying a general viewpoint on issues. But that function has been eroding as candidates can appeal directly to people without reference or commitment to party. Indeed, a candidate's independence from his or her own party is often presented during primary and general elections, as admirable.

The decline of parties may also be seen in the continuing fall in the number of voters who identify with a particular party. To an increasing extent, voters describe themselves as *independents*. They are voting less often by party label, instead choosing candidates on an office-by-office basis and splitting their votes among Democrats and Republicans. Without television, *ticket-splitting* would be lower, and candidates would have to stay more closely tied to their parties. The parties would thus be stronger and more important, though still not as important as they once were.

Voter Turnout

Finally, we must consider the relationship between television and political participation—specifically in turning out to vote and in engaging in other political activities. Of the major democratic societies, the United States has the lowest voter turnout in the world. In recent presidential contests, about half of the people who could legally vote actually cast ballots. In state and local elections, the turnout usually is even less. Turnout in primaries and in popular votes on issues such as referendums and initiatives is also generally quite low. The decline has been constant and has become most pronounced in the television age.

The decline in voting is controversial. Nonvoting has been explained by various theories. Among them are:

1. Voters who choose not to vote are basically content with the way the country is being run and feel no need to vote.

2. Registration requirements are cumbersome, and casting a ballot is too time consuming.

3. Since Americans are highly mobile and many change their residences every few years, they are often unable to meet the voting residency requirements.

4. Only a few issues are hot enough—war and depression are examples—to make people feel the stakes require them to vote.

5. Americans hold elections on more occasions for more offices (president; senator and representative; state governor, lieutenant governor, attorney general; county and local officials) and on more proposals (bond issues; state constitutional amendments; recalls; contests dealing with referendums and initiatives) than citizens in other countries, and they get tired of voting.

6. People feel powerless to effect change or do not believe that the major political parties give them any meaningful choice.

The role television plays in nonvoting depends to a large extent on which explanation one accepts, so it is difficult to generalize on this subject. Television, however, seems to have contributed to nonvoting in at least one additional way: namely, its early projections in presidential contests of the winner. On election night, the networks compete to be the first project winners on the basis of their analyses of exit polls and early returns. Since the polls on the East Coast close before those on the West Coast because of differences in time zones and winners can be declared before westerners have gone out to vote, some westerners probably decide voting is not worth the effort. To them it seems that a winner for the presidency has been declared. Failure to vote for a presidential candidate in the western states also often means failure to vote in contests for other offices being contested at the same time.

Television may have contributed to nonvoting in such cases, but even if television had not been invented, radio would be making the same projections. Newspapers, of course, have always been slower and were never able to print projections before the polls had closed.

Political Participation

With its emphasis on theatrics, on visual images rather than substantive commentary, and with its adversarial approach to political leaders, television is sometimes accused of encouraging cynicism about politics and turning Americans away not only from voting but from political involvement altogether. Is there truth to this charge? Not much. From the 1960s until the present—the period during which television became a central part of the lives of most Americans—the nation has witnessed much political activism. Notable examples are the civil rights movement, protests against the war in Vietnam, and activities promoting women's rights and environmental protection. In fact, it can be argued conversely that television has sparked active participation in political life.

Like political parties, interest groups have learned the importance of manipulating television to promote their goals. In the 1960s television footage of peaceful demonstrators attacked by police with water hoses and clubs in Birmingham and Selma, Alabama, helped to galvanize public opinion in support of civil rights. Television coverage of anti-war protests in the late 1960s and early 1970s also made many aware of the strength of opposition to American involvement in Vietnam. Some interest groups became particularly adept at staging media events early and lively enough to make the evening news. Groups that have mounted impressive demonstrations attracting television coverage include animal rights activists, pro- and antiabortion forces, anti–nuclear power organizations, opponents of white domination in South Africa, and groups opposing Soviet restrictions against Jewish emigration.

But even without television, such groups may have attracted the public attention through other media. In this century alone, successful media campaigns to publicize such causes as the franchise for women, prohibition, collective bargaining, and veterans' benefits all met with some success in the pretelevision age. It is reasonable, therefore, to assume that the more recent success of some interest groups in achieving their goals would have resulted without television.

Governmental Institutions

All levels of government—national, state, and local—have devised means of using and dealing with television. For the federal government, only the federal judiciary has sought to avoid this medium. Cameras are not permitted in the Supreme Court. Justices never discuss specific decisions publicly and make only infrequent appearances on television.

The Presidency

Recent presidents have all been extremely well-aware of the impact of television. But even before television became a principal means of communication, governmental leaders understood the necessity of reaching audiences. Many of the developments we associate with the television age originated in an earlier era.

Before television, presidents traveled to rally support for their programs. A notable example was Woodrow Wilson's national tour in 1919 to try to persuade Americans to support ratification of the Treaty of Versailles, which was in trouble in the Senate. Presidents have also traveled to demonstrate interest in local communities and to generate news stories about them in those areas.

Without television, presidents would still hold press conferences and meet informally with reporters to attract attention, and newsreel films would still focus on presidential activities. Presidents would also speak directly to the American people through radio speeches, as Franklin Roosevelt did in his "fireside chats." Through the use of the radio, the president could bypass the press, which has sometimes served as an intermediary to the people. To be sure, the press could comment on what the president said, but radio assures the president much the same direct link as television.

It is sometimes said that television is capable of forcing a president's hand because of its agenda-setting capacity. Television is said not to influence opinions so much as to dictate the topics that people deem important. When a respected television anchor decides to focus on environmental issues, for example, public opinion will be persuaded to consider the subject.

Often overlooked, however, is the influence the president has in setting the agenda by, in effect, compelling television to report stories. When the president wants to publicize an issue, he may summon a press conference, address a group, or denounce an individual. This ability to influence the public was equally potent in the pretelevision age. Thus, Woodrow Wilson set the agenda when he called for the

United States to join the League of Nations; Franklin Roosevelt set the agenda when he introduced his New Deal programs of economic recovery; and Harry Truman set the agenda when he highlighted the Marshall Plan (named for Secretary of State George C. Marshall) to provide economic aid to a war-ravaged Europe. Were there no television, presidents might set the agenda anyway in the manner of these presidents.

Without television, executive departments, agencies, and bureaus would continue to use the existing media. Even in pretelevision times, government organizations carefully used print and radio journalists to promote a favorable image. J. Edgar Hoover, the first director of the Federal Bureau of Investigation (FBI), for example, successfully cultivated journalists, supplying them with information in return for sympathetic comments. Hoover, director from 1924 to 1972, also destroyed the reputations of some journalists critical of the FBI.

Congress

And what of Congress? How would it fare without television? Most noticeably, its composition would be different. The present system benefits *incumbents*, those legislators already in office. In the 1990 congressional election, most incumbents who sought reelection won. Only fifteen of these incumbent representatives lost their seats in the House, and only one of these thirty-one incumbent senators lost his seat in the Senate.

The major reason incumbents generally win is that they receive much more than their challengers in campaign contributions from PACs. And the percentage of PAC funds has risen for congressional incumbents—from 56.8 percent in 1977–1978 to 79.1 percent in 1989–1990. PACs favor incumbents since the latter are in a position to act on policies of immediate benefit to them.

Incumbency, then, has obvious advantages. Incumbents have time and power to build huge campaign chests. A legislator would have to be involved in a major public scandal to have his or her tenure in office threatened, and even one so involved may weather the storm of controversy.

To be sure, incumbents have advantages other than PAC contributions for television ads that serve to strengthen their bids for reelection. But since money for television is so vital in conducting political campaigns, it is a major factor in incumbent success. So, without television, we would likely have a Congress in which there were many more new faces after each election.

With a diminished influence of incumbency, the economic composition of Congress would change. Currently wealthy politicians have a clear advantage because legally a candidate can spend unlimited personal funds on his or her campaign. The Senate is sometimes described as a millionaire's club because of its millionaire members, such as John Danforth, the late John Heinz, and Jay Rockefeller.

Incumbency affects not only the economic composition of Congress, but its social composition as well. Without television and the heavy costs it imposes on campaigning, women and members of minorities would have a better chance for congressional seats. In the 1991–92 Congress, for example, only two women—Nancy Kassebaum and Barbara Mikulski—served in the Senate, with ninety-eight men. Although the number of minority members of Congress—particularly blacks—has increased since the 1960s, this development can be attributed largely to gains in the right to vote achieved by southern blacks and to the migration of blacks to northern cities. Areas without a large black electorate rarely elect a black to office. Since the role of television in political campaigning benefits incumbents and most incumbents are white males, women and blacks continue at a disadvantage.

To be sure, television is not the only reason women and minorities find it hard to get elected. Some people will not vote for a woman or a member of another race for reasons of prejudice, too. But it is reasonable to assume that there would be more women and blacks in Congress had television never been invented.

On the other hand, television has stimulated interest in the work of Congress and made it more public. Hearings sometimes take place before the American people—for example, the hearings against organized crime conducted by Senator Estes Kefauver from Tennessee in 1950, the Watergate hearings in 1974, and the Iran-Contra investigations in 1987. Yet it was not coverage but issues that generated public concern.

Even before television, congressional hearings sometimes were subjects of intense national attention. Examples include investigations of military activities by the Union Army during the Civil War, corruption in the Warren Harding administration, the munitions industry in the 1930s, and war profiteering in World War II. Televised hearings have certainly produced celebrity status for some members of Congress, like Estes Kefauver (organized crime) and Sam Ervin (Watergate). But a member of Congress could achieve fame from a congressional investigation even before television. It was Truman's work as chair of the Senate's Special Committee to Investigate the National Defense Program, for example, that contributed to his selection by President Franklin Roosevelt as Democratic vice-presidential candidate in 1944.

Without television, then, Congress would have experienced some profound changes, most notably in its composition. But many aspects of the political behavior of its members would be much the same because of the importance of particular issues and the structural foundation of the separation of powers established by the framers.

Public Policy

Since television plays so prominent a role in determining how political issues are perceived by government leaders and the public, there is much concern about the way issues—particularly foreign policy, terrorism, and domestic affairs—are treated by television.

Foreign Policy

Perhaps the most controversial example of the relationship between foreign policy and television was coverage of the Vietnam War. Had there been no television, would there have been no protest movement in the United States against the Vietnam War—a protest movement that undermined the ability of U.S. political leaders to pursue the war? There is little evidence to indicate yes.

In the past other media representatives were attacked for much the same reasons that television has been criticized during wartime. During the Crimean War, for example, the British foreign secretary, Lord Clarendon, complained that "three pitched battles gained would not repair the mischief" done by the correspondent of the London *Times* on the scene.

Antiwar protest movements have generally emerged over time even before the television era. Draft riots occurred in northern cities during the Civil War. Antiwar movements existed during the War of 1812, the Mexican War in the late 1840s, the Spanish-American War of 1898, and even the Korean War in the early 1950s. In fact, continuation of the Korean War was a major issue in the presidential election of 1952. The experience of the United States and other countries indicates that antiwar movements are increasingly likely to emerge as wars drag on and become more devastating. France, which had sustained unprecedented casualties in World War I, experienced a mutiny in 1917. Russian dissatisfaction with the same war contributed to a revolution in 1917, which toppled the czarist government.

Without television, the same war weariness would have occurred over Vietnam. The major reason the protest movement generated support against American continuation of the war was because the war seemed endless. Many Americans who had supported the use of combat forces initially became disillusioned because it seemed the United States was not doing enough to win the war. To be sure, many Americans were moved by some television pictures portraying images of U.S. soldiers as murderers and torturers of innocent civilians; but often viewers were not made sympathetic to the cause of the antiwar movement by these reports. When Morley Safer of CBS furnished films of marines burning the homes of Vietnamese peasants, the overwhelming public response condemned Safer, not the marines. There is much evidence to suggest that it was war weariness rather than television that nurtured the protest movement.

But television may have some impact on the way military policy is made because of the power of its pictures. Against much opposition, President Reagan in 1982 sent marines into Lebanon to strengthen the existing government there. When a terrorist bomb at a U.S. installation took the lives of 241 marines, the gory pictures on television undermined support for the president's action. Within five months, the United States withdrew its troops from Lebanon. Even without the television pictures, however, the loss of the marines would have encouraged political leaders to withdraw, as there has been little popular support for intervention in the first place.

It seems that political leaders are so wary of media coverage in general and television coverage in particular that they *act* as if television shapes public opinion. In Great Britain, Prime Minister Margaret Thatcher barred journalists from reporting military developments as British forces moved to retake the Falkland Islands, a British possession off the coast of Argentina that had been seized by Argentina in a long-standing dispute. Taking a possible cue from Thatcher, American authorities kept U.S. journalists from covering the intervention of U.S.

troops in Grenada in 1983 to topple the Marxist regime there. In subsequent military interventions, moreover, journalists were restricted. When U.S. armed forces invaded Panama in 1989, a pool of journalists that had been selected to cover U.S. military interventions was delayed in performing its job. Journalists—both print and electronic media—also complained about government restriction of their work during the 1991 war with Iraq.

Since the Vietnam War, U.S. military interventions usually have been short. Some observers believe that television has increased pressure to make interventions short lest pictures on television of killing and destruction undermine popular support of U.S. foreign policy.

But changing assessments of world politics and what constitutes threats to U.S. national security are more significant than television in the reluctance to use military power. The nation has clearly experienced a *post-Vietnam syndrome*, as it is called—a widespread reluctance to use armed forces anywhere unless briefly and successfully. In this regard, the administration of George Bush let it be known in advance that if U.S. military power were used against Iraq to force that country out of Kuwait in 1991 it would be swift and decisive.

The charge is sometimes made that television helps to undermine democracies by allowing critiques of their weaknesses that would never be permitted in a dictatorship. It has been pointed out, for example, that television was permitted to cover the devastation produced by U.S. and South Vietnamese military actions but not the atrocities of the Viet Cong; the filming of the Palestinian *intifada*, or uprising, in areas occupied by democratic Israel but not the use of poison gas against the Kurds in dictatorial Iraq; the killing of civilians in El Salvador but not the torture and denials of human rights in Cuba.

Two points need to be made here. First, the lack of opportunity to cover stories is not unique to television. It is usually the case that dictators prevent journalists of *all* media forms from covering stories that might depict them in an unfavorable light. Second, television critiques are not limited to democracies. Where direct coverage has not been permitted, television journalists have interviewed scholars and analysts, emigré representatives, and refugees to get their stories on acts of repression. The atrocities committed by the Pol Pot regime in Cambodia, in which millions died, were reported. Stories about the Iraqi use of poison gas have been widely recounted, and pictures have been shown on television. And for decades, the Soviet Union and other communist societies were portrayed in ways that those societies often found to be provocative.

Terrorism

The use of television by terrorists has become a subject of great controversy. The term *terrorist* itself is a controversial word, and it is often said that one man's terrorist is another man's freedom fighter. But if *terrorism* is defined as acts of violence against private individuals for political purposes, then the people who hijack aircraft, intimidate passengers and crew, and place bombs in places that are sure to kill and injure civilians are surely terrorists. The hijacking of TWA Flight 847 in 1985 gave extraordinary television exposure to the hijackers and their representatives, who appeared day after day on television interviews to argue their cause. Critics say that without television, terrorists would not be able to get the publicity they desire, and so acts of terrorism would be reduced. But television representatives respond that journalists should be free to report the news as they see it, and in fact that a free society demands they do so.

Here it would appear that the critics of television make the most convincing points. Terrorism is often described as a tactic of the weak. A strong power can rely on the conventional use of military power, but weaker countries and so-called substate actors, like guerrilla units, must use different tactics to achieve their goals. And they have found that terrorist attacks can undermine public confidence in democratic governments. They have even confessed that getting their message on television is a central objective of their policy.

Terrorists can manipulate television by giving it what it needs—drama, danger, and great pictures—to achieve high viewer ratings. Hostage-taking has been an ideal technique for terrorists because of its television appeal. Since 1985, many Americans have been held hostage in Lebanon. Terrorists have played on American public opinion by showing pictures of the hostages begging their governments to give the terrorists what they want. These emotional appeals are hard for the U.S. government to counter with reference to security interests. Although executives of TV news programs say they are taking steps to minimize propaganda opportunities for terrorists, competition between networks continues to tempt them to carry terrorist messages. And so, for example, in 1989 Americans saw a videotape of the hanging of William Higgins, an American military officer in a United Nations peacekeeping mission in Lebanon.

If television coverage of terrorist acts were restricted, an important component of the terrorists' strength would be diminished. Terrorist acts would not cease, but they would decline. Yet, one can reasonably argue that imposing restrictions on television broadcasts, even in cases of terrorism, undermines democracy. As in foreign policy areas, democracies are vulnerable to manipulation by enemies.

Domestic Affairs

Finally, if television had not been invented, would domestic policy be different? Probably not, if we consider the character of public policy in nineteenth and twentieth century America.

Often neglected in the extraordinary attention given to television is the enormous impact that other media have had on public policy. Among books, for example, consider Harriet Beecher Stowe's novel *Uncle Tom's Cabin* (1852). It was said to have so inflamed public opinion about slavery that Abraham Lincoln commented, when introduced to the author, "So you're the little woman who wrote the book that made this great war." Upton Sinclair's *Jungle* (1906), exposing conditions in meat-packing plants, helped provoke government regulation of the food industry. Michael Harrington's *Other America* (1962) generated so much attention to poverty in America that it provided the philosophical underpinning of Lyndon Johnson's War on Poverty, which he initiated in 1965.

Print journalism, too, has been particularly important in influencing public opinion. *Muckrakers* was what President Theodore Roosevelt called journalists who specialized in articles about corruption in government, the mistreatment of immigrants, the evils of capitalism, and the conditions of the poor. Much Progressive-era legislation was inspired by such newspaper and magazine reporting.

Although our times have been described as the television age, they might better be characterized as the communications age. The information Americans receive comes not only from television. There are 1,500 daily and 7,600 weekly or semiweekly newspapers in the United States, with sales of approximately 60 million copies daily. In addition, the United States boasts 400 million radios, 60,000 magazines and journals, and more than 55,000 new books annually.

Even when we recognize the power of other forms of communication, we should not neglect the compelling power of events themselves. After all, there have been wars and rebellions long before most men and women could even read. People will always seek to know about such events, by whatever means. Although television highlighted the civil rights movement of the 1960s and the women's movement of the 1970s and 1980s, these movements would have occurred anyway. By the time that the civil rights movement became prominently featured on television, various forms of racial discrimination were already being criticized. Racism as public policy had been thoroughly discredited by the example of Nazi Germany, which carried it to its logical extreme. Supreme Court decisions after World War II began to support civil rights of blacks. The bus boycott in Montgomery, Alabama, mobilized economic power for equal treatment. In the civil rights movement, a constellation of forces came together. Television may have brought visual images to the general population, but the issue of civil rights would have appeared on the national agenda anyway.

A similar observation could be made about the women's movement, as indicated by such political activity as marches and demonstrations in favor of the Equal Rights Amendment and in opposition to the exploitation of women through pornography. It is well to recall that what has in the past few decades become known as the women's movement has a history going back at least to the middle of the nineteenth century. Over many years suffragists mobilized a successful public campaign in favor of voting rights for women that culminated in the adoption of the Nineteenth Amendment in 1920. In the 1960s the women's movement was renewed by the character of the workplace, in which women were underpaid; the increase in the number of divorces, which had a negative economic impact on women; and the spirit of the times, which led many groups, sensing that they were being treated unfairly by both government and society, to assert their right to equal treatment. Laws benefiting women were enacted because of these and other factors, not because the movement was shown on television.

Conclusion

Television has had a profound impact on the American political system. It has contributed to changing the character of political campaigns and weakening political parties. It has altered the way government leaders communicate to people as well as the way interest groups appeal for public support.

But without television, much of the American political system would be the same. Presidents would still have to use techniques of mass persuasion to win people to their programs. Public policy matters would still be fought out on the basis of competing interests, with each group using all vehicles of mass communication.

Although television has had an impact on the American political system, critics of television have exaggerated that influence. There is much to be learned about television from the events in Eastern Europe in 1989 and 1990. In most of these communist societies, control of the mass media was nearly total. There were no private television or radio stations and no independent publishing houses. An underground press existed, but when the writers and publishers of underground works were identified, they often received harsh prison terms or other punishment. Still, the people of Eastern Europe well understood that the information they got on television could not be believed. And when the communist regimes showed signs of weakness and the Soviet Union indicated that it no longer wished to pay the price of empire, they toppled like falling dominoes. The leaders of those communist governments learned that people are not so gullible as to believe all or much of what they see through the mass media in general and television in particular. It is a lesson that critics of the television media in free societies might well heed.

Sources and Suggested Readings

On the general impact of the mass media or television in American political life, see Austin Ranney, *Channels of Power: The Impact of Television on American Politics* (New York: Basic Books, 1983); and Thomas R. Dye and Harmon Ziegler, *American Politics in the Media Age*, 3d ed. (Pacific Grove, Calif.: Brooks/Cole, 1989).

On political campaigns, elections, and political parties, see Kathleen Hall Jamieson and David S. Birdsell, *Presidential Debates: The Challenge of Creating an Informed Electorate* (New York: Oxford University Press, 1988); and Thomas E. Patterson, *The Mass Media Election: How Americans Choose Their President* (New York: Praeger, 1980).

The impact of television on public opinion is considered in Shanto Iyengar and Donald R. Kinder, *News That Matters: Television and American Opinion* (Chicago, Ill.: University of Chicago Press, 1987). On criticisms of the media, see

Tom Goldstein, ed., *Killing the Messenger: 100 Years of Media Criticism* (New York: Columbia University Press, 1988); and Steven Starker, *Evil Influences: Crusades against the Mass Media* (New Brunswick, N.J.: Transaction Publishers, 1989). On bias in television coverage, see C. Richard Hofstetter, *Bias in the News: Network Television Coverage of the 1972 Election Campaign* (Columbus, Ohio: Ohio University Press, 1976); and Michael Parenti, *Inventing Reality: The Politics of the Mass Media* (New York: St. Martin's Press, 1986).

On government institutions and television, see Stephen Bates, ed., *The Media and Congress* (Columbus, Ohio: Publishing Horizons, 1987); and C. Don Livingston, "The Televised Presidency," *Presidential Studies Quarterly* 16, no. 1 (Winter 1986): 22–30.

On war and television, see Peter Braestrup, *Big Story: How the American Press and Television Reported and Interpreted the Crisis of Tet 1968 in Vietnam and Washington* (New Haven, Conn.: Yale University Press, 1983). For terrorism and television, see Robert Kupperman and Jeff Kame, "When Terrorists Strike . . .: The Lessons TV Must Learn," *TV Guide* 37, no. 38 (September 23, 1989): 18–22.

JOY E. ESBEREY

5 | What If There Were a Parliamentary System?

It does not require improbable flights of fantasy to imagine the leaders of the newly independent states in North America adopting a parliamentary system of government.[1] The American colonists' rebellion against King George III was not part of a grand design to establish a "utopian" democratic state. On the contrary, one could argue it was as much a war *for* the British system of government as it was a war *against* the British monarch and his advisers. It was a war against "colonial" subordination. The colonists who objected to taxation by a government in which they had no representation demanded the rights and liberties of Englishmen, rights acquired by Englishmen during centuries of struggle to control the autocratic tendencies of the monarchy. Out of this struggle the Westminster model of parliamentary government evolved as the institutionalization of these ideals.

The Westminster (named for the section of London where the Parliament building is located) system of parliamentary government is an example of *constitutional monarchy*.[2] It is a system in which the legitimacy of the monarch or *Crown*, as a legal entity, remains unchallenged and forms the basis of all political power and authority. At the same time extensive restraints limit the ability of any individual monarch to use these royal powers. Because these restraints and practices have not been collected in one comprehensive, authoritative document, the parliamentary system is said to have an *unwritten constitution*, but "unwritten" should not be confused with "ineffective." The Westminster system sometimes appears rather old-fashioned, even comic, because it operates behind a surface of colorful historical terminology and procedures, but it is a highly effective decision-making system.

At its core is the notion of *parliamentary supremacy* or *sovereignty*, a concept encompassing more than the related institution (the legislature) or the process (lawmaking). The absolute monarchs had been more than just lawgivers; they played a leading part in religious matters (becoming after Henry VIII, the head of a state church), commanded the army, managed the royal household and the public domain, and even personally dispensed justice to their subjects. All these activities were considered part of the royal *prerogative* (activity subject to no restrictions).

The first dimension of the struggle to control this autocratic power resulted in the acceptance of the constitutional principle, the *rule of law* (the belief that no one, royalty included, should be above the law). To combine this principle with monarchy required that all royal actions be based on advice and that the advisers, rather than the sovereign, be held responsible for royal actions (*accountability*). The second dimension involved hearing grievances from those required to help finance royal activity such as wars. Thus began the royal practice of summoning prominent subjects to an assembly at which problems were discussed and consent given to the levying of taxes. While the monarch originally appointed his advisers and summoned to the legislature those of his own choosing, these prerogatives were subsequently restricted as subjects gained the right to choose those who sit in the legislature and the legislature the right to control the selection of those who would advise the sovereign (*privy councilors*).

It was on this foundation that the modern parliamentary system, characterized by a fusion of power and representative, responsible government, was built. The growth of democracy, by which the right to participate in selecting representatives (the *franchise*, or right to vote) was gradually extended to most of the adult population, did not change the substance of the system. When we talk of parliamentary supremacy then, we mean:

1. that there is no higher power in the land than Parliament (the legislature) acting lawfully (i.e., according to rules it has established for its own behavior)

2. that Parliament in this sense is the monarchy acting on the advice and with the consent of the elected representatives in the legislature

3. that no Parliament can bind or restrict the activities of any subsequent Parliament.

The Westminster Model

Institutional Elements

Elections and the Electorate

The electoral system is based on the representation of geographical areas rather than of population, which provides democratic legitimacy to Parliament but also reveals its pre-democratic origins. The country is divided into territorially based *constituencies*, each of which is entitled to elect one person to a seat in the legislature. To win a seat a candidate has to gain one more vote than any other candidate.

The Legislature as Lawmaker

For historical reasons, reflecting a distrust of the people but an inability to deny them representation, the legislature is *bicameral* (having two chambers or houses). The older, nonelected chamber is supplemented by an elected "lower" House, which gradually came to dominate. While both chambers are made up of individual members, activity tends to be dictated by a limited number of roles that reflect the historical struggle to wrestle control of power from the monarchy. Members came to be identified as supporters or opponents of the sovereign; thus the distinction among members who act as advisers to the sovereign (government *front benchers* or *ministers*), those who consistently support the activities of these advisers (government *backbenchers*), and those who consistently oppose these advisers (*the opposition*). This terminology also reflects the structure of the meeting place, where the groups are seated facing one another, and the adversarial nature of the parliamentary process.

The Legislature as Executive

A distinguishing feature of the Westminster system is that the political dimension of the executive function is carried out by members of the legislature (*ministers of the Crown*) within the principle of ministerial responsibility. Traditionally the monarch had delegated to selected individuals the day-to-day tasks involved in managing his personal and public domain, such as control of financial matters, the maintenance of the king's peace, and relations with foreign monarchs. While most of these activities continued to be carried out by appointed officials (*civil servants*), the practice developed of having one member of the legislature take charge of, and thereby become responsible for, the activities of these officials, structured within government departments. These ministers were simultaneously members of the government and of the legislature with both legislative and executive responsibilities. In the former role, they introduced legislative proposals concerning the activity of their department; in the latter role, they had the responsibility of supervising the implementation of these laws and policies. As part of the process of individual accountability, each minister appeared regularly in the legislative chamber to answer questions on this policy area and could face a vote of no-confidence if the members were not satisfied with the performance of his department.

When restrictions were imposed on the right of the sovereign to choose personally his or her own advisers, the practice of ministers interacting individually with the monarch also declined; royal advisers began to meet regularly together as the Privy Council. As governments became more active, individuals with similar policy interest or outlook chose to serve only if like-minded individuals were also appointed; the formation of the government assumed its collegial aspect. In the legislative context this meant that a vote of no-confidence directed at an individual minister could provoke the resignation of all ministers (*collective responsibility*). From this situation of executive responsibility assumed by a team of loosely connected individuals emerged the modern system of cabinet government: the party with the majority of seats in the legislature is invited to form the government, selects from within its own ranks individuals who will become ministers, and presents the monarchy with a list of candidates to approve. This cabinet monopolizes the powers of government for as long as it maintains the confidence (voting support) of the House.

A specific British historical circumstance (the inability of the earlier Hanoverian kings, who came from Germany, to speak the English of their subjects) produced a situation where one minister assumed responsibility for chairing council and cabinet meetings and, as cabinet and monarchy diverged, the added task of being a go-between: conveying to the monarch the views of the cabinet and to cabinet the views of the monarch. Until late in the eighteenth century it was asserted that this "prime" minister was no more than "first among equals," and the collective nature of the cabinet was stressed. When the position was combined with leadership of a modern political party, however, the individual attracted more public attention, and the *prime minister* assumed the status of chief executive and *head of government*.

A nonelected office—the *head of state*—was retained as the personal embodiment of the whole system. This is basically a symbolic position despite a residual political dimension. As head of state, the monarch fills an important cultural role; being above politics and increasingly held in high regard, monarchs provided continuity and unity to the system.

Administration

As the role of government increased, the number of individuals employed to implement policy grew and the task of administration became more specialized. From a position based on royal selection, or *patronage*, the management of policy implementation evolved into a complex, organized administrative structure. At first the only change was for royal patronage to give way to political patronage, as government ministers appointed friends, supporters, and relatives to paid government employment or sold administrative positions to the highest bidder. With a more extensive role in the affairs of the people and as the incompetence and corruption of the patronage-based appointments became unacceptable, a system whereby individuals obtained their position on merit became the norm. These reforms created a public service that was both professional (individuals expected to stay in the service throughout their working life) and permanent (employed during good behavior), but retained its politically subordinate status. The higher civil service existed to advise the political actors and to carry out their orders. They were expected to do so impartially (showing no preference for one party or another) and anonymously (not publicly associated with a policy or action) and consequently could not be held politically accountable for any action.

The prerogative powers of the monarchy to dispense justice were also limited, with the administration of justice passing into the hands of nonelected officials trained in law. To maintain impartiality, lawyers operated as a self-governing profession and the judiciary was appointed from among these practicing lawyers and on their advice. These judges were influential in the control of the court system in cooperation with the relevant departmental officials. The department was concerned with the legal form of statutory law and supervising the administration of the law. As the department was headed by a minister, the judicial process can be said to be politicized. This does not mean that the judiciary had an independent political role: its activities could all be subsumed under the heading of *adjudication*—the application of general laws to individual cases. In the course of hundreds of specific case decisions, judges could give the law a different meaning from that intended by Parliament, but any time the interpretation was seriously out of step with the intentions of the legislature Parliament could amend the relevant statute or pass a new one to reaffirm its view.

Operating Practices and Principles

Government and Opposition, or, Responsibility in an Era of Party Politics

The political system created was seen to be a vehicle by which voters could achieve the political ends they desired. If they wanted changes in the laws, or new laws, they had an efficient process by which to act. If, on the other hand, they wished to prevent change, to lower or refuse taxes, the same system could be used to prevent action. The views of the voters were expressed indirectly through periodic elections and through the central role of their elected representative within the process. The growth of political party organizations, first in the legislature (to increase effectiveness in lawmaking) and later in the constituencies (to ensure election or reelection), was not seen to undermine the parliamentary system. Rather it was believed that organization facilitated democratic control, for the voters were able to choose between alternative sets of ideas (*party platforms*). Thus the winning party (the one with the most seats in the legislature) was said to have a *mandate* (democratic legitimacy) for implementing its ideas. The system did lead to the virtual disappearance of the independent candidate (one without party affiliation) but not to the neglect of voter interests. Although elections had turned into contests between parties, they were a battle that had to be fought and won in individual constituencies, and therefore the popular view could always prevail over party interests where they diverged.

The role of the "official" opposition is one of the most distinctive features of the legislative process in the Westminster system. To allow democratic choice while at the same time protecting the stability of the system, the decision-making process maintained its adversarial or con-flictual nature, and the two sides became a mirror image of each other. The function of the opposition is not merely to oppose—to offer regu-lar and detailed criticism of all government proposals and activities. It also tries to present itself to the electorate as an alternative—a govern-ment in waiting—even to the extent of creating a "shadow" cabinet of subject-area spokespersons to confront the ministerial expertise of the government. Nevertheless, the growth of party politics is generally held to have restricted the ability of the legislature to hold the govern-ment to account. By definition, the opposition is a minority and there-fore lacks the numerical strength necessary to impose its will on the governing majority; it is restricted to drawing the attention of the elec-torate to the government actions and to persuading the electorate that opposition policy alternatives are more beneficial. By such actions the opposition attempts to ensure that it will win the next election. To defeat the government between elections it must persuade government backbenchers to act against their own front bench, a difficult though not impossible task.

It is one of the paradoxes of the Westminster model that a system which developed as a struggle to control the prerogative power of an absolute monarchy has ended up as a system in which the remnants of this prerogative power are believed to be the final safeguard of democ-racy. The head of state is expected to act on his or her own initiative (without a responsible adviser if necessary) to defend the interest of the people where the legislature fails to do so.

The ability to do so lies in those political acts that still require royal participation to be valid. The monarch calls and dissolves the legisla-ture and must sign any act of Parliament for it to become law. The monarch also invests the government with the seals of office, thus providing the cabinet with a legal status. On the basis of these func-tions, the monarch is held to have the responsibility of ensuring that the system will always have the capacity to get legislation authorized and to pay its bills. A government that is unable to do so will be dismissed, and if a replacement is not readily available within the existing legislature, the House can be dissolved and new elections called. Such an act is seen as preserving rather than undermining par-liamentary democracy. Normally a member of the legislature will be willing to advise the monarch so to act and accordingly will take the "political heat" if the action is unpopular. In the last resort the monarch would be expected to act independently to ensure that the people's view prevails over that of the elected representatives, if they should diverge.

Two Sides, Not Just Two Parties

It is often suggested in political science literature that the Westminster model exemplifies a two-party system, a view that is not completely accurate. The system does have the dual characteristic of government and opposition, and cooperation between groups or parties across the floor rarely occurs (except in periods of national emergency), but this does not preclude cooperation between parties on the same side of the House. It is also argued that only single-party government can ensure that the system works at maximum efficiency and according to the wishes of the people. In practice, while postelectoral coalitions between parties to form a government are rare, semi-permanent preelection coalitions are not uncommon. They have usually consisted of a dominant large party and a regionally based subordinate small party, but two small parties can forge a formal alliance to gain office. If these coalitions are publicly identified before the election, the rights of the voters are not impinged upon. The opposition can contain as many parties as the people choose to support, although only the largest of them will be designated the "official" opposition and be given the advantages in terms of parliamentary organization that accompany this status. While these parties may all work together to bring down the government, they are concerned to keep a reasonable distance from each other so as to enhance their own subsequent electoral chances. Situations have occurred in which a government is kept in office because a party in the opposition does not wish to improve the electoral position of a rival opposition party.

Federalism and the Westminster Model

The concentration of power in an efficient central government apparatus would appear to be incompatible with a *federal* structure, where *jurisdiction* (authority to enact and administer laws) is divided between two levels of government. Nevertheless, in Australia and Canada we have two examples of this combination, and we can therefore add a federal dimension to our Westminster model.

Within parliamentary systems the validity of the upper chamber of the legislature has tended to be undermined by its undemocratic nature, and the general tendency has been toward unicameralism. Even where bicameralism continues, upper chambers have declined to a subordinate role in which they can delay but not veto the actions of the lower House. Such is the case with the House of Lords in Britain. The change is justified with the argument that the popular House elected on the principle of "one person, one vote" should have a monopoly of legitimate power.

In a federal parliamentary system some modification of this pattern has been necessary. There traditionally the lower or "popular" House has been supplemented by a federal house or council of states representing the units (states or provinces) of the federation. Usually a distinctive electoral system is used for the federal chamber, which can differ from the lower House in the qualifications for membership, the franchise, the size of the constituency, and/or the length of the terms. The units of the federation are usually granted equal representation in the council of states irrespective of size, wealth, or population and have powers equal to those of the lower House. As a consequence some device for resolving conflict between the houses is required, either *joint sessions* (in which the interests of the numerically superior popular House will eventually prevail) or a *double dissolution* (which will force both houses to seek reelection and allow the people to decide).

Institutional Elements of an American Model of Parliamentary Government

Let us assume that a parliamentary system had been introduced into the United States after the American Revolution and in the same form as that described above, with only those modifications necessitated by the establishment of a republic to replace constitutional monarchy. Let us further assume that similar parliamentary systems were adopted by the individual American states as well as the national government.

The Location of Sovereignty

The break with the link to the monarchy would mean that the Crown could no longer be the legal embodiment of sovereignty. The obvious solution would be to transfer abstract sovereignty to the people while leaving the exercise of these powers to the parliamentary system and the rule of law.

Institutional Changes

Very little change would be necessary in the basic position and structure of the lower House of the legislature (the present House of Representatives), the electoral system, and the nonelected administrative elements. The thirteen colonies that had had a separate existence prior to the Revolution would form the basis of the federal system and would have insisted upon equal representation in the federal chamber. Because these states had different histories and social compositions, they would also have insisted on controlling the process by which their representatives were selected (as is the case in Switzerland).

Again the concern for states' rights and for stability might have encouraged the notion that a Council of States should have a longer term than the national House or even that it should have staggered elections—say, a third of the members being selected every two years, as the Senate in fact operates. But such devices would create difficulties for responsible government inasmuch as the will of the people expressed through state representatives would have lagged behind the will of the people expressed through national representatives. It is probable, therefore, that pressure would have developed for both houses to have similar limits to their term. The fact that an election can be called whenever a government resigns means that the houses would remain permanently coordinated.

The problem of institutionalizing the executive function in the American model would have been the main issue the framers faced, an issue that offers no easy solution. The problem lies not with the symbolic elements of the office but with those prerogative powers still retained by the head of state. It would not have been possible to transfer these powers to the people in the same way as the symbolic sovereignty had been transferred. In the post-Revolutionary period, suspicion of executive power was such that the constitution makers would not likely have allowed the cabinet to exercise the powers of the head of state. By opting for a republican system they ruled out any form of hereditary office. Direct election of the head of state by the people would have required a stronger commitment to popular democracy than existed at that time. It is likely, therefore, that the American parliamentary system would have introduced a head of state elected by the representatives of both houses.

To provide necessary continuity it is possible that the term of office of the head of state would have been longer than that of the legislature; this would be particularly important if the head of state were to retain the power to summon and dissolve parliament. On what grounds should we assume that this would be the case? There is no structural reason why the legislature might not have a fixed term (as in the Norwegian parliamentary system). What might have worried American constitution makers was a situation in which a fractious opposition could prevent the government from operating effectively while at the same time refusing to assume the responsibilities of office, thereby creating chaos or stalemate. The head of state would need the necessary tools to ensure that such a situation could not occur: power to dissolve parliament at least once between elections might suffice, especially if the maximum length of time any parliament could sit was fairly short, for example, three years.

Similarly, it seems unlikely the framers would have left it to the head of state to decide when a government had or did not have the confidence of parliament. This problem could be solved by requiring that a government resign if defeated on a specific vote of confidence. This would remove the possibility of a government propped in office by the head of state but lacking the support of the legislature.

The American parliamentary system would have been established before the development of disciplined parliamentary parties took the choice of who should govern out of the hands of the head of state. Assuming again that the framers would have been reluctant to entrust such a task to any single individual, it is likely that the legislature would also have been given the task of selecting the individuals who would assume ministerial office. The natural tendency to prefer to work with people who share one's attitudes and ideas and the need to give the collegiate or collective nature of the government real substance would have ensured the emergence of "slates" of candidates— and thus the first stage of the transformation to a party-based system. If the cabinet was to meet and operate as a collective body, then it would need a chair to handle the organizational problems. It is not necessary that any one individual assume this responsibility; the task could be rotated among the ministers or combined with one of the less-onerous *portfolios* (the offices and functions of ministers of state or members of the cabinet). However, we can assume that in the first decades of the American system the cabinet would have operated in its classic form, with the "prime" minister performing this merely coordinating role. The emergence of the prime minister as a leadership figure with the responsibility of head of government would await the development of the party system and changing attitudes toward the role of the government in society.

The Political Process

Political Culture and the Political Process

The way a political system works depends very much on what the people think about the system and its role in their lives. There exists in the United States a political culture, what Gunnar Myrdal termed an "American Creed," that is both "significantly different from that found elsewhere" and so widely shared and deeply held within the nation that it has taken on the characteristics of religious belief. Benjamin B. Ringer further notes that Myrdal was "convinced that Americans are almost universally conscious of the Creed and accept it as a valid and idealized normative standard and framework for the governance and treatment of people." This culture is not merely a product of "differences of geography and historical experience," claims David Mervin, but also of "constitutional arrangements and political institutions." According to Myrdal, the ideals and practices that constitute the creed were

> written into the Declaration of Independence, the preamble of the Constitution, the Bill of Rights . . . [and] have thus become the highest law of the land. The Supreme Court pays its reverence to these general principles when it declares what is constitutional and what is not. They have been elaborated upon by all national leaders, thinkers and statesmen.[3]

While we must therefore try to imagine how this creed might have influenced the way the parliamentary system worked in the United States, we cannot ignore the probability that the creed would have been influenced, in turn, by the existence of the parliamentary system. It helps to divide the creed into those elements that reflect a negative attitude toward government, and which therefore would be in direct conflict with the belief system associated with the Westminster model, and the more positive elements, which present less of a problem.

Negative Elements of the American Creed

There is a direct conflict between the principle of parliamentary supremacy and a suspicion of government, especially when political power is concentrated. The advocates of both alternatives have clothed self-interest in the garments of higher law. As M. J. C. Vile noted, "Like most of the men of wealth and property in the eighteenth century, the framers of the Federal constitution . . . were frightened by two spectres: autocratic and democratic. They wished to avoid the tyranny of one man or of many."[4] Similar views would have been found among the men who created the parliamentary system, but they would have disagreed on how best to solve the problem.

The authors of the U.S. Constitution were, as Mervin has pointed out,

> intent upon constructing political mechanisms that would allow for the essential minimum level of government without encroaching on their hard-won liberties. There was to be no all-powerful central state apparatus, and political leaders were to be given no blank cheques: on the contrary, they were to be hedged in by a complex, decentralized and fragmented system designed to prevent any one leader or group of leaders from becoming excessively powerful.[5]

By contrast, the advocates of parliamentary supremacy put their faith in their own control over the levers of power. Once the prerogative had been tamed and they had become the controlling force in Parliament they had nothing to fear from the one or the many. Thus both groups could be said to consider, as Vile puts it, "the nature of the constitution to be a vital factor in maintaining freedom and the rights of the individual, as well as ensuring order and stability in society." But only the constitutionalists believed that individual rights must be entrenched and protected by a judicial system raised to the status of a branch of government. Alexander Hamilton claimed that the judiciary was the "least dangerous" branch of government, but one may well ask why the framers were not more fearful of what is, after all, another type of arbitrary power. Vile has asked of the modern Supreme Court: "How is it that nine non-elected judges with life tenure can wield this power in the most election-conscious nation in the world?"[6] It is not enough to suggest that the framers did not foresee the phenomenal growth of government yet to come; it is necessary to emphasize that an enthusiasm for liberty and for democracy are not the same thing. The constitutionalists do not appear to have asked how government activity could be democratically controlled. They asked only, Is government activity really necessary? They denied the argument that only a vigilant democratic government can ensure liberty.

The battle between these differences of emphasis would not likely have been settled by the introduction of the parliamentary system and would have continued up to the present day. What would have been less likely, though, is the sanctification of the negative approach to government. Without the protection provided by institutionalization, the consensus would have been difficult to sustain. There was a contradiction between the socioeconomic openness of the new American society and the antidemocratic elements of the creed. The adversarial aspect of the parliamentary system demands competition and active expression of discontent: while those who control the levers of power might wish to suppress it, the opposition needs it to fuel their challenge. We would therefore expect that some of the most dominant negative characteristics of the creed would have been either less widely supported or not developed at all. Consider, for example, the idea, as Vile puts it, that

> there must be a minimum conformity enforced by the state, and yet it is conformity with a liberal ideal. No ideas can be tolerated that threaten the basis of that liberalism or that seem to introduce the germ of a divisive force into the community. Thus the tendencies towards a sharp polarization of ideas must be consciously resisted.

With a parliamentary system, it would not have been necessary to ask, as Robert B. Dishman has, "Surely, then, we have as much right to judge—and to criticize—the institutions by which we meet our social needs as the gadgets and machines by which we satisfy our physical wants?" Let us look briefly at an example to demonstrate the validity of Dishman's argument that "social institutions, given a favourable environment, gradually acquire a life and, in a sense, a will of their own." While the social and economic forces confronting any government tend to be worldwide, their form and impact are shaped by those social institutions.[7]

Under a parliamentary system of government, it is unlikely that Americans would be as suspicious of government as they are, even considering that many who came to the country did so to escape repressive regimes.[8] They could not have equated democratic government with the autocratic governments they left behind; it is far more likely that they would have seen in democracy an opportunity to improve their conditions. Certainly later migrants from Europe who went to countries with parliamentary systems like Australia, Canada, and New Zealand included many who saw the possibilities of government as well as those who feared government.

It is instructive to compare the negative attitude to government expressed in the creed by the constitutionalists to explanations of general inaction in the United States in the face of the Great Depression of the 1930s. James T. Patterson suggests that an important explanatory factor is the "lack of experience with or confidence in governmental answers to public problems," even among those who had most to gain from government activity. Labor leaders, for example, actively distrusted government, which had long sided with big business. Reformers, pointing to the lack of a well-trained and respected civil service, doubted the government could cope with large-scale problems. The poor, divided and isolated, could not imagine how government could help them. Other explanations emphasize lack of coherence among government programs and leaders, an uncertainty and dissonance among political institutions, and unwieldy procedures for decision making.[9]

It seems the antigovernment element of the creed was sustained by its institutionalization. Fearing the power of government, the founding elites set up a political system that would make any government difficult and coherent activity virtually impossible. Thus when activists tried to use the political machinery to introduce reforms, they inevitably failed. It proved equally impossible to control the machinery or to hold one officeholder to account for the failures—they were inherent in the system. Popular distrust or distaste for government activity was therefore justified and in turn came to reinforce and sustain the negative elements of the creed.

The Positive Elements of the American Creed

A parliamentary system would have made it possible for the U.S. government to act effectively and with relative efficiency. Those groups believing the machinery of democratic government can and should be used to redress both economic and social inequalities would have periodically succeeded in using the political structure to advance their ends. To the extent that they were successful, they would have further undermined suspicion of government. Of course, if they failed or if their efforts had been clumsy, they might have reinforced doubts about the virtues of government, but there is no reason failure would have been inevitable. The abundance of America's resources meant that reformers would be working in ideal circumstances.

The positive elements of the creed would have flourished in an American parliamentary system. Myrdal elaborated the positive elements as:

> the ideals of the essential dignity of individual human beings, of the fundamental equality of all men, and of certain inalienable rights to freedom, justice and a fair opportunity [which] represent to the American people the essential meaning of the nation's early struggle for independence.

No doubt individualism and freedom would be highly prized, but they would be challenged by other abstract goals, especially human dignity and equality. The awareness of human beings "created equal but everywhere unequal," as Henry Fairlie has summarized the dilemma, would have served to remind some Americans that the Declaration of Independence was not only about liberation from autocratic tyrants.[10] There is a positive side to liberty as well as a negative one. An important catalyst might well have been the democratic forces unleashed by the French Revolution. The elitists in a parliamentary system would have been less successful in holding the forces of democratization at bay; they could only fight a continuous rearguard action to restrain the progressive forces anxious to use political processes for equalitarian ends.

Democracy, in this sense, reflects a positive attitude toward the political. Stein Ringen has claimed that "to be democratic is to be 'optimistic' about the possibility of politics; that we have created this [democratic] state to use for our benefit." This positive view puts freedom and individualism in a different context. As individuals we are free to use the political machinery "to achieve things we want by acting together, instead of each individually relying on his or her own efforts." As individuals we accept restraint on our freedoms as long as we are confident that the process whereby these restraints are formulated and implemented is under our control: that we have "equal access to participation in the political process and equal power to influence it."[11] That is, as long as the method and means were legitimate, active government might well have been acceptable to the majority of the American population, even to those who would have preferred inaction.

Those individuals in the new nation who believed that giving substance to equality was important would have been able to create effective vehicles with which to "sell" these views to the electorate. The parliamentary system would not guarantee their success. Certainly in the days of the open frontier the conditions were such that any suggestion that achievement of equality needed anything more than absence of restraint might have lacked general appeal, but indentured laborers would have found it attractive. As industrialization increased, the workers in sweatshops and the residents of crowded urban ghettos would have provided more fertile ground for the idea. Defenders of the inevitability of negative government have not found it difficult to find statistics showing how much better off the poor in the United States are than the poor in other countries or how the material standard of living of the poor today is higher than that of yesterday's poor, but these academic comparisons have less relevance in practical politics. Voters tend to judge the system according to their expectations and their position relative to others within their immediate experience. There is considerable ambiguity in the rather grandiose ideas of "individualism" and of "human dignity" in the American Creed and the view commonly expressed in the 1930s that "relief should be given grudgingly, if at all, in order to discourage . . . [the undeserving poor] from malingering."[12] Activists would not have been slow in stressing these ambiguities to win political support to their party alternative.

The general acceptance in the American Creed of one specific ideology—liberal capitalism—would thus have been challenged, and ideology would have played a greater role in American politics. *Ideology* is here defined (by Vile) as a "system of thought in which a number of ideas about the nature of the political system and the role of govern-

ment are logically related to each other, and developed as a con-
sciously held guide to political action."[13] With a parliamentary system
of government it would have been difficult to prevent a sharp polarization
of ideas as rival parties battled for the right to form the government.

The Political Process

We will now consider the way in which beliefs, attitudes, and opinions
affect the will to act and the means available to deal with problems that
require a political solution. As Chapter 9 states, "Widely shared troubles do not automatically become national issues. For a problem to
reach the national political agenda, somebody has to define it, articulate it, measure it, and propose solutions." And Mervin reminds us that,
under a presidential system of government, "it is monumentally difficult to galvanize the American political system into action." At the
same time we should realize that the modern American political process is not a system in which elected individuals play a dominant role
in the articulation and aggregation of interests. It is widely acknowledged that the dominant force in the presidential system is the organized group and that the system is best described as pluralistic, that is,
as Vile explains, a system in which "large numbers [of groups], of
varying sizes and importance, [battle] . . . for their interests in a society
where no group dominates" and in which "politics is a continually
changing pattern of group activities and interactions."[14]

Would this situation have arisen under a parliamentary system?
Probably not, despite the fact that groups are also very active in contemporary parliamentary systems. Vile notes that "interest groups
thrive in the fragmentary character of the governmental system" and
"provide a co-ordinating link between the institutions" in a system
characterized by a separation of powers and checks and balances.[15] In
a parliamentary system of government this coordinating function is
provided in a more coherent way by the disciplined parliamentary
party, and the extension of these parties into extraparliamentary or
constituency-based parties makes them "purpose built" vehicles for the
aggregation of interests and the legitimizing of policy proposals.

The Development of Political Parties

One would expect the development of political parties in the American parliamentary system to have paralleled that of the Westminster model. For the nineteenth-century elite, individualism within the legislature would have given way to loose groupings and then to a situation in which a parliamentary group reached out into the constituencies, creating a party organization as a means for winning elections. A second type of development would reverse this process: groups working outside parliament would create a constituency-based party as a means of effectively influencing the policy-making process. This goal requires that the individual members of parliament accept party authority and vote accordingly. To the extent that voters know in advance that their representatives would be bound by party discipline and that the parties themselves are organized so that control flows from the grass roots (the constituency members) upward, this development is not necessarily undemocratic. A party, meeting in representative assembly, debates and votes on policy proposals so as to formulate a party platform. This platform would be submitted to the voters during an election campaign, so that a vote for a candidate endorsed by the party could be considered a vote for the policies advocated by the party. An electoral victory would be interpreted as a mandate to introduce the policies concerned, and these policies would be subjected to further scrutiny by the parliamentary representatives of the party (meeting as a caucus) and to public debate during the legislative process. The voters could continue to express their views on these matters through their members of parliament. If the governing party attempted to introduce a major policy measure that had not been raised during the election, it would be subject to considerable pressure to call an election so that the views of the electorate could be expressed. Much more usual is the situation in which the government, under pressure from caucus and the constituency organizations, chooses to modify or even drop the proposal completely.

What, then, would the American parliamentary party system have come to look like? Vile argues that American politics can be understood only if we remember the strength and influence of sectional, ethnic, and racial loyalties, which undermine the possibilities of class politics and reinforce individualism as the dominant philosophy.[16] But we have already noted that pluralism based mainly on occupational or socioeconomic groupings has been able to overcome these divisions and displace individualism, and we argue that with the fusion of powers that characterizes the parliamentary system, the coalescence of groups into parties would produce substantial political rewards.

Strong pressure for party politics would have come from those groups outside the founding and economically dominant elites. The first mass-based parties owed their origins to the frustrations that workers and their unions felt over their inability to achieve better wages and conditions through bargaining with owners and employers. Most European labor or worker parties were created to provide a better means of achieving these goals (and as such should be distinguished from the more elitist, ideologically focused socialist parties). Where these groups of blue-collar workers formed a substantial majority of the electorate, their views could not be ignored.

Some people are surprised to find that more than one-third of British working-class voters have traditionally supported the Conservative party, but there is a simple explanation. The Conservative party needed working-class constituencies to gain a parliamentary majority and was therefore forced to offer policies that went a long way toward meeting the practical needs of the workers, thus splitting them off from the more radical workers who supported a labor or socialist party. This approach to the lower classes may have been paternalistic, but it involved acceptance of the need for government intervention—government-sponsored programs—that benefited workers groups and thus helped maintain stability. The Conservatives could use their control over the levers of power to steal the more moderate policies of their opponents and thereby keep power and prevent more radical reforms. This strategy is a good example of the way in which the strength of the parliamentary system can be used to control rather than exercise power.

This technique is not restricted to class politics; agriculture offers another interesting example. In Britain, where large estates put land-ownership beyond the grasp of the agricultural laborers, and in Australia, where widespread use was made of itinerant workers, labor parties drew significant support in rural areas. In countries where land was relatively easily available and where small holdings and family farms were the norm, this group formed a natural constituency for conservative or liberal parties, or, if the agricultural sector was predominant, farmers often formed agrarian parties to protect their interests.

How would this process have developed in the United States? We might have found both situations operating, depending on where we looked. We would expect to find right-of-center agrarian parties operating in those states in the American heartland where agriculture was the mainstay of the state economy. Individual owners who supported minimalist government in principle would nevertheless have had an active interest in transport and marketing policies and might have supported proposals such as government-guaranteed loans for farm investment. Farmers in the less competitive areas might have supported a party that offered subsidies or protection from competitors. Those who felt that the family farm embodied the essence of the American Creed would have rallied to an agrarian party organized to defend this interest against cattle barons in the past or agribusiness in the present. The sharecroppers in the Deep South or the Oklahoma farmers in the Great Depression would seem to be a natural constituency for party activists who would encourage them to use the opportunities of the political process to improve their conditions. The ranch hands of the cattle country might have been too committed to the individualistic philosophy to respond to the call to organize, but they would have been the exception to the rule. The struggle for better wages for itinerant agricultural workers, a struggle that in recent years has produced confrontation and supermarket boycotts, would certainly have taken on a party political dimension. Given the extent of the United States and the diversity of its agricultural base, it is likely that these developments would have been clearest at the state level, but as the size of the agricultural sector declined in the face of urbanization and industrialization, farmers would have found that what they had in common could be more important than these differences, and some form of national party organization to represent their interests at the federal level might well have followed.

The separation of church and state that characterized the establishment of the independent nation reflected historical necessity. The English monarch as head of a state church had gone. Colonists who had moved to America to escape religious persecution would certainly have opposed any attempt to establish a new State church, but religion would not have ceased to be a relevant dimension of political life. In the absence of class, religion could well have been called into play to provide the coordinating factor that cut across sectionalism and ethnicity. Immigrants from different parts of Europe, settling in different parts of the country, might have been politically socialized by their church and could have used the formation of a political party as a means of establishing and defending church-supported policies—a church-based education system, for example, against those who wanted to establish a secular public education system. As the forces of secularization became more dominant and as the growth of Marxism as an ideology increased the sense of threat, Christian parties might have coalesced into Christian Democrat or Christian Social parties, parties that link individuals from all social strata in defense of a particular way of life. The contemporary growth of the Moral Majority and similar groups would have reinforced this trend.

Our examples so far are basically of pragmatic parties mobilizing people with a common interest to protect or to assert politically. As such they differ from organized groups only in their willingness to pursue and exercise public office. Would we have also found ideological parties in the American parliamentary system? The ideological party could have been the catalyst for the whole process. The argument that there is no class in America and therefore no basis for ideological parties is only partially valid. Class in the sense of hereditary privilege and rigid social strata was largely absent and, where present, relatively easily destroyed by the upward mobility possible in a frontier society. Nevertheless, there were landowners and laborers, entrepreneurs and workers, rich and poor in nineteenth-century America as much as anywhere else, and consequently the environment existed to support this type of party system. The appeal would have been greatest to the trade unionists struggling to improve the conditions of workers in the face of an open immigration policy and in the urban and industrial areas. It would have been relatively simple for them to follow the European lead and create a labor party to be the political arm of the trade union movement. With this type of financial and membership support, such a party could well have been expected to make a strong electoral showing in industrialized and urban areas of the United States. Had it been strong enough to win a majority of seats, such a party could have used the machinery of government to achieve benefits and security for workers. Even if it had not secured a majority of seats in the legislature—and this is quite likely at the federal level because the electoral system tends to favor rural areas—its presence on the political scene as a visible and effective opposition, and its potential as a coalition partner, could have influenced policy making in a number of areas of domestic policy.

The Structure of Political Parties

What would the American party system have looked like at the end of all these developments? One would expect the federal parties to have become associations of state parties and regional groupings to have emerged where sectional interests were the dominant factor. It is probable that the parliamentary systems at the state level would have maintained the two-party dominance characteristic of the Westminster model. We might also find, especially in rural areas or the smaller states, that one-party dominance would develop, reflecting the homogeneity of the population. At the federal level though, and possibly in the larger or more diversified states, a multiparty system would seem most likely. This development would have had two further consequences: first, a need to modify the conflictual elements and develop a higher degree of cooperation, possibly even a situation where coalition government became the norm; and, second, demands for a change to the electoral system to produce a closer relationship between popular vote and the distribution of seats in the legislature. This move to proportional representation would also have been demanded by the larger cities, which would remain underrepresented in the national legislature without a change in the electoral system. The combination of these changes would have ensured that the multiplicity of parties did not constitute a threat to national unity or the continued existence of the country.

The Machinery of Government

We would expect that during two centuries of practice, in the various states and at the national level, the American parliamentary system would have developed a wide variety of adaptations to the structures and processes of government. Obviously there is only room to explore a few of the possibilities here, so we will concentrate on those which offer the greatest contrast with the existing presidential model.

The Head of State

One cannot imagine there having been any serious opposition to George Washington as the first president in a parliamentary system. His lack of political ambition, his "national" profile, and his role in the War of Independence guaranteed not only that he would be offered the office but that he would establish a good model for his successors. It is unlikely, though, that many other individuals who actually became American presidents would have been content to follow in his footsteps; perhaps only the other military men like Ulysses S. Grant and Dwight Eisenhower. Where else might the American people have looked for a personal symbol of popular sovereignty? The earlier years would have been more difficult. Frontier heroes such as Daniel Boone and Davy Crockett would have seemed too flamboyant, explorers such as Meriwether Lewis and William Clark too little known, lawyers and clergy too dull. Because of long distances and poor communications it would have been difficult for individuals to gain a national reputation even among the politicians who would decide the election.

In the twentieth century the problem would be reversed. Some parliamentary systems have used the head-of-state role to express the importance of minorities in their national identities: we could imagine a situation in which Martin Luther King, Jr., could have been president. Would former movie stars such as Shirley Temple Black or Ronald Reagan have been tempted to abandon practical politics in favor of prestige? In the euphoria over the space program success, John Glenn or another prominent astronaut might have accepted the honor. Would it be too far-fetched to imagine a Roosevelt or Kennedy dynasty with the office passing from one family member to another? Because of the limited power of the office, there would be little to fear from a semi-hereditary succession. Much would depend on how important a role the president would play in the formation of the government.

The Legislative-Executive

The growth of political parties brought a new and important actor onto the parliamentary stage—the party leader. Originally chosen to be the party's main spokesperson and agent in coordinating the work of the legislature, the leader became an important figure in his own right. The president, in carrying out the responsibility of ensuring there would be a government that had the confidence of the legislature, would have to discuss the alternatives with the party leaders who, in turn, would have had more say in the membership of the cabinet. In the democratically oriented parties, the party conference or caucus would have insisted on the right to elect the ministers, but the more elitist parties would have allowed their leader to name his own team.

In practice, regardless of the circumstances, the choice would have been strongly influenced by objective factors. There would have been strong pressures for a cabinet that not only represented all major geographical regions but also reflected ethnic, racial, and religious diversity. We would have seen great rivalry between the frontier states and the eastern establishment, and a government in which New York had more representatives than California and Texas would face serious electoral consequences. We would also expect to find certain groups and regions anxious not only to be represented in the cabinet but also to control policy areas they felt to be crucial to their welfare—for example the agricultural portfolio to the Midwest, forestry and fisheries to New England or the Northwest. Could you imagine the reaction of Texas voters if an energy portfolio was created without a Texan at its head? Such pressures would lead inevitably to an increase in the size of cabinet,[17] an increase that could become dysfunctional in terms of cabinet's capacity to operate effectively as a collective decision-making body.

It is likely that in the early years of the Republic, ministers would have been drawn from the landowners and the professions. By the late nineteenth century, however, we would expect the cabinet to reflect the occupational diversity of the nation. A variety of factors could decide which specific individuals make it to the cabinet. Some would force themselves in by sheer weight of their personality, others by family influence or professional prominence, but the great majority would climb to office via the party ladder. All would have had long years of service in state or national legislatures; many would have been ministers at the state level. In the mid-twentieth century the growth of the media has offered individuals greater opportunity to gain national attention, and as government becomes more complex we have seen more "prominent" outsiders joining the cabinet. The cabinet established by George Bush during his first year in office is the closest any modern American cabinet has come to having a parliamentary style in that it is formed mainly of individuals with political experience.

Of course in an American parliamentary system they would all, including George Bush, still be members of the legislature. The trend toward appointing outsiders would not have affected the principle of responsible government, which required every member of the cabinet to participate regularly in the work of the legislature and to be available on a daily basis to answer questions concerning the activity or inactivity of the department. These individuals would have had to find a constituency either during a general election or at a by-election created specifically for that purpose. No individual, no matter how well connected or expert, could stay in the cabinet if he or she failed to win a seat.

The Legislative Process

Once selected, working in cooperation with senior department public servants, the cabinet team monopolizes the preparation of draft legislation (*bills*). They meet as a group on a weekly basis to approve the specific form in which party policy is to be transformed into public policy. Each individual minister is then responsible for having his or her department prepare the necessary legislation or regulation and for presenting and defending it in the legislature.

The whole emphasis is on a cohesive, rational, and coherent policy-making process, as can be seen if we consider how Prime Ministers Reagan or Bush might have handled the budget-making process in the parliamentary system. Elected to office on a platform promising reduction of the deficit and tax cuts, the prime minister would so far as possible have placed into the key portfolios individuals who were strongly committed to this financial strategy. The cabinet as a whole would have discussed in detail the areas where cuts were to be made, and the minister of finance would also have described where he would make the necessary tax cuts while still raising sufficient revenue to meet the government's commitments. While the actual details would have been worked out by the public servants, members of parliament in private discussions with ministers and in caucus would also have had an input. The process culminates in the preparing of the budget that is presented to the legislature for approval. A revenue budget, which is optional, would have been necessary because the Reagan government wanted to make changes in the existing tax structure. The defense of the proposed changes in the debate that follows the budget speech would involve a number of cabinet ministers. A government unable to get legislative approval for these changes would be forced to resign. In a similar fashion, the whole of the government spending plans—department by department and program by program—is presented for legislative approval in the expenditure budget. For the Reagan government, this would have meant explaining and defending all the specific policy cutbacks made necessary by the tax cuts and justifying continued spending on defense.

It is unlikely that the U.S. federal cabinets would ever have achieved the same degree of central control or dominance that has characterized the British experience. Cohesion is more difficult in a federal system where regional loyalties challenge party loyalties, and the large number of units in the American federation, as well as the size of the population, would have made control precarious. However, our description would be accurate for most of the state governments.

Obviously the position and activities of the ordinary member of parliament would in these circumstances be very different from that of the member of Congress. In particular we would stress that the notion of "responsible government" inhibits legislative activity. As Vile notes:

> Members of Congress . . . enjoy great powers without responsibilities . . . [the system] allows them to wallow in carping criticism and to engage in other negative tactics free from the anxiety of ever having to shoulder the responsibility of government. . . . [In the Westminster system, the opposition] are guided by their own previous experience in the various ministries and their expectation that one day they themselves may have to administer the policies now under debate.[18]

Getting a bill through the legislature does not involve "wheeling and dealing" with individual members. The government House leader has the job of seeing that there are enough of the party's members present in the chamber to get the bill approved, but he or she will not have to be concerned about how they will vote. All the legislation due to be voted on will have been discussed in the weekly caucus meeting. A member who disagrees personally with the policy might be allowed to abstain from voting, as long as abstention does not endanger the majority. Only if the matter were one in which there was strong and united constituency opposition to the specific issue could a legislator vote against the party without penalty.

This does not mean that ordinary backbenchers are reduced to the status of mere ciphers. The point of the legislative debate is to draw the attention of the public to the weakness of the government's proposals and to demonstrate clearly why the opposition believes it should form the next government. Because the public expects the legislative process to be rational and coherent, less moderate behavior could rebound on the opposition. In any policy area the legislature would normally consider only a single bill or related package of bills. Amendments could be offered to the bill at any stage in the process, but no one would expect a separate bill of the same subject to be introduced: legislative time is a relatively scarce commodity. The bill would also go through both houses in the same form and in sequence.

In the parliamentary system the executive is dominant only if the legislature wants it this way, and this in turn depends on the attitudes of the electorate. If the electorate wants an efficient government, and this seems to be a major concern of the American taxpayer, then the parliamentary system makes it a possibility. The final link in this chain of efficiency is that between the legislative/executive and the administrative process. Because the bill that will establish the framework for policy delivery has been drafted by the department that will implement it, coherence is inherent in the process. The procedures for implementation and potential difficulties will have been considered prior to legislation. Where necessary, affected communities and groups will have been consulted and their concerns addressed. Of course nothing ever works to perfection, but the possibility exists to a higher degree in the parliamentary system. Maximum efficiency requires a concerned and active electorate that will keep the elected representatives in the legislature on their toes and the executive under control. Just such an electorate already exists in the United States but has been frustrated by a political structure that could be neither used effectively nor controlled.

Federal Influences

At the national level the most significant structure would be the Council of States. While this chamber would not rival the present U.S. Senate in its power and prominence, it would have played an influential role in an American parliamentary system. In particular, it could have ensured that the national government was not as powerful as the various state governments. Because it was a representative elected body, the council would not have been completely dominated by the lower House in the way that the British House of Lords and the Canadian Senate (both appointed bodies) have been. It is also likely that because of the large number of units in the federation and the strength of regional loyalties, it would not have been divided strictly on party lines as happened to the Australian

Senate: there the same parties dominate in both houses and the MPs and senators meet in a joint caucus to establish party strategy. We would anticipate that in the United States there would have been a greater number of parties at all levels and that different party coalitions would have come to exist at the state and federal levels (as is the case in Germany and Switzerland). Thus America might have been the first Westminster-style parliamentary system to attempt to hold a government responsible to two houses. It is very likely that a distinction would have been necessary between matters entirely within the federal jurisdiction, where the Council of States could only delay legislation and would not provide the basis for a motion of no-confidence, and matters of concurrent jurisdiction in which the federal government was operating along the jurisdictional margins; then the council would be able to defend the interests of the states by defeating a government.

The second major development would have been the growth of intergovernmental relations, mainly in the form of interministerial and first ministers' conferences. The strength and timing of this development would have depended on development in the Council of States. If this institution failed to protect state interests from the actions of a majority-dominated lower House, then we would expect intergovernmental conferences to have emerged to remedy the deficiency. In all probability the necessity would not have arisen as long as the federal government kept a low profile on the domestic policy field. If, however, as happened in Australia and Canada, the federal government assumed the responsibility for redistributing income between the richer and poorer states, we would have found intergovernmental relations flourishing.

The development of this new policy structure could also have produced pressure to redraw state boundaries so as to create a smaller number of more effective units—effective in the sense of being able to resist or repulse efforts to increase federal intrusion on domestic policy. Thus under a parliamentary system we could foresee a federation of twenty units rather than fifty. The drive for these boundary changes would have been supported by those parties that would have been stronger in the larger unit and opposed by those which would be weaker. Twenty strong state governments would have proved very effective vehicles for defending states' rights and for keeping the American system comparatively decentralized.

Public Policy

Minority Rights

The preference for the protection of democracy through the electoral process also extends to the question of human and minority rights. Would an America with a parliamentary system have been as concerned with rights? Would the condition of minorities have been improved, worsened or unchanged by these circumstances? As we have indicated, the presidential system protects liberty by limiting the power of government. By creating a system in which all action is difficult, the framers hoped to minimize any restraint on the freedom of individuals. More liberty was seen to be a direct consequence of less government. With the addition of the Bill of Rights, the presidential system established the machinery for the strong protection of a limited number of rights. In keeping with the individualistic element of the American Creed, there is no collective machinery for delivering the benefits that the Constitution provided. Each individual is expected to spend his or her own time, money, and effort to secure these rights in daily life. The courts provide the arena for this battle, but for the system to work each individual needs an adequate knowledge of how the system works and equal access to the system—conditions that seldom exist in practice.

The Westminster system approached the same question from a perspective in which anything is allowed that has not been made illegal by an act of Parliament. Rights or liberties are thus drawn very widely but rest for their protection upon the exercise of restraint by the majority. There is no reason why rights should be less well protected in a parliamentary system; however, it is an effective vehicle for intervention and could be used to restrict rights where circumstance or public opinion favors such an action. We must, however, balance our fear of such a situation with the recognition of the fact that the system also allows swift and effective action to protect or extend rights. If legislation is introduced to achieve this end, the remedy will apply to everyone in the category concerned and not just the individuals who bring a specific case to court. Further, the same government that introduces the legislation also controls implementation and is in a better position to see that changes are made.

The question of whether this legislative protection of minority rights is effective was discussed extensively in Canada when the federal government introduced a limited Bill of Rights (applying only to the federal level of jurisdiction) in 1960. It was raised again in the 1980s when another federal government succeeded in winning the consent of the provincial governments to the entrenchment of a Charter of Rights and Freedoms in the revised Canadian Constitution.[19] The reformers conceded that the parliamentary system had had a good record of protecting rights in homogeneous societies, but they were less confident that the system could act as effectively in heterogeneous societies. The argument is based on the possibility of a majority monopolizing government institutions and using them to protect its own interests and hence discriminate against minorities.

The parliamentary solution does not presume that people are motivated by lofty ideals, although it does provide an opportunity for those who are idealists to take a lead. It responds also to pragmatism and self-interest and to concern for the disorder that overt discrimination creates in a democracy. Any combination of these motives can lead to a situation in which a majority party is prepared to introduce legislation to protect the rights of disadvantaged groups and to set up the machinery to enforce it. In most Westminster model countries human rights codes have been passed and human rights commissions (staffed by bureaucrats and exercising quasi-judicial powers) established to enforce these codes. The code and commission approach has the virtue that it seeks to eliminate the problem through education and conciliation and not merely to punish offenders.

It is noticeable that in assessing the advantages of judicial review (Chapter 6) over parliamentary supremacy in the area of rights there is a tendency to exaggerate both the virtues of each approach and the supposed differences in effectiveness between them. With regard to the latter it is instructive to observe that citizens of Japanese origin were deprived of their civil rights and liberties in both the United States and Canada during World War II, despite the existence of an entrenched Bill of Rights in the former and its absence in the latter. While we can perhaps dismiss this example as atypical, because it happened in wartime, it is not an isolated case. A look at the record suggests that until the 1930s, the U.S. Supreme Court was equally unsuccessful in protecting the rights of non-Protestants, religious minorities, blacks, women, Native Americans, or trade unionists. The decisions handed down by the Court in cases in which rights issues were raised were, until the early 1960s, notable for restricting the equality guaranteed by the Constitution. Alan Westin suggested that "in its record between the late eighteenth century and 1937 the Supreme Court demonstrated a greater willingness to protect the interests of property holders, slave owners, big business and similar conservative groups in their defence of private property and free enterprise." The fact that after 1937, and especially in the 1960s, the courts began to issue decisions which benefited blacks, religious minorities, political dissenters, women, consumers, and environmental groups, should not blind us to its earlier record. If anything, the history of the U.S. Supreme Court reveals that social change tends to precede judicial change.[20]

Enfranchisement of the Black Minority

The introduction of the parliamentary system would in no way have altered the commitment of the American people to what Myrdal describes as the "ideals of the essential dignity of the individual human being, of the fundamental equality of all men, and of certain inalienable rights to freedom, justice and a fair opportunity." The fact that such ideals were expressed in broad general terms meant that the more progressive elements in society would be able to work within the framework of this belief system to radically transform the position of the black minority. Such a transformation would not have required an environment in which the majority of white people throughout the United States accepted the equality of American blacks. It only required a situation in which the smaller minority, who actively and violently opposed the reforms, were isolated from the silent majority who may have believed nonwhites to be inferior but would have rallied to support the American Creed in a head-on confrontation. Myrdal points out that the devices that the southern states used to deprive blacks of their constitutional rights by indirect means reflected an awareness that "the white man . . . does not have the moral stamina to make the Negro's subjugation legal and approved by society. Against this stands not only the Constitution, which could be changed, but also the American Creed, which is firmly rooted in the American hearts."[21]

Clearly the rulings of the Supreme Court in rights cases testing the Fourteenth and Fifteenth amendments played a major role in the disfranchisement of the blacks, but it does not follow automatically that in the absence of an activist court the legislators in the southern states would have taken more overt and drastic measures. It does not matter that, even in the aftermath of the Civil War, the majority of the white population did not accept or welcome blacks as equals. What does matter was that in a number of states blacks could vote on an equal basis with whites.[22] We would expect the legislature in the parliamentary system to have played a role similar to that of the Congress, which during Reconstruction took the lead in ensuring that the blacks in Southern states were given their civil rights.

We must therefore begin our policy fantasy in the Reconstruction period. Rather than a conflict between a president and Congress, such as characterized actual events, we would have seen a confrontation in the national parliament between the majority party government of the Radical Republicans and the opposition party of President Andrew Johnson, which was supported by the Democrats. In its enthusiasm for a harsh reconstruction for the South, the government would have granted to the southern blacks the full franchise at state and at national level. This development would have made it increasingly difficult for northern and new states to avoid enfranchising their own blacks. In an effort to prevent the southern states undoing these reforms, parliament might even have initiated a constitutional reform along the lines of the Fifteenth Amendment (proposed in 1869). In any event, legislation similar to this amendment would have given the franchise—de facto—to all black men who did not have the right to vote in 1869.

We can assume that the debate would have been complex as each side sought to find a way to present the issue that would call forth the greatest degree of public support. The Johnsonian party would have appealed both to the minority who responded to the accusations that the reforms were intended to create black domination in the South and to the larger group that could be reached by an appeal to states' rights. As president, Andrew Johnson provoked a constitutional crisis; as leader of the opposition he would not have been able to veto the proposals or even force them to be watered down. Without the barriers of the presidential system, the proposals of the Radical Republicans could not have been stopped, although they might have been reversed if the Johnsonians had won a subsequent election. As this did not happen, we can assume that the reformers would have continued their efforts and that the substance of the Reconstruction Acts of 1867 and the Civil Rights Acts of 1866 and 1875 would have become law, albeit in a different form.

We cannot presume that this reforming impetus would have continued even without the intervention of the Supreme Court. What we do know is that the way would have been open for blacks and reformers to use the party system and parliament to develop new rights and to protect the rights they already possessed. In the decades that followed this process could have involved fighting a rearguard action to maintain their status against those who would have turned back the clock. It could also have been an opportunity for further progressive legislation, so that by the turn of the century civil equality, if not economic and social equality, could have been a fact.

The key to subsequent development must be sought in the party system. Although blacks were never likely to be a majority nationally, they did constitute a sizable minority in a number of states in the immediate postwar period even if they lacked the means to dominate.[23] Their voting power would only be effective in alliance with elements of the white community. A parliamentary system of government would have provided these coalitions with an opportunity to limit the activities of the Ku Klux Klan and similar organizations through legislative control of the machinery of law enforcement and to restrict the violence that spread throughout the South and undermined the reform movement. While the federal government might have been restrained from further direct intervention because of concern over states' rights, the political party would have provided a direct and less public channel for exerting pressure on their state counterparts. To the extent that activities toward disfranchising blacks at the state level would win or lose votes for the party elsewhere, we would expect internal party pressure to be exerted to prevent it. In an attempt to weaken some of the opposition, reformers might have turned their attention to the less controversial aspects of minority rights, concentrating, for example, on improving the quality of separate educational facilities rather than aiming directly at desegregation.

Ringer suggests that "the most natural alliance would seem to have been with the poor whites, whose own poverty, illiteracy, and powerlessness generally matched that of the blacks."[24] In a capitalist system, however, these two groups were rivals rather than natural allies. The jobs and earnings of the poor whites were threatened by a new wage-earning black population when more workers meant cheap labor. The only chance of an alliance between blacks and poor whites would have been in a system where a strong trade union movement or a labor party was active in the defense of workers' conditions and wages. An alter-

native alliance could have formed among blacks, reforming northerners, and the new business interests trying to establish themselves in
the South. Even the paternalistic alliance that did emerge for a while
between some of the old plantation owners and former slaves would
have had a certain naturalness to it. The important thing is that there
were a number of white groups in the South that could have used the
support of blacks to establish or protect their own interests and would
have had to make concessions to blacks to achieve this end. If these
groups had all ignored black voters, the way would have been open for
formation of a black party that could win enough seats in the legislature to hold the balance of power. In this position blacks would be able
to extract further concessions in exchange for keeping one of the white
parties in office. White parties would then find it more politically
advantageous to absorb blacks into their own party. The parliamentary
system would, in these circumstances, tend to reward the moderates
and marginalize the extremists. Of course, all these developments depended on blacks continuing to be able to vote. Without a vote, and
without a Supreme Court to limit the actions of the extremists, blacks
would probably have ended up in the same dependent and subordinate
position as the Native Americans. With the vote, it would have been
difficult to keep them in a subordinate position. In a local government
election or in a single district in a state or federal election, black
candidates would have won representative status and thus exerted pressures and traded favors, keeping the issue alive until the tide of world
opinion moved decisively toward minority rights. Instead of a brief
period of progress followed by a hundred years of discrimination and
suppression, we would have seen movement, even growth, throughout
the whole period.

Whatever the degree of success in the nineteenth century, the black
minority would have had a completely different position by the beginning of the twentieth century. Any movements formed to improve the
socioeconomic position of the blacks would have focused on reforming the system from within, using the party machinery and the vote
rather than the courts and the streets. Groups such as the National
Association for the Advancement of Colored People (NAACP), the
Montgomery Improvement Association, or the Southern Christian
Leadership Conference might all have developed to confront specific
incidents of discrimination or disadvantage. They would also have
formed links with and given support to political parties. If the main

political parties had neglected to promote further advancement for minorities, an umbrella party could have been created and financed by these groups to deal with the problems in a more comprehensive way. Alternatively, separate links might have developed between occupational groups such as the Brotherhood of Sleeping Car Porters and the American Labor party.

The spearhead of the movement to give blacks a higher political profile would have come at the national and local level. In the rural areas of the South and the big conurbations of the Northeast, the concentration of black voters would have created a situation in which black candidates would have won mayoralty elections and had considerable success in the whole range of elected positions at the local government level. Repeating this success at the national level would have been difficult but not impossible. We would anticipate that in constituencies where the vote of the black population was significant, all the major parties would run black candidates, thereby ensuring an important black presence in the lower House of the legislature. On the other hand, blacks would have had much less success in elections for the Council of States. The size of the electorate would have removed the advantages of population concentration[25] and worked to the disadvantage of the minority.

How might the careers of black activists such as A. Philip Randolph and Martin Luther King Jr. have developed in these circumstances? It is not hard to imagine Randolph, from his position as president of the Brotherhood of Sleeping Car Porters, becoming a leading figure in developing a black section within the trade union movement. From here it is a short step into Labor party politics, if not a career in the legislature. Dr. King's career would have been even more spectacular. His middle-class background and education would have made him an attractive candidate to mainstream parties as well as black parties. He would have been an effective political leader gaining for his people by the legislative route benefits that could only be dreamed of during protest and civil disobedience.[26]

So far our fantasy has considered the efforts of a minority to gain recognition and equality in an environment in which they were always dependent for success on the goodwill of a proportion of the white population. There is an alternative scenario in a system where the parliamentary government operates in association with federalism. In these circumstances the black minority could have used the strategy that has worked for some French-speaking Canadians, a strategy based on establishing areas in which they would form a majority at the state level. Rather than a movement away from the Deep South, we might have seen extensive black migration into areas like South Carolina, Mississippi, and Louisiana, where the potential existed for achieving a majority. In these conditions we would have seen a number of black parties competing with each other to form the government. With the levers of power in their hands, blacks could develop socially and economically along lines of their own choosing. Given the lack of resources, these states might have lagged behind neighboring states, but the black population would have gained in terms of human dignity and self-reliance.

There is no need to assume that these states would have remained disadvantaged. It is probable that the federal government would have seen moral or political advantage in providing financial aid to these state governments. This assistance could have been provided directly through fiscal transfers or indirectly through providing tax advantages to those in the private sector who could finance investment. Federal loans could have helped subsidize improvements in education and skills development. Why would the federal government have acted in this way? The direct political advantages would have been small, and given the large number of states in the United States, these black states would not have carried much weight at intergovernmental conferences. If we accept however, that Americans do actually support the positive aspects of the American Creed, then many federal politicians could have supported this development as exemplifying the American Dream unfolding as it should. Other state governments might have seen practical advantages in encouraging this development as an alternative to more extensive reforms within their own jurisdictions. In both these arenas, individuals would have been concerned for national stability and interested in any development that would diffuse the tensions of the racial situation.

What grounds have we for such an optimistic view of developments? Our first ground for hope was the incongruity between the American Creed and the minority situation. The second leg of the argument emphasizes the dysfunctional role of the Supreme Court. In the parliamentary system a court that challenged the decisions of a majority government would provoke a political controversy which could be settled only by a constitutional reform restricting the powers of the courts. Third, at various times in the century in which American blacks were denied their constitutional rights, president, Congress and the Court tried to so something to change the situation. On each occasion they were frustrated by the checking power of the other branches. This situation would not arise in our parliamentary America. If we consider how much was achieved with everything in the political system working against the change, there can be no doubt that, with a system which facilitated change, the position of minorities would have been improved.

The Welfare State

Our fantasy in this section concerns the interaction of disciplined parties, the parliamentary machinery, and the decentralized federal framework in the specific circumstances of the welfare state. (See Chapter 9.) Our scenario is based on the assumption that American parties would not have been restricted to blindly duplicating the solutions developed in the class-based conditions of Western Europe. Our parties will draw on the American Creed to work out their own distinctive solutions to problems of industrialization, solutions that reflect the greater potential of the New World and a stronger commitment to the market economy. We would find neither a "liberal" consensus in a system of weak parties nor a two-party system dominated by a sharp ideological polarization. Instead, the Americanized parliamentary system would present in adversarial relationship, two opposing perspectives on the possibilities of politics. Each view would be reflected by one strong party, with smaller parties advocating the more extreme form of the position. Complete polarization would be prevented by the existence of nonideological parties able to attract electoral support away from either side. Because of the size and complexity of the American nation, there would be a variety of government-forming party combinations depending on the economic conditions. The contrast would be stronger and tensions greater in those states where mining, heavy industry, and manufacturing coexisted with agriculture and a service sector, where strong urban centers were balanced by powerful rural constituencies—for example, New Jersey, New York, Pennsylvania, Ohio, Illinois, and Michigan. Because of the federal division of powers and the strength of localism, we would expect the early attempts to deal with the problems created by industrialization and uneven development to be sought at the local or state level. At the same time party links between the state and federal levels would encourage attempts to seek national solutions where local efforts proved inadequate or impossible.

We can look first at party development within the anti-interventionist side. Here we would find those who place their faith in economics and disparage political parties which share the belief that "if we were only free individually to pursue our own good, we would together inadvertently . . . advance our common good," as Ringen puts it. Included would be smaller parties that denied the legitimacy of the notion of "economic policy" and would restrict the role of the government to external relations, defense, and law and order. The core would accept a limited role for the state in economic matters, including, says Ringen, "protecting the market against monopolization and . . . [balancing] market imperfections."[27]

The key party in the pro-interventionist camp would be the socialist party with a small communist party on its extreme left. These groups, suggests Ringen, "instead of setting their trust in the invisible hand of the market . . . advocated the method of politics, whereby central planning is used for coordination of economic activity and far-reaching authority to regulate markets and redistribute income is entrusted to the state."[28] Since neither group would likely win a majority of seats in the legislature, nor would they be able to work together, the way would be open for the growth of more moderate parties that could bridge the ideological gap, enter into coalitions with either side, and thereby dominate the government formation process.

Religious parties form obvious center parties because they draw support from all regions, occupations, and economic groups. They are pro-interventionist to the extent that they favor social policies that address the basic needs of the people but anti-interventionist in their opposition to the growth of a public bureaucracy to deliver these benefits. Their commitment to policy delivery through church and voluntary organizations would provide natural links to the other center parties, the agrarian and small business parties. In those states where religion failed to play this pivotal role, we would expect the social democratic party to fill the gap.

The diversity of the American population and varied economic development, even in the smaller states, would have created great pressure for compromise as the struggle for electoral support forced parties to broaden their position to attract support away from their rivals. The first "political" efforts would have produced legislation to improve conditions in the workplace: legislation setting health and safety standards, limits to age and hours of employment, and minimum wage levels. Why would this type of legislation have been possible in the nineteenth and early twentieth century with a parliamentary government when it was not possible in the presidential system? Two factors point to the essential difference: restrictions on court action, and the better representation of the interests of labor.

We have noted above the prominent role the judicial branch played in protecting the rights of property against efforts to improve the working coalitions of the people. Both Vile and Patterson have noted the ability of elite groups to block in the courts legislation that they could not prevent in the legislature.[29] Of equal importance is the fact that even without a trade union–based labor party government, workers would have been influential in the American parliamentary parties. They would have been effectively represented in the religious, agrarian, and social-democratic parties, forcing the liberal and center parties to at least appeal to the non-unionized and craft workers. All parties would have actively sought the support of the growing body of white-collar workers in the service industries.

What is to prevent the losers in this contest from voting with their feet? We highlight here the difficulties reformers face in trying to improve working conditions at the state level in a federal system. A state government seen to be creating an environment harsh on entrepreneurs and investors would face a movement of money and jobs out of the state. Further, efforts to improve the conditions of the workers could be undermined by an immigration policy that fed a constant flow of cheap labor into the workplace. Under these circumstances, state governments concerned might attempt to use the intergovernmental relations machinery to establish voluntary common minimum standards. Where this failed, they might put pressure on their state representatives in the national legislature or on members of their political party in other states to fill the gap and could even resort to a constitutional amendment if the matter were outside federal jurisdiction. Because the pressure for the change would come from the state level, these reforms would not be opposed on the ground that they undermined states' rights. The situation most likely to have provoked this change in attitude was the economic convulsion of the Great Depression: it highlighted both the inability and the unwillingness of the private sector to cope and helped legitimize, at least in principle, the political alternative, even as it created economic circumstances in which the government would be heavily handicapped.

The anti-interventionist compromise would base its appeal on the idea of "safety net": a guaranteed minimum standard and a right to basic education and health care through programs that would be cost effective because they were selective and targeted. The opposition would attack the proposals as inadequate, as delivering inferior services to the disadvantaged and socially divisive. The government would defend itself by stressing that its policies make the best use of the taxpayers' money.[30]

During times when the economy showed a steady growth or boom and it was possible for the market to deliver a reasonable standard of material goods to a growing number of people, the safety-net approach would have general support, but it would face tough opposition. Every day during the legislative session, government ministers would face a barrage of questions concerning situations where the safety net had failed and attacking the moral basis of their policy options. The opposition would criticize their failure to address institutionalized inequalities and unequal opportunities. The pro-interventionists would continually hold out before the people the possibility of using politics to prevent the powerful from exploiting the weak. To the extent that the means they propose to achieve these ends echo the European tools of state ownership and centralized planning, they would be unlikely to win an electoral majority, even in hard times or depressed areas. These means are not compatible with the American Creed or the structure of American federalism. To be electorally successful the pro-interventionists would need to create means that were compatible with market forces, means that would appeal not only to the older generation who retained vivid memories of the hard times of the 1930s but also to the younger generation raised in affluence and seeing a greater sense of purpose. Might we have seen at a much earlier stage the idea Julian Le Grand and Saul Estrin have recently advocated, of "decoupling" capitalism and markets? Would this innovation have allowed our governing party to offer economic democracy (a program to maximize economic opportunity, guarantee a minimum income, and enable workers to own and run their enterprises) as an end of political democracy? Imagine a charismatic young party leader on the campaign trail rallying support of those wanting, as Ringen puts it, "to gain control over the material circumstances of their lives," who would appeal to us to make use of the powers of government to achieve these ends together.[31] Not the powers of some distant autocratic government, of some authoritarian central bureaucratic state, but our own power—"we, the people."

Once elected, the party of economic democracy would have to deliver. Coming into office in these circumstances would closely resemble the situation Kermit Gordon describes as characteristic of the early days of a new administration in the presidential system:

> A renewal of government energies and a resurgence of hope. . . . The new President has a blank sheet upon which to write. . . . The new Congress . . . welcomes the impetus to the legislative process which is generated by the presidential initiatives. . . . The public seems . . . to nourish the hope that the new leaders . . . will find the therapies for the nation's ills. . . . The voters expect new diagnoses, new strategies, and new initiatives. . . .[32]

The difference in the parliamentary system is that the voters already know the proposed remedies and have legitimized the intentions, and their expectations will extend throughout the government's term of office.

The ministers would be able to draw on the experience and knowledge base of the civil service in drafting legislation and implementing their policies but will have depended on their party "think-tanks" for the innovations themselves. What might some of these ideas be? If capital and owners threatened to leave a state because safety standards were too exacting, minimum wages too high, environmental protection laws too restricting, the government could respond by establishing laws that provided support for workers and/or areas which wished to establish cooperatives or community ownership. Instead of nationalization or state ownership it could support popular capitalism by providing infrastructure, tax concessions and advisory support.

Rather than punitive tax levels to "rob the rich to help the poor," legislation could offer differential tax rates. The citizens would be left with a free choice of how to spend their income, but their choices would have different tax consequences. If I choose to make my money available for capital investment at a time when this investment is needed, it would attract no tax. If, on the other hand, I choose to use the money in a nonproductive manner, such as indulging in the "possessions of celebrities," I would be required to pay tax. Employers might be required to make direct contributions to the costs of education in return for the increased level of skills in the work force that education makes available to them.

Have we strayed too far from policy making in the American parliamentary system? It would be very difficult to substantiate a claim that the introduction of a parliamentary system would have produced this or that specific policy change. What we have tried to suggest is that the more effective governing machinery would have encouraged people to formulate innovative alternatives, to seize the opportunity that the system offered through the party system of making changes, of taking our destiny into our own hands.

This system would not eliminate poverty. It would not end the problem of single-parent families struggling to survive in a workplace not geared to their needs. It would not solve the problem of workers and employers alike in the declining heavy industries of the East or the problem of automobile and garment industries facing intense competition from abroad. It does provide a vehicle for collective action, for effective action. More important, it provides a vehicle in which the opportunity of a small group of the people to frustrate the will of the democratic majority is limited. In discussing the factors contributing to the relatively limited response of the American affluent society to the problems of poverty, Patterson has stressed those groups that have a strong vested interest in preventing reforms:

> Lobbies such as the Chamber of Commerce, the National Association of Manufacturers and the Farm Bureau Federation drew their strength from employers and large commercial farmers who profited from keeping poor people in their place. . . . [They remind us that we cannot] ignore the role played by purposeful interest groups that had good reasons for resisting generous welfare.

The ability of interest groups such as these, and their trade union counterparts, to inhibit policy action is more limited in a parliamentary system. As Vile has explained, in a presidential system "interest groups thrive in the fragmentary character of the governmental system . . . in the vacuum created by weak parties."[33]

Again we would stress the greater capacity of the parliamentary system for intergovernmental cooperation. We can only briefly touch on the financial aspects of social policy. Obviously by allowing most of the activity to take place at the state level we increase the probability that some citizens will be able to achieve a much higher standard of living than others merely by living in a richer state. Market forces would create large movements of people out of poorer states into richer states, putting pressure on services and resources and causing inflation in the price of real estate and services. The government and people of the richer states might therefore be held to have as much direct interest in improving conditions in the poorer states as the people who live there. The voters might be prepared to accept an increase in taxes to allow transfer payments to these "have-not" states to help maintain basic standards. Some economists would argue that this system is inefficient, but it depends on how you define efficiency.

The parliamentary system as we have outlined it gives the citizens in a democracy a wider range of choices than Albert Hirschman's famous trilogy—exit, voice, and loyalty.[34] It adds the possibility of effective action while retaining the virtues of decentralized decision-making and local initiative. It offers the possibility of preserving individualism through collective action. Unfortunately it does not work on its own. It requires an informed electorate, an active electorate, an electorate that keeps a close eye on its elected representatives and demands that they in turn keep a close eye on the government. It requires that the political parties are themselves democratically organized and allow for and encourage a high degree of participation. It requires that public servants be prepared to serve the electorate and not substitute their own judgment for that of the people's legitimate wishes. It is in this sense a system ideally suited for the American political environment.

Foreign Policy and Defense

If, as Vile suggests, the frustrations that the executive branch faces in domestic policy force a president to succumb to the "temptation to spend more and more of their time and effort on foreign policy,"[35] can we assume that the legislative-executive of a parliamentary America would be too involved in domestic policy to do justice to foreign affairs? We must emphasize that the distinction between foreign and domestic policy is alien to the Westminster model. This area of royal prerogative power came under parliamentary control in the same way as all other areas. Although the head of state remained symbolically commander in chief of military forces, the functions associated with it, such as declarations of war and treaties, were firmly in the hands of the elected government.

The American cabinet would have made decisions in the foreign policy area in the same way, using the same processes of collective cabinet scrutiny it would have used to consider an agricultural subsidy or an amendment to the Fishing License Act. External Affairs would have been considered a prestigious portfolio, held by one of the senior ministers in the government. The Defense portfolio would, at least in peacetime, have had a lower profile. Nevertheless, the efficiency of the cabinet system of decision making would mean that the new nation had available the political means of developing a rational and coherent foreign stance and of putting it into practice, if it so desired.

In the aftermath of the War of Independence, we might expect the new regime to have shown a distaste for external relations. It might even have happened that isolationism would have emerged as the dominant guiding principle as early as the late eighteenth century. Two factors make this development improbable. First, the American parliamentary system was to operate within a federal framework in which states' rights were very strongly expressed. Public policy initiatives in areas of domestic policy would naturally be considered part of the jurisdiction of the state governments. A federal cabinet that became active in domestic policy would inevitably have upset their state counterparts, often members of their own party. The easiest solution to this problem is for the national government to concentrate on foreign policy. Rather than a hierarchical pattern whereby individuals moved from local government, to state politics, and into federal politics, we would have seen career differentiation. Individuals whose main interest was in the domestic sphere would stay in state politics, while those more interested in foreign policy would opt directly for the national level.

The Republic had emerged in troubled times and almost immediately faced problems with the boundaries between itself and the remaining British territories on the continent. But troubled times are also interesting times for individuals interested in international affairs. The American Revolution was the first in a century of revolutions, and the new government could have played an active role in these developments. The revolution in France in 1789 and the revolutionary war that followed (1789–1801), the accession of the Corsican general Napoleon Bonaparte to supreme rule in France, and the Napoleonic wars (1802–15) all contributed to an atmosphere of expectations and tensions that could have found echoes in North America. George Washington may have wanted to keep America out of these events, but as head of state he would have had less say than the men who formed America's first cabinets. While the original rebellion had been essentially conservative in nature, there is no reason to assume that it would have stayed that way. Flushed with the pride of victory over the British, a new group might have come to power committed to a vision of supporting revolutionary change elsewhere. Change as violent as the French Revolution might have worried those who feared the specter of the masses, but the revolution was also against autocratic and hereditary power. Vile has noted that: "Change and innovation [is] built into U.S. culture . . . [in] the desire to create a new society, to develop its economy, to move to higher standards of living or a better life,"[36] and such feelings would have lent a cloak of legitimacy to an active foreign policy.

Our fantasy will consider two possibilities. We will create a new scenario of events that did not happen but might have with the right catalyst—a strong and effective national government. Second, we will rewrite an event that did occur to show how the existence of a parliamentary government would have drastically changed the event.

It does not require much imagination to suggest that the national legislature could have attracted a group of young radicals dedicated to an eighteenth-century version of Manifest Destiny to justify territorial expansion. We might also have found an earlier expression of the principles of the Monroe Doctrine without the clause that committed the United States not to interfere with existing European colonies in the Americas. The Monroe Doctrine philosophy that there was an essentially different political system in the Americas could have been a battle cry rather than a statement of fact. Rather than merely warning Europeans not to attempt further expansion in the Americas, the United States might have played an active role in helping the peoples of colonial America throw off the imperial yoke. Might we have seen by the end of the nineteenth century a truly "new world" in the Western Hemisphere, a world of flourishing liberal-capitalist nations.

In practice the new Republic would have lacked the military

strength in the eighteenth century to take on any of the imperial powers in direct conflict. But the turmoil on the European continent, not just at the turn of the century but also as a result of liberal-inspired revolutions in 1830 and 1848, would have meant that their attention was turned inward and opportunity for expansion beckoned not just to the West but also northward.

To the north of the new Republic lay the sparsely populated territory of Quebec. What could be more natural than that the newly independent nation would want to help liberate the people of Quebec?[37] The presence of large numbers of Empire Loyalists in the adjacent British territories, "traitors" who had failed to support the revolutionary cause, would have encouraged the presentation of the war as a natural completion of the American Revolution. Did not the French colonists also suffer from the same lack of representative and responsible government that had led to the original upheaval?

Failure need not have ended the dream. There were a number of other incidents in the next half century that could have encouraged the American government to active intervention or expansionist activity to the north. The revolt of the French Canadians led by *les Patriotes* is a case in point. The revolutionaries produced their own resolutions in the style of the Declaration of Independence and likewise threatened secession. The aim: to establish a secular democracy. And a parliamentary system of government with a separation of church and state meant that a newly independent Quebec would have been easily incorporated into the federal structure of the United States.[38]

The successful incorporation of Quebec would have stimulated further activity. We can turn our attention to the other side of the continent where a boundary dispute continued between the United States and the British over a West Coast colony. If James K. Polk had won the 1844 election as potential prime minister rather than president, his twin concern for the annexation of Texas and the recognition of American rights in the Oregon territory might have been realized. Polk's campaign slogan "54°40 or Fight" might have become a reality. In the subsequent peace treaty, the Americans might have gained the whole of Vancouver Island and the lower mainland of British Columbia. Once Alaska had been purchased from the Russians in 1867, the expansionist thrust could have led to the United States gaining control over the whole West Coast. The uprising of the French-speaking Metis led by Louis Riel in central Canada could have led to further intervention and another state joining the union. With three key areas in the United States, the intervening territories would have been under strong economic pressures to succumb. A truly continental nation might well have been achieved by the end of the century.

Our scenario depends for its success on a British government too involved in other affairs to be willing to wage a constant battle to keep colonies that cost more than they yielded. More important, it requires an American government able to develop and sustain continuity and momentum in foreign policy. Under a presidential system of government this was impossible; with a parliamentary government it would have been probable. It would depend on the ability of the "expansionist" party to sell its policy to the electorate and its ability to achieve these objectives without excessive cost. By appropriating for the American government some of the profits from the exploitation of formerly Crown land in these new states, the latter problem might have been solved.

Simultaneously, events in the Southwest may have encouraged an even more adventurous foreign policy. With the European powers caught up in the struggle against Napoleon, the colonies of Central and South America were ripe for revolution. With American encouragement would the great republican confederation which Simon Bolívar tried to set up for Colombia, Venezuela, Ecuador, and Bolivia (1818–30) have survived to become the core of a United States of the South? Would the American interest in Mexican affairs have been limited to the war of 1846–48 and the annexation of territory? Would the American government have given the liberation movement of Benito Juárez greater support and helped develop a democratic government strong enough to withstand the French invasion of the early 1860s? There is nothing in our fantasy that would bring us into conflict with the element of the American Creed discussed above. This was not interventionist government in the sense of bureaucratic interference with the freedoms and rights of American citizens. This was American citizens using their government machinery to bring the benefits of the American "way of life" to the whole Western Hemisphere. If it is improbable, it was unfortunate for all the people concerned.

For the second element of our fantasy, we will take a much more narrow focus and consider the events of 1917–20, concerning the American involvement in World War I, the Paris Peace Conference, and the creation of the League of Nations. While a number of British

politicians had shown interest in the creation of an international organization, there is little doubt that Woodrow Wilson was the driving
force behind the League. His concern to keep the United States out of
the war had not reflected a lack of interest in the events. As early as
1917 he had revealed his vision of the postwar world—his crusade to
make the world safe for democracy. And in 1918, he announced his
Fourteen Points, which included a proposal for the League of Nations.

There was little enthusiasm for the League among the British and
French leaders at the peace conference, so it is likely that without
Wilson the idea would never have got off the ground. In a parliamentary America, however, it is unlikely Wilson would have been prime
minister. His victory in 1912 was owing to a split in the Republican
vote between William Howard Taft and Theodore Roosevelt, an unlikely occurrence in a parliamentary election. But even if Wilson had
survived that hurdle, his victory in 1916 had been by a narrow margin
and the Republican party won a majority in both houses of Congress in
1918. As leader of the opposition, Wilson would have had no status to
launch his grand scheme. The United States would still have entered
the war—the sinking of three American ships in 1917 guaranteed
that—but the subsequent events would have changed dramatically.

Let us assume that Taft would have formed the government and that
Senator Henry Cabot Lodge, chair of the Senate Foreign Relations
Committee, had become minister for external affairs; Senator Warren
Harding would also be a member of the government. All these men
had a strong commitment to keeping America out of foreign entanglements. Harding was to campaign for president in 1920 on a pledge to
"return to normalcy," and he had consistently opposed Wilson's inter-
nationalism. A speedy return to isolationism would have followed the
signing of a peace treaty. With no interest in winning support for the
League, the Republican government at the conference would not have
had to make concessions to the British and French. In cooperation with
the British government, they might have been able to avoid French
occupation of the Rhineland. They might even have signed a separate
peace with Germany if the French had been difficult. With less oppressive treaty terms the new Weimar Republic in Germany might have
avoided some of the problems that led to National Socialism and the
rise of Hitler.

Alternatively we can imagine that an election of 1918 took the opposite course—that the idea of the League of Nations had caught the

imagination of the American people and the Wilson Democrats returned to office with an impressive majority. Without a need to placate the Senate and the exhausting efforts to win popular support that interrupted Wilson's visit to Paris, the American leader might have been able to keep a firm control of the course of events. With his League firmly established and the American leadership clearly demonstrated, he might indeed have been able to undo many of the harmful terms of the peace treaty. If the League had been able to work as intended, fascism in Italy, the Japanese expansion in Manchuria and China, and German rearmament might have been avoided.

Other problems would have had to be faced. The significance of the Russian Revolution might have been overlooked in the pressures of ending the war, but it would have demanded attention soon afterward. Would the American people have been persuaded that this revolution, too, was a step on the road to freedom and justice? Or would the violence of the method have blinded Americans to the justness of the cause—rebellion against an oppressive tyranny? How the situation in Russia might have developed if the American people had rallied to the cause of the Russian people rather than the aristocracy would make another interesting fantasy. The American people have shown their compassion for others by opening the doors to the poor and the oppressed, but this was not the only way. If the American government had been willing to take its radicalism one step further and put the establishing of democracies abroad higher on the agenda than the maintenance of the rights of states to manage their own internal affairs, we might be living in a very different world. Of course, America would have been accused of imperialism, but that has happened anyway.

Conclusion

We have looked at a representative cross-section of aspects of American politics and government that would have been changed with the introduction of a parliamentary system of government. Because of the immensity of the task we have not tried to impose an artificial cohesion on the transformation, and we have raised difficult issues and different possibilities in the separate sections. Similarly, we have chosen examples from across the whole time frame of American history. Obviously, if the early historical experience had been different, it is unlikely that the events we describe or the individuals we mention in the later period would have taken place. Thus we are asking you to suspend logic as well as to use your imagination.

We have concentrated on the strengths of the parliamentary system as a political vehicle. In doing so we have not exaggerated the potential that a parliamentary system offers in a democratic environment. We do not wish to suggest that the parliamentary system is a magic wand that can cure all ills. It will have its costs, and these must be weighed against its benefits. Similarly, we have chosen to present a series of activist scenarios because it made a more vivid picture, but activism is not inevitable. It is our view, however, that an America with a parliamentary system of government would not just have been a different place. It would also have been an America in which practical politics would have more closely reflected the beliefs and ideals of the people.

Notes

1. Trying to imagine the course of events in the United States if it had had a parliamentary government, is a more involved process than one might imagine. First, there is more than one model of a parliamentary system. Second, parliamentary systems have been strongly influenced by the American presidential system: these elements must be eliminated from the model. Third, we must decide if other features of the American system should be ignored: for example, a written constitution, a bill of rights, a political role for the judiciary, federalism—all elements that did not exist in the original English or Westminster model. The Canadian version of this model now incorporates all these features and a number of others that can be considered examples of the Americanization of the system, but we cannot assume that these features would have developed in North America without the stimulus of the presidential system. It would have been useful to consider how these combinations would have changed subsequent events, but limits of space preclude such an investigation. You may think that this has already been done elsewhere in the volume, but all other chapters explore change holding the presidential system constant. This chapter changes this core element, thus creating the possibility of changing all other elements substantially. Where we appear to be going over ground already covered in other chapters you should be aware that we are approaching the issue from a completely different angle. Finally, it should be noted that the Westminster model is very complex, and we are presenting a highly simplified version.

2. There are a number of terms that can be used to refer to the hereditary head of state in the Westminster system. As well as the specific individual—king or queen—a number of abstract terms exist—"monarch," "monarchy," "royalty," "sovereign"—and we will treat them as synonymous. The terms "the Crown" and "sovereignty" have political or legal connotations, which means that they are distinctly different from the individual.

3. Gunnar Myrdal, quoted in David Mervin, *Ronald Reagan and the American Presidency* (New York: Longman, 1990), p. 3, see also p. 2; Benjamin B. Ringer, *"We the People" and Others: Duality and America's Treatment of Its Racial Minorities* (New York: Tavistock, 1983), p. 241; Gunnar Myrdal, *An American Dilemma* (New York: Harper and Bros., 1944), pp. 4–5.

4. M. J. C. Vile, *Politics in the USA* (London: Hutchinson, 1987), p. 19. See also H. G. Nicholas, *The Nature of American Politics* (Oxford: Oxford University Press, 1986), p. 10.

5. Mervin, *Reagan and the American Presidency*, p. 16.

6. Vile, *Politics in the USA*, pp. 18, 247; Alexander Hamilton, *Federalist 78*, 1788, in Alexander Hamilton, James Madison, and John Jay, *The Federalist Papers*, ed. Clinton Rossiter (New York: New American Library, 1961), p. 465.

7. Vile, *Politics in the USA*, p. 75, see also p. 19; Robert B. Dishman, *The State of the Union* (New York: Charles Scribner's Sons, 1965), p. 1.

8. Mervin, *Reagan and the American Presidency*, pp. 15–16.

9. James T. Patterson, *The Welfare State in America: 1930–1980*, BAAS Pamphlet in American Studies (Durham, England: British Association for American Studies, 1981), pp. 10, 11. See also Charles Peters and Nicholas Lehmann, *Inside the System* (New York: Holt, Rinehart and Winston, 1979), p. 4; Robert L. Peabody, ed., *Cases in American Politics* (New York: Praeger, 1976), p. 8; Mervin, *Reagan and the American Presidency*, p. 15.

10. Myrdal, *American Dilemma*, p. 4; Henry Fairlie, *The Spoiled Child of the Western World* (London: Sheldon Press, 1975), p. 237.

11. Stein Ringen, *The Possibility of Politics: A Study in the Political Economy of the Welfare State* (Oxford: Clarendon Press, 1987), pp. 3, 19, 9.

12. Patterson, *Welfare State in America*, pp. xx, 10.

13. Vile, *Politics in the USA,* p. 75.

14. Mervin, *Reagan and the American Presidency,* p. 15; Vile, *Politics in the USA*, p. 27.

15. Vile, *Politics in the USA*, p. xx.

16. Ibid., pp. 25–48.

17. In the Westminster model there is no fixed number of government departments or portfolios, and the prime minister, with the tacit support of the legislature, can reorganize the administrative structures at will. In the American system it is probable that the number and subject field of departments would be controlled by the legislature.

18. Vile, *Politics in the USA*, p. 20.

19. See R. I. Cheffins and P. A. Johnson, *The Revised Canadian Constitution: Politics as Law* (Toronto: McGraw-Hill Ryerson, 1986). See also Peter H. Russell, "The Political Purposes of the Canadian Charter of Rights and Freedoms," *Canadian Bar Review* 61, no. 1 (March 1983): 30–54.

20. Alan F. Westin, "The United States Bill of Rights and the Canadian Charter" in *U.S. Bill of Rights and the Canadian Charter of Rights and Freedom*, ed. Willaim R. McKercher (Toronto: Ontario Economic Council, 1983), pp. 35–36.

21. Myrdal, *American Dilemma*, p. 4; Myrdal, quoted in Ringer, *We the People*, p. 4.

22. Ringer, *We the People*, p. 175.

23. Ibid., p. 204.

24. Ibid., p. 203.

25. The single-member, simple majority electoral system gives concentrated groups more seats in an elected chamber than it does to the same number of voters widely dispersed throughout the country.

26. See Alonzo L. Hamby, *Liberalism and Its Challenges* (New York: Oxford University Press, 1985), pp. 148, 166.

27. Ringen, *Possibilities of Politics*, p. 1.

28. Ibid., p. 2.

29. Vile, *Politics in the USA*, p. 131; Patterson, *Welfare State in America*, p. 10.

30. Ringen, *Possibility of Politics*, p. 13; George P. Shultz and Kenneth W. Dam, *Economic Policy beyond the Headlines* (New York: W. W. Norton, 1977), p. 3.

31. Saul Estrin and Julian Le Grand, "Market Socialism," in *Market Socialism*, ed. Julian Le Grand and Saul Estrin (Oxford: Clarendon Press, 1989), p. 1; Ringen, *Possibility of Politics*, p. 3, see also p. 8.

32. Kermit Gordon, ed., *Agenda for the Nation* (New York: Doubleday, 1969), p. 3.

33. Patterson, *Welfare State in America*, pp. 9–10; Vile, *Politics in the USA*, p. 114.

34. Albert Hirschman, *Exit, Voice, and Loyalty: Responses to Decline in Firms, Organizations, and States* (Cambridge, Mass.: Harvard University Press, 1970).

35. Vile, *Politics in the USA*, p. 200.

36. Ibid., p. 76.

37. For evidence that the liberation of Canada was certainly no mere theoretical concern during the War of 1812, see John Fitzmaurice, *Quebec and Canada* (London: C. Hearst, 1985), p. 7.

38. Ibid., pp. 15, 16.

Sources and Suggested Readings

While there are a large number of introductory texts on the British parliamentary system, they generally provide more detail on English politics than may be necessary. A better place to start would be a simple introduction to the Canadian system: W. L. White, R. H. Wagenberg, and R. C. Nelson, *Introduction to Canadian Politics and Government* (Toronto: Holt, Rinehart and Winston, 1990). The comparative dimension is well treated in Ronald Landes, *The Canadian Polity* (Toronto: Prentice-Hall, 1991), where both the British and Canadian parliamentary systems are compared to the presidential system. It has the advantage over books that have been published more recently in which the American influences on the parliamentary system dominate discussion. For a detailed study of the working of the parliamentary process, C.E.S. Franks, *The Parliament of Canada* (Toronto: University of Toronto Press, 1987) is very useful. Alternatively, you may gain a good insight into the differences between the two systems from books on the presidential system written by an English author or for a British audience, for example, M.J.C. Vile, *Politics in the USA* (London: Hutchinson, 1987). In the policy area, Benjamin Ringer, *"We the People" and Others: Duality and America's Treatment of Its Racial Minorities* (New York: Tavistock, 1983) gives a more than comprehensive overview of the minority problem; James T. Patterson, *The Welfare State in America: 1930–1980* (Durham, England: British Association for American Studies, 1981) gives a brief factual overview; and Stein Ringen, *The Possibility of Politics* (Oxford: Clarendon Press, 1987) gives a challenging examination of the issues.

The presidential and parliamentary systems are compared in Don K. Price, "Parliamentary and Presidential Systems," *Public Administration Review* 3, no. 4 (Autumn 1943): 317–34; Howard A. Scarrow, "Parliamentary and Presidential Government Compared," *Current History* 66, no. 394 (June 1974): 264–67, 272; and R. Kent Weaver, "Are Parliamentary Systems Better?" *Brookings Review* 3, no. 4 (Summer 1985): 16–25.

Proposals to modify the U.S. political system so that it adopts some of the features of a parliamentary system are considered in Donald L. Robinson, ed., *Reforming American Government: The Bicentennial Papers on the Committee on the Constitutional System* (Boulder, Colo.: Westview Press, 1985); James L. Sundquist, *Constitutional Reform and Effective Government* (Washington, D.C.: Brookings Institutions, 1986); and James Q. Wilson, "Does the Separation of Powers Still Work?" *Public Interest*, no. 86 (Winter 1987): 36–52.

NEIL B. COHEN

6 | What If There Were No Judicial Review?

Who decides what the Constitution means?

(a) Congress
(b) The President
(c) The Supreme Court
(d) The electorate

Most students, indeed most citizens, would not find this a difficult multiple-choice question. The vast majority of respondents to this question would pick (c)—the Supreme Court. Of course the Supreme Court decides what the Constitution means! This answer seems so obvious that most people would not waste any significant time mulling over the various possibilities.

Certainly, the Supreme Court is *an* interpreter of the Constitution. But how did the Court get that role? Is it assigned by the Constitution, or did the Court assume this role for itself? Also, is the Court not only *an* interpreter of the Constitution, but *the* interpreter? That is, does the Supreme Court have the final say over what the Constitution means? The answers to these questions are not at all obvious, but they are important to pursue in order to understand the role played by *judicial review*—the power of the federal judiciary to strike down federal and state laws that are inconsistent with the Constitution.

What if there were no such thing as judicial review? It is hard to imagine American government without it, but would life really be so different without judicial review? Would it be better? Worse? A little of both perhaps? To answer this question, an understanding of the development and role of judicial review is essential.

The Idea of a Written Constitution

The American system of government centers on a written constitution. As more fully described in Chapter 1, the Constitution of the United States is a complex document that fulfills several disparate roles. First, it is a philosophical document, eloquently expressing our beliefs about ourselves as an organized society. Second, the Constitution is a structural document, establishing the three branches of the United States government, defining the powers of each branch and the net of checks and balances connecting them, and marking the boundaries between the federal government of limited powers and residual power of the states.

Third, and most important for the purposes here, the Constitution is a legal document that establishes an array of fundamental legal rules for the nation. As a legal instrument, the Constitution is *law*. That is, it provides a set of enforceable norms governing those people and institutions within its ambit.

Not only is the Constitution law, but it is a very special type of law. Article VI of the Constitution states that the Constitution "shall be the supreme Law of the Land." Thus, when the Constitution is in conflict with any other law, such as a statute passed by Congress, the Constitution must prevail. It is the Constitution's status as "supreme Law," specified in this *supremacy clause*, that gives the document its special place in American legal and political life.

Who Decides What the Constitution Means?

While the Constitution may be supreme law, it is not self-executing. That is, it does not interpret itself or enforce itself. Accordingly, some person or institution must be empowered to interpret the Constitution. At the very least, each branch of the federal government has a need to conform its conduct to the dictates of the Constitution. In addition, and more controversially, mechanisms are needed to deal with disputes between branches of the federal government and between the federal government and the states.

These concerns are not just abstract and hypothetical. Rather, they reflect the complex allocation of political power among the branches of the federal government and between the federal government and the states. Several types of clashes over the meaning of the Constitution can arise. After all, while all the actors in each branch of government take an oath to conform their conduct to the Constitution, those actors and, therefore, their branches, may disagree as to the conduct mandated by the Constitution. In other words, all the parties may be attempting in good faith to act "constitutionally" but disagree as to what that entails. Several examples of such conflict that have actually occurred spring easily to mind:

• What if Congress passes a law it believes constitutional, but one or both of the other branches disagrees? This conflict is best exemplified by the most famous of all Supreme Court decisions—*Marbury v. Madison* (1803)—discussed below. In such a case, who decides whether the law is in conformity with the Constitution?

• What if Congress passes a law it believes constitutional but a party affected by the law claims is in violation of the Constitution? This is probably the model for the vast majority of constitutional disputes concerning federal laws. In such a case, who decides whether the law is in conformity with the Constitution?

• What if the president takes action he believes constitutional but that another branch believes to be in violation of the Constitution? This paradigm, while occurring less frequently, does occasionally arise. A good example is provided by the dispute concerning President Jimmy Carter's abrogation of various treaties with Taiwan without the advice or consent of the Senate (see *Goldwater v. Carter* [1979]). In such a case, who decides whether the action is in conformity with the Constitution?

• What if the president takes action he believes constitutional but that a party affected by the action claims is in violation of the Constitution? For example, what if the president issues an executive order mandating that federal agencies adopt affirmative action hiring plans resembling quotas? This paradigm recurs with some frequency. In such a case, who decides whether the action is in conformity with the Constitution?

• What if a state passes a law that an affected party believes to be in violation of the Constitution? In such a case, who decides whether the state law is in conformity with the Constitution?

The answer to these questions seems obvious today. Of course, it is the judiciary that decides these issues. But why? How did the judiciary achieve this power? Was it inevitable? Could we exist any other way?

It is not at all obvious that the judiciary should have such a critical role in constitutional interpretation, and it may not have been obvious during the political debates concerning the Constitution that the judiciary would have such a role. To understand the development of that role, it is essential to turn to the bedrock case of American constitutional jurisprudence—*Marbury v. Madison.*

Marbury v. Madison

The story of *Marbury v. Madison* starts with a dispute about political patronage. It begins with the presidential election of 1800. As a result of the election of Thomas Jefferson as president, the United States faced for the first time a phenomenon with which we are familiar today: a change in the controlling political party. John Adams, the outgoing president, was a Federalist, while Thomas Jefferson was a Democratic-Republican.

The lame-duck Federalist administration spent much of its final weeks in power doing what comes naturally for political parties about to leave office—filling jobs with loyal party faithful. Indeed, the outgoing Federalists established many new positions in order to create additional vacancies to be filled. Among the positions created were several justices of the peace for the District of Columbia.

On March 3, 1801, only hours before the Federalists were to go out of power, William Marbury was confirmed as justice of the peace. (Until the Twentieth Amendment went into effect in 1937, presidents were inaugurated on March 4.) Accordingly, his commission was signed by President Adams, who entrusted it for delivery to John Marshall. Marshall, who himself had just been named chief justice, was still serving as Adams's secretary of state at the time. In his hurry, Marshall failed to deliver Marbury's commission, along with those of several other appointees.

After Jefferson's inauguration, James Madison, his close friend and the new secretary of state, refused to deliver the commissions to Marbury and the other appointees. Thus, the stage was set for Marbury's attempt to use the court system to wrest the commission from Madison.

Marbury decided to start at the top; he brought his suit against Madison in the Supreme Court of the United States. Whatever other motivations Marbury had for this unusual first step in litigation, one reason was certainly the identity of the chief justice—John Marshall himself. Not only was Marshall a Federalist, but he was the man responsible for Marbury's failure to receive his commission. Apparently the primitive judicial ethics of the time did not require Marshall to disqualify himself!

We tend to think of the Supreme Court as an *appellate* court; that is, one which hears appeals from decisions made by lower, or inferior, courts. Why did Marbury believe that the Supreme Court could hear his case even though he was not appealing an inferior court decision? Marbury believed that he could bring his lawsuit in the Supreme Court because the Judiciary Act of 1789 (passed by Congress and signed by President George Washington) gave the Supreme Court original jurisdiction to issue *writs of mandamus* (orders to public officials commanding them to do their duty). *Original jurisdiction* is jurisdiction to hear cases originally—that is, not on appeal from some other court.

The Constitution, however, also speaks about the Supreme Court's jurisdiction. Article III, section 2 of the Constitution states that the Supreme Court has original jurisdiction over only a few types of cases, and Marbury's lawsuit was not of the type included in the list. Thus, the stage was set for conflict. Which would be given precedence—the statute giving the Supreme Court original jurisdiction to hear Marbury's complaint, or Article III of the Constitution, denying the Court jurisdiction?

Marshall did not waste the opportunity to embarrass Jefferson and Madison, who were, of course, his political opponents. In the Supreme Court's opinion in *Marbury v. Madison*, Marshall first indicated that Marbury's commission was wrongfully withheld, that he was entitled to a remedy for that wrong, and that a writ of mandamus against Madison was the appropriate remedy.

Having embarrassed the Jefferson administration, though, the Supreme Court did *not* issue the writ of mandamus! The reasoning behind the Court's refusal to issue the writ constitutes the classic statement of the court's claim to the power now known as judicial review.

The court noted the conflict between the grant of original jurisdiction in the Judiciary Act and the Constitution's limit of the Court to appellate jurisdiction. Citing the Constitution's supremacy clause, the Court indicated that a statute inconsistent with the Constitution could not be considered a law. But what gave the court the right to decide that the Constitution and the statute were inconsistent? After all, Congress and the president take oaths to obey the Constitution; Congress had passed the statute and the president had signed it. Why did not their implicit determination that the statute did not violate the Constitution deserve greater respect? Indeed, why was the decision of Congress and the president—the branches given roles in law-making by the Constitution—not final?

The answer given by John Marshall was deceptively simple. According to his opinion for the Court, the dispute facing the Court was, essentially, no different from many other lawsuits in that the parties disagreed as to the law governing the situation. In such cases, observed Marshall, "it is emphatically the province and duty of the judicial department to say what the law is." Here, too, it was the court's job to determine which party's version of the law actually governed the situation. Marbury, relying on the jurisdictional statute as the governing law, was claiming that the Court had original jurisdiction to hear the case; Madison, relying on Article III of the Constitution, was claiming that the Court did not have original jurisdiction to hear the case. The Constitution, as supreme law of the land, has priority; therefore, it prevails. Accordingly, the Court ruled that it had no original jurisdiction to hear Marbury's complaint and dismissed the suit.

Thus, the court used a traditional case-specific role—determining the governing law in a case between litigants—to create a systemic power—the authority to definitively interpret the Constitution for the entire government. In *Marbury*, then, through very simple reasoning, the Supreme Court asserted that it has a very critical power—the power to overrule lawmaking done by the other branches of the federal government on the grounds that, *in the Court's opinion*, those branches acted inconsistently with the Constitution.

The *Marbury* case was quite controversial. Indeed, even to this day the debate continues as to the proper scope of judicial review of decisions by courts over the other branches of the federal government. The idea that the judiciary could determine the constitutionality of decisions by state governments has been less controversial, though. The reason for the greater acceptance of this latter sort of judicial review is that it requires only recognizing the supremacy of the federal Constitution over state laws without the additional intrabranch supremacy issues that are raised by judicial review of decisions of the other branches of the federal government.

What If There Were No Judicial Review?

Is the power of judicial review, claimed by the Court in *Marbury*, legitimate? Was the case correctly decided? Could the court have legitimately decided that it did not have the power to overrule lawmaking by the other branches? Although judicial review has been a part of the American political and legal system continuously since the *Marbury* decision in 1803, the answers to these questions are surprisingly difficult.

The text of the Constitution nowhere contains explicit authority for the Supreme Court or, for that matter, any part of the judicial branch, to overrule constitutional judgments made by the other branches. Yet, it cannot be said that John Marshall invented the doctrine of judicial review aided only by logic and insight. *The Federalist Papers*, the classic contemporaneous commentaries on the Constitution, provide strong support for the concept of judicial review: In *Federalist 78*, Alexander Hamilton wrote: "Limitations [on legislative authority] can be preserved in practice no other way than through the medium of courts of justice, whose duty it must be to declare all acts contrary to the manifest tenor of the Constitution void." Nonetheless, the fact remains that the idea of judicial review is not firmly based in constitutional text. If the matter were being decided today before a court comprised of *strict constructionists* (i.e., those who claim they are merely construing the words of the Constitution and not inserting their own values into their interpretation), would a power of judicial review over the acts of other branches of the federal government be found? What about judicial review of state laws?

Possible Benefits

The idea of judicial review has become an ingrained, if not always popular, part of the American political system. What if that power of the judiciary were suddenly taken away—or had never been asserted in the first place? Certainly our political and legal system would be quite different. Would the changes be for the better or for the worse? As creatures of the status quo, it would be easy to surmise that our system would be worse without judicial review (as I ultimately believe; see below), but it is also possible that the absence of judicial review might have some positive results.

For one thing, in the absence of a judiciary to whom the buck can be passed, Congress and the president might take more seriously their oaths of office to obey the Constitution. Now, Congress and the executive, as the branches that must face the electorate, have the flexibility to take politically expedient, yet unconstitutional, actions without doing irreparable damage to constitutional government because they know that the courts, through use of judicial review, can undo the damage without having to face the electorate. A good example is provided by President Franklin Roosevelt's letter to Representative Samuel Hill in 1935 urging him to support a controversial bill to regulate the bituminous coal industry notwithstanding any doubts about its constitutionality caused by the Supreme Court's series of decisions invalidating various New Deal initiatives:

> All doubts should be resolved in favor of the bill, leaving to the courts, in an orderly fashion, the ultimate question of constitutionality. . . . I hope your committee will not permit doubts about constitutionality, however reasonable, to block the proposed legislation.

President Roosevelt essentially asked Representative Hill to abdicate his oath to obey the Constitution because the courts would correct any constitutional violation. If there were no judicial review, of course, unconstitutional statutes would nonetheless be fully operative. Thus, a request such as President Roosevelt's could not be made. One can hope that, in such a regime, the political branches would rise to the occasion and choose to obey the Constitution rather than bring about an irremediable violation of it. After all, apparently Representative Hill was prepared to follow his oath and attempt to conform his conduct to the Constitution—at least before he received President Roosevelt's letter. As President Andrew Jackson earlier observed, "Each public officer who takes an oath to support the Constitution swears that he will support it as he understands it."

There is certainly no significant body of evidence that members of Congress would ignore their constitutional oaths in the absence of judicial review, while there is some evidence that they would act in good faith. There are a few matters over which the Constitution makes Congress, not the Court, the final arbiter. One such provision is Article I, section 5, which provides, "Each House shall be the Judge of the Elections, Returns and Qualifications of its own Members." While the Court has ruled that Congress's unreviewable power under this provision is limited to ascertaining whether the members have met requirements set forth in the Constitution, within that sphere the houses of

Congress are answerable to no one. Nonetheless, with the possible exception of a controversy involving Representative Adam Clayton Powell—the House of Representatives refused to seat him in 1967 because of reports that he had, among other things, wrongfully diverted House funds for the use of himself and others—there is no indication that Congress has misused or abused this power even though it is not checked by judicial review. Thus, there is reason to believe, or at least to hope, that an unreviewable Congress would rise to the occasion and take its constitutional responsibility seriously.

A second possible benefit from the absence of judicial review is more subtle. At present, in our system in which the judiciary is the final interpreter of the Constitution, the process of constitutional interpretation is a *legal* process. It is presided over by lawyers and debated in courtrooms and in legal briefs. Thus, neither the setting of the debates nor their language is accessible to the average person. As a result, great constitutional debates take place, for the most part, in what is essentially private, rather than public, discourse.

If there were no judicial review, the democratic branches would be the final arbiters of the Constitution. The democratic branches—the executive and the legislature—are peopled by politicians. Their debates are open and accessible to the public, not conducted in the esoteric language of lawyers or in the absence of media coverage.

If there were no judicial review, then, the public might well be more involved in constitutional decision making than it is now. At the very least, the process of constitutional decision making would be more open. Constitutional debates would involve the public, and constitutional principles would be more widely known and understood. Perhaps the public perception of the Constitution would cease to be that of a musty document on display at the National Archives and would become an appreciation of the central principles of our nation.

Finally, if there were no judicial review and the Constitution were thus solely in the hands of the political branches, there might be a greater likelihood that the document would be interpreted in light of present-day concerns. Politics does not revere the past nearly as much as law does. Accordingly, the Constitution might more likely be a living, dynamic document in the absence of judicial review. While there would certainly be risks inherent in allowing temporal controversies to shape the interpretation of an eternal document, the benefits flowing from a contemporary interpretation of the Constitution not unduly bound by the dead hand of the past might well outweigh those risks.

A good example of this phenomenon might be provided by controversies concerning gun control and the Second Amendment to the Constitution. One obstacle to federal (and, perhaps, state) gun control legislation is the Second Amendment, which states "A well regulated Militia, being necessary to the security of a free State, the right of the people to keep and bear Arms, shall not be infringed." Although tempered somewhat by the introductory statement of its underlying motivation, the language of this constitutional provision is nearly absolute. A strict constructionist judicial interpretation of this provision could result in the voiding of strong gun control legislation. Yet, if constitutional interpretation were left in the hands of Congress and the president and they were able to overcome the other political obstacles to passage of such legislation, those political actors might be more likely than the courts to place the prohibitory language of the Second Amendment in the historical context of the amendment's introductory statement and, thereby, find the prohibitory language inapplicable to our present-day gun control problem.

Possible Detriments

The detrimental effects of the absence of judicial review would likely be more pronounced, however, than the benefits. The harms would be both structural and legal.

The structural harm would be twofold. The first aspect of this harm would be intrafederal. It would spring from the fact that the judiciary would have a greatly diminished role in the federal government. Without its judicial review power, the Supreme Court in particular would be left with little to do other than reviewing lower court opinions for mistakes and interpreting ambiguous statutes. The three-part checks-and-balances scheme of our federal structure would be composed of two stars and one bit player. Indeed, the judiciary would have no ability to serve as a check on the other two branches at all—it would be merely an organ for interpreting and enforcing their will.

The second aspect of structural harm would be in the realm of federalism—that is, the relationship between the sovereignty of the federal government and that of the states. If there were no judicial review of state legislation, then the legislature and governor of each

Separate views in terms of states would separate the United States

state would have the final view as to the constitutionality of a state law. Even assuming that those local officials would exercise this authority both knowledgeably and in good faith—an assumption of questionable validity—the views of the officials in one state might well differ significantly from those in another state. This disparity could result in the adoption of a statute in one state that was rejected in another because of the second state's view of the statute's constitutionality. We would, essentially, have a Constitution whose meaning differed from state to state. Clearly, this situation would not be desirable.

The absence of judicial review would have even more serious consequences for our constitutional society. Indeed, it is likely that the result would be particularly pernicious. When adherence to constitutional limits is most important, such as in restraining overreaching political majorities from trampling on the rights of legitimate minority interests, the absence of judicial review would encourage flouting of those limits. Indeed, the absence of judicial review would be most likely felt when its presence was most seriously needed. Would *de jure segregation*—segregation by law—for example, ever have been eliminated in the absence of judicial review of state lawmaking?

Of course, the members of the judiciary are not the only participants in the government who have a duty to conform their actions and conduct to the dictates of the Constitution. The president, all the members of Congress, and most state officials take oaths of office to obey the commands of the Constitution. Yet, the democratic nature of those branches would create a powerful incentive to interpret that oath at times in politically popular ways rather than according to the dictates of the Constitution.

Members of Congress and the executive branch who take their oaths seriously would be the object of enormous pressures to take popular actions even when those actions are inconsistent with the Constitution. The pernicious effect of this pressure need not be intentional violation of the Constitution by these decision makers. Instead, the result could easily be an atmosphere that creates an incentive for those decision makers to convince themselves that their actions are not inconsistent with the Constitution. In other words, the lack of judicial review might bring about a great deal of self-delusion in the other branches of government.

A good example is provided by the recent flag-burning controversy, described in Chapter 1. The Supreme Court, in *Texas v. Johnson* (1989), had decided that a Texas statute criminalizing flag burning violated the First Amendment. After a fierce political outcry, Congress passed a statute disingenuously designed to get around the *Johnson* decision. Few serious students of the Court's opinion believed that the new statute was constitutional and, to no one's surprise, the Supreme Court struck it down.

There was great political pressure on all members of Congress to undo the effect of *Johnson.* Could it be that those who supported the statute were engaging in some wishful thinking in convincing themselves that the new statute would pass constitutional muster? If so, a very likely scenario, it would be an example of senators and representatives unintentionally violating the Constitution—they believed they were acting in accord with the Constitution, but were wrong.

In the absence of judicial review, this type of self-delusion would not only be more likely to occur but would be more dangerous. In *United States v. Eichman* (1990)—the second flag-burning case—the Supreme Court corrected the error of the other two branches. If there were no judicial review, however, the error would go uncorrected. Thus, if there were no judicial review, there would be great potential for the development of a jurisprudence of wishful thinking. When the public desire to do something is strong, the branches of government most directly accountable to the people would be more likely to conclude, in good faith, that the politically expedient solution is also the constitutional solution. Thus, the absence of judicial review would likely bring about, however unintentionally, a triumph of present politics over continuing constitutional principle.

A similar phenomenon might also occur in cases in which the legislative or executive branches wished to act in a constitutionally questionable manner. Indeed, precisely such a method of conduct was urged by President Franklin Roosevelt's letter to Representative Hill. At best, this would be another example of delusion; more realistically, though, it appears to be a species of not-so-benign neglect of the Constitution.

We would have a system in which Congress and the president gave lip service, but nothing more, to their oaths concerning the Constitution. Essentially, the Constitution would be a dead letter except when the actions of the political branches were consistent with it. Of course, when the actions of the political branches are consistent with the Constitution, a constitutional enforcement mechanism is unnecessary. It is precisely for those occasions in which political leaders are tempted to opt for popular, rather than constitutional, solutions that judicial review is most needed as an enforcement mechanism.

Finally, the absence of judicial review would undermine one of the most important, but least understood, roles played by the Constitution—the role of antimajoritarian counterweight to oppression by the majority. Majority groups and coalitions constituting majorities control legislatures and elect presidents. The Constitution (especially the Bill of Rights), however, not only empowers majorities but also, and at least as important, protects minority interests from overreaching majorities. Thus seen, most of the limitations on governmental power contained in the Constitution are antidemocratic. They place limits on what may be accomplished through majority vote of democratically elected legislators. These limits prevent the majoritarian branches from, for example, mandating Christian prayer in the schools even if such legislation is desired by a majority of the populace. Without judicial review, lawmaking and constitution interpreting would be in the same hands—the hands of the majority. The result would likely be that the majority's views would prevail over those of the minority even in situations in which the Constitution, as it would be interpreted by people not facing political pressures, places limits on the majority.

In sum, I fear that if there were no judicial review many of the rights granted to individuals by the Constitution would be illusory. Only popular rights, and rights of the popular, would be protected, because the political system would protect them from intrusion. Unpopular rights, and rights of the unpopular, would wither. The Constitution's aim to protect enduring ideals of individual rights from transitory majoritarian passions would be vitiated.

This likelihood was well expressed by Supreme Court Justice David Souter in his 1990 Senate confirmation hearings:

> There is no question about it. If [the Supreme Court did not enforce fundamental rights, no matter how repulsive the acts protected may be to the majority], there would be no point in having a Bill of Rights. If that were not the case, there would be no point in having any substantive protection for civil liberties. We would leave the entire issue to whatever majoritarian impulse there might be at the time, and we would have a vastly different society from the one which the framers of the Bill of Rights intended us to have.

Conclusion

What if there were no judicial review? The situation is so foreign to our experience that it is hard to imagine. One thing seems certain, though—life would be quite different.

In some ways, the absence of judicial review might result in a better political system. For example, Congress and the president might take more seriously *their* oaths of obedience to the Constitution if the judiciary did not serve as a backstop to prevent constitutional violations. In addition, in the absence of judicial review the public might be more involved in constitutional decision making than is now the case. Finally, there might be a greater likelihood that the Constitution would be interpreted in light of present-day concerns, making it a more vital and responsive, yet still enduring, document.

The enormous damage that would flow from the absence of judicial review would greatly outweigh these potential benefits, however. Our system has worked quite well with the delicate system of checks and balances among the three branches of the federal government. Yet, in the absence of judicial review, the judiciary would not be a check on the other two branches: it would merely serve to interpret and enforce their will. The other branches that by their nature, are more responsive to temporal political pressures are more likely to overreach in favor of political majorities, with serious consequences for minority interests. It is in these situations that judicial review assures adherence to constitutional limits. The absence of judicial review would encourage flouting of those limits, resulting in the triumph of present politics over continuing constitutional principle. In addition, the absence of final, federal judicial review would result in a Constitution whose meaning differed from state to state.

Fortunately, judicial review, while not inevitable, has become an integral part of the American political structure. We can be thankful to the framers of the Constitution for providing the system that allowed it to develop and to the judiciary that has effectively and responsibly nurtured it.

Sources and Suggested Readings

The literature about judicial review is extensive. Some indication of the views of the framers can be found in *The Federalist Papers*, especially numbers 78–

82. A convenient modern edition is edited by Clinton Rossiter (New York: New American Library, 1961). Of course, the primary source of American judicial review doctrines is the decision of the Supreme Court in *Marbury v. Madison*, 1 Cranch 137 (1803). A good guide to that seminal case is provided by William W. Van Alstyne, "A Critical Guide to *Marbury v. Madison*," *Duke Law Journal* (1969): 1–47.

The political theory underlying judicial review is explored in a number of modern works. Particularly useful books include Raoul Berger, *Congress v. The Supreme Court* (Cambridge, Mass: Harvard University Press, 1969); Alexander M. Bickel, *The Least Dangerous Branch: The Supreme Court at the Bar of Politics*, 2nd ed. (New Haven, Conn.: Yale University Press, 1986); Alexander M. Bickel, *The Supreme Court and the Idea of Progress* (New Haven, Conn.: Yale University Press, 1978); Charles L. Black, *The People and the Court: Judicial Review in a Democracy* (New York: Macmillan, 1960); Jesse H. Choper, *Judicial Review and the National Political Process: A Functional Reconsideration of the Role of the Supreme Court* (Chicago, Ill.: University of Chicago Press, 1980); John H. Ely, *Democracy and Distrust: A Theory of Judicial Review* (Cambridge, Mass.: Harvard University Press, 1980); Learned Hand, *The Bill of Rights* (Cambridge, Mass.: Harvard University Press, 1958); Robert H. Jackson, *The Struggle for Judicial Supremacy: A Study of Crisis in American Power Politics* (New York: Knopf, 1941); and Leonard Levy, *Judicial Review and the Supreme Court: Selected Essays* (New York: Harper and Row, 1967).

Helpful articles and shorter works include John B. Attanasio, "Everyman's Constitutional Law: A Theory of the Power of Judicial Review," *Georgetown Law Journal* 72 (1984): 1665–1723; Jan G. Deutsch, "Neutrality, Legitimacy and the Supreme Court: Some Intersections Between Law and Political Science," *Stanford Law Review* 20 (1968): 179–261; and Eugene V. Rostow, "The Democratic Character of Judicial Review," *Harvard Law Review* 66 (1952): 193–224.

GLEN JEANSONNE

7 | What If There Had Been No Slavery?

"Five score years ago, a great American, in whose symbolic shadow we stand today, signed the Emancipation Proclamation," civil rights leader Martin Luther King said in a stirring speech he delivered to the March on Washington for Jobs and Freedom in 1963. He added:

> But one hundred years later, the Negro still is not free; one hundred years later, the life of the Negro is still sadly crippled by the manacles of segregation and the chains of discrimination; one hundred years later, the Negro lives on a lonely island of poverty in the midst of a vast ocean of material prosperity; one hundred years later, the Negro still languishes in the corners of American society and finds himself in exile in his own land.

In his speech King pointed to the evils of slavery as still influencing the conditions of black people in America. King and other African-American leaders have often noted that however difficult other immigrant groups found life in the United States, none had to endure the special legacy of slavery.

To understand the impact of slavery, we should ask ourselves whether the condition of blacks in America would be different today if slavery had never existed. To be sure, we can only speculate. But such speculation will compel us to consider matters often neglected when the African-American experience is evaluated.

The Condition of African-Americans

African-American men and women were freer in 1992 than when King spoke these words in Washington. Legal protection has been extended through numerous civil rights laws, executive orders, and Supreme Court decisions. In a legal sense *segregation*—the separation of people on the basis of race—has vanished, educational opportunities have increased, voting participation has expanded, and the number of African-American officeholders has increased from fewer than two hundred in 1965 to more than seventy-three hundred in January 1990. In 1988 Democrat L. Douglas Wilder became the first African-American elected governor of an American state when he defeated Republican J. Marshall Coleman in Virginia, a state in which African-Americans constitute less than 13 percent of the electorate. Democrat David Dinkins defeated incumbent Edward Koch in the primary and Republican Rudolph Guiliani in the general election to become the first African-American mayor of New York City. African-American mayors were also elected in Atlanta, New Orleans, Detroit, Cleveland, and New Haven, Connecticut. These victories were made possible by changes in African-American registration and white attitudes. Four times as many African-Americans were registered to vote in 1980 as in 1960; moreover, African-Americans won electoral victories in areas where they constituted far less than one-half the voters. An African-American, Clarence Thomas, sat on the Supreme Court, and there were more than four hundred African-American federal judges, over 15 percent of them appointed by President Jimmy Carter. Colin Powell, a four-star general, became in 1989 the first African-American to serve as chairman of the Joint Chiefs of Staff. There was a rising African-American middle class, and African-American entertainer Bill Cosby had the top-rated network television program in 1990. Racial attitudes in the South had changed so remarkably that since 1974 more African-Americans have moved into the South than out of it.

Yet King's speech remains poignant because for many African-Americans the promise of the Emancipation Proclamation is still unfulfilled. African-Americans lag behind whites in nearly every economic and educational category: employment, white-collar positions, per capita income, high school graduation, college attendance, graduate and professional school enrollments. In 1988 almost six of every ten African-American families with children under age eighteen were headed by a single parent, virtually all women, while for whites the figure was only two out of ten. Life expectancy for whites in 1987 was 75 years, for African-Americans, 69.4 years. The annual death rate for African-Americans was 50 percent higher than for whites, with the greatest single disparity death by homicide. In 1987 the African-American homicide rate was six times higher than that for whites. Homicide was the leading cause of death for African-American males ages fifteen to twenty-four, and one of every three deaths of African-American males ages twenty to twenty-four was a homicide. African-Americans constituted 12 percent of the population but 44 percent of murder victims. The crime wave was largely intraracial; 95 percent of African-American homicides were committed by African-American perpetrators. African-American males ran a dangerous gauntlet from cradle to grave: high rates of infant death, educational dropout, drug abuse, alcoholism, arrest, incarceration, and chronic unemployment. In a population 12 percent African-American, 27 percent of AIDS (acquired immune deficiency syndrome) victims were African-American. In 1990, 23 percent of African-American men in their twenties were in prison, jail, or in the court system, compared to 6 percent of whites. There were more African-American men in their twenties under court control than African-American men of all ages in college.

Poverty is endemic in the African-American community. African-Americans constitute one-third of the poor, three times their proportion of the population. In 1982, 29 percent of all African-American males between the ages of twenty and sixty-four were either unemployed or were not in the labor force at all. By 1988, unemployment for all races had declined, but African-Americans were still 2.5 times as likely to be jobless as whites. Their duration of unemployment was longer than whites, and they had less savings to subsist on.

The African-American family is in crisis. Since 1960 the divorce rate for African-Americans has risen more than 400 percent, and African-Americans separated without a divorce at a rate five times higher than whites. The United States has the highest teenage pregnancy rate among Western nations. African-Americans constitute 15 percent of teenage girls, yet 29.3 percent of births to teens under twenty were African-American; 35.2 percent to teens under eighteen; and 57.3 percent to teens under fifteen. Nationally, 90 percent of African-American teens giving birth were unmarried. This virtually doomed the parents to becoming school dropouts and welfare recipients and doomed their offspring to a life of poverty.

How has racism, and its twin scourge, poverty, endured in a nation where equality under law is presumed and where the creed of the Declaration of Independence professes that "all men are created equal"?

A Brief History of Race Relations

In reality, African-Americans have never been free or equal in America. The basic guarantees of citizenship and civil rights were denied to them for much of America's history. Section 2 of Article I of the Constitution recognized the existence of slavery by directing the inclusion of "three fifths of all other Persons" (i.e., slaves) in the enumeration that was to form the basis of apportionment and taxation. Slavery was not totally abolished until the Thirteenth Amendment was ratified in 1865. African-Americans were not guaranteed citizenship until the Fourteenth Amendment was ratified in 1868; hence, they were excluded from constitutional protection under the Bill of Rights. Since they were not considered citizens in many states, African-Americans could not vote, hold office, or participate on juries. The amount of property they could own was severely limited; in fact, as slaves they *were* property, although there were small numbers of free blacks in the North and the South. In most southern states slaves could not be taught to read or write; in some, slave marriages were not recognized.

American slavery began in the 1600s as a convenience to white planters who lacked sufficient labor to hoe and pick cotton and plant and harvest labor-intensive crops such as tobacco, indigo, and rice; it soon degenerated into a system of inherited servitude based on skin color. Since African-Americans could not attend school and most were manual laborers, the concept developed that they were intellectually inferior; race itself became a stigma, that is, blackness was equated with stereotyped inferiority. In colonial America there was some opposition to slavery, and the authors of the Constitution made it possible for Congress to halt the slave trade after 1808 but not to abolish the institution of slavery. Since slaves and free African-Americans were not citizens unless the individual states made them so, they did not enjoy civil rights protected by the federal government. *Civil rights* in the United States are rights designed to protect persons from arbitrary treatment by the government or by other individuals. Such rights may concern employment, voting, housing, or access to public facilities. Over time the variety of rights has been gradually extended. For example, until 1920, when the Nineteenth Amendment was ratified, women were not entitled to the right to vote in all states.

Emancipation and the Civil War Amendments

African-Americans obtained political rights before economic benefits. Two periods—the Civil War era and the civil rights era (1954–68)— saw the greatest expansion of African-American political rights. Abraham Lincoln's Emancipation Proclamation of 1863 abolished slavery in the states in rebellion. The Thirteenth Amendment, ratified in 1865, prohibited involuntary servitude, as slavery was called, in the United States. Freed slaves, however, still relied on state laws for most civil rights. While legally free, they remained economically dependent. Most southern states enacted laws, called *black codes*, which limited the rights of freed slaves to vote, serve on juries, possess firearms, and change jobs freely.

The Fourteenth Amendment, ratified in 1868, was designed to establish permanently the rights of freed slaves. Its provisions included the following:

> All persons born or naturalized in the United States, and subject to the jurisdiction thereof, are citizens of the United States and of the State wherein they reside. No State shall make or enforce any law which shall abridge the privileges or immunities of citizens of the United States; nor shall any State deprive any person of life, liberty, or property, without due process of law; nor deny to any person within its jurisdiction the equal protection of the laws.

This amendment has become the most important basis for civil rights for all United States citizens, not just African-Americans. Without slavery, the Civil War, and the consequent necessity to define the rights of the freed slaves, it may not have been enacted.

The Fourteenth Amendment has played a critical role in the development of constitutional law. Originally, the Bill of Rights (the first ten amendments) applied only to the federal government. These amendments, which specify the rights of citizens, protected Americans only from actions by the national government, not acts by the states. However, the *due process* clause and *equal protection* clause of the Fourteenth Amendment have been interpreted by the Supreme Court to "nationalize" nearly all of the Bill of Rights, applying them to the individual states. This *incorporation* of the rights of the first ten amendments to state citizenship has been gradual. Although it is not clear that such applicability to state action was intended by the authors of the Fourteenth Amendment, the ramifications have been enormous. All Americans enjoy more protection because it was thought necessary to specify the rights of African-Americans and because judicial interpretation subsequently incorporated a wide variety of rights into constitutional law.

The Fifteenth Amendment, enacted by Congress in 1869 and ratified in 1870, prohibited any state from denying the vote "on account of race, color, or previous condition of servitude."

The Retreat from Equality

In the decade following the end of the Civil War, Congress enacted five major civil rights statutes enumerating the rights of the freed slaves. The most elaborate was the Civil Rights Act of 1875, which made it a federal crime to discriminate in public accommodations. However in the *Civil* Rights *Cases* of 1883 the Supreme Court declared the law unconstitutional on the grounds that the Fourteenth Amendment applied to government action only and did not prohibit discrimination by private individuals. A decade earlier, in the *Slaughterhouse Cases* (1873), the Court had narrowly interpreted the *privileges and immunities clause* of the Fourteenth Amendment.

These limitations delayed the extension of true civil rights to African-Americans for nearly a century. The South proceeded to restore white supremacy by a variety of devices. By 1910 every former Confederate state had succeeded in disfranchising African-Americans by some state statute. The most effective mechanism of disfranchisement was the white primary, by which states defined political parties as private organizations that were free to restrict their membership to the white race. Other devices included discriminatory literacy tests and the necessity of paying a tax, called a *poll tax*, to vote.

A system of racial segregation, enforced by race and custom, developed in the southern states, encompassing every facet of life. In the northern states, segregation was often based on custom and habit rather than law, relative isolation facilitated by the small numbers of African-American families living there. Throughout the old Confederacy a system called *Jim Crow* developed, named for a famous actor who entertained with blackface makeup. African-Americans were denied access to white schools, parks, restaurants, hotels, hospitals, railroad cars, and buses or were confined to specific areas within them.

In 1890 Louisiana passed a law segregating railroad cars, euphemistically entitled An Act to Promote the Comfort of Passengers. In 1892, Homer Adolph Plessy, who was seven-eighths white, deliberately tested the law by taking a seat in the "whites only" coach and was promptly arrested. The U.S. Supreme Court in 1896 upheld the constitutionality of the Louisiana law on the grounds that it was not discriminatory, since whites were separated from blacks as much as blacks were separated from whites. This case, *Plessy v. Ferguson*, remained the law for fifty-eight years. Although the case concerned segregated transportation facilities, it was also applied to the custom of creating separate schools for white and African-American students.

Segregation

Without slavery and the subsequent attempts to preserve racial separation the nation would have developed a much more efficient educational and economic system. Slavery did not just place African-Americans in bondage; its legacy dragged down the social and economic development of all Americans. A dual social and economic system developed for whites and for African-Americans. It was carried to inane limits in some states; African-Americans had to swear on separate bibles in court and use separate telephone booths. The economy, particularly in the South, was stunted by wasteful duplication of effort. Businesses and factories were compelled to construct separate rest rooms and waiting rooms. Without the legacy of slavery, America could have invested more, with increased efficiency, in its human and material infrastructure. The nation would have developed a better trained work force and resources would have been allocated more rationally. Economies of scale could have been practiced in businesses and educational institutions that served a wider public.

Deliberately retarding the progress of African-Americans meant smaller markets for businesses and wasted individual talents that could have been utilized in education, business, the arts, medicine, and the professions. It restricted the cultural offerings available to all Americans, prevented talented athletes and entertainers from exhibiting their abilities, and deprived millions of the opportunities to enjoy them. The poverty imposed by a restricted economic climate increased crime and required higher taxes. It lowered standards of living for everyone. It is no accident that the South, where the dual economy was most pervasive, was the most backward region of the nation. The intellectual superiority imputed to whites and the inferiority imputed to African-Americans had devastating effects. It encouraged white supremacist groups such as the Ku Klux Klan. It increased color consciousness, white guilt, and stereotypes of inferiority. Fewer extremists, white and black, would have emerged from this era to plague modern social institutions with their violence and hostility. Without this dual system there would have been fewer differences between white and black student achievement and a larger African-American middle class, and African-Americans would have had an earlier start in establishing businesses, accumulating wealth, and bequeathing it to their offspring. African-American philanthropy would be more firmly established, and more African-Americans would have earned graduate degrees and medical and law degrees. The attempts to rectify discrimination by reparations in the form of racial quotas would have been unnecessary and would not have developed.

Renewed Progress toward Equality

African-Americans and their white allies worked to rid America of institutionalized racism, and progress was gradual but persistent. In 1944 the United States Supreme Court ruled in *Smith v. Allwright* that the Texas white primary (which excluded blacks on the grounds that only whites could join the Democratic party) was a violation of the Fifteenth Amendment. The court rejected the claim of the state of Texas that the Democratic party was a voluntary association and ruled that it was acting as an agent of the state.

Since education has been a key to economic success in America, African-Americans sought equal educational opportunity. In the *Gaines* case in 1938, the Supreme Court ordered Lloyd Gaines admitted to the law school at the University of Missouri because Missouri had no separate law school for African-Americans. Under the *Plessy* requirement that separate facilities were legal only if equal, Herman Sweatt, an African-American, was ordered admitted to the University of Texas law school because the law school created for African-Americans by the Texas state legislature was inferior. In the same year (1950) as this decision, known as *Sweatt v. Painter*, the Supreme Court ruled in *McLaurin v. Oklahoma State Regents* that separate facilities provided for an African-American plaintiff studying in the graduate school of the University of Oklahoma were unequal.

Not all progress occurred in the courts. During the Great Depression of the 1930s, the programs of the New Deal brought increased employment opportunities to African-Americans. During World War II, the demand for labor in war industries attracted African-Americans to northern cities. Largely at the insistence of African-American leaders, President Franklin Roosevelt created a Civil Liberties Unit in the Department of Justice and a Committee on Fair Employment Practices to eliminate discriminatory employment by the federal government.

In 1948 President Harry Truman by executive order abolished segregation in the armed forces. Truman's call for civil rights legislation in the Democratic platform at the national convention in 1948 provoked a walkout by some southern delegates. Subsequently South Carolina governor, J. Strom Thurmond, was nominated as a candidate for president by the States' Rights Democratic party, called the *Dixiecrat* party because its principal support was in the South. Thurmond's candidacy did not prevent Truman from winning the election, but Congress refused to enact Truman's civil rights program. Without slavery and its legacy of institutionalized segregation, the entire issue of civil rights for minorities would have been less pronounced. Opposition to civil rights for African Americans divorced from the legacy of white supremacy would not have been the divisive force that it became in American politics. The politics of race that pervaded the late 1950s and 1960s would have been muted.

The administration of Dwight D. Eisenhower (1953–61) witnessed the flowering of the movement of civil rights for African-Americans and an acceleration in the pace of change. The *Brown v. Board of Education of Topeka, Kansas* decision of 1954 was a watershed in the movement. In the *Brown* case the Supreme Court considered anew the issue of segregated public education and overturned the precedent set by *Plessy*. It was the opening salvo in an era sometimes termed the Second Reconstruction (1954–68).

In a unanimous opinion, Chief Justice Earl Warren cited the findings of social scientists, chiefly psychologists and sociologists, among them Kenneth B. Clark and Gunnar Myrdal, the latter a Swede who had written the influential study, *An American Dilemma* (1944). Warren concluded that "in the field of public education the doctrine of 'separate but equal' has no place. Separate educational facilities are inherently unequal."

The ruling had implications far beyond public education. Just as slavery had once been the law of the land and had been overturned, so the whole system of legalized segregation was brought into question. The gates were opened for a flood tide of change.

Certainly the subsequent history of the 1950s and 1960s would have been far different without the shadow of the history of institutionalized racism. African-American activism would not have developed on the scale it did without the existence of a system of discrimination. White conscience would not have been pricked, nor would the ensuing decades have experienced much of the tumult that occurred. From the *Brown* decision onward America would be preoccupied with overturning a legacy of prejudice.

Martin Luther King and Civil Disobedience

In December 1955, in Montgomery, Alabama, Rosa Parks, an African-American seamstress, violated a local segregation statute by refusing to give up her seat on a bus to a white rider. She was arrested and fined $10. Blacks then boycotted the Montgomery bus system for an entire year, until bus segregation was outlawed by a federal court injunction, rapidly followed by a Supreme Court decision that struck down the Montgomery statute as a violation of equal protection of the laws. The boycott made a national figure of the Reverend Martin Luther King, Jr., its leader. King used peaceful civil disobedience to promote change, aided by the National Association for the Advancement of Colored People (NAACP) and the Congress of Racial Equality (CORE) in addition to the group he founded, the Southern Christian Leadership Conference (SCLC).

Civil disobedience, a form of protest, is the peaceful breaking of laws regarded as immoral or unjust. People who engage in such activity are willing to accept legal punishment for their offense, in the hope that public opinion will be swayed by their actions to their point of view. The ultimate goal of civil disobedience is to have elected public officials repeal the bad laws and enact good ones.

Civil disobedience had been used in America on a limited basis before, for example, by draft resisters and by some labor unions, but its use on a massive scale was a product of the civil rights movement. Without the necessity to overturn racist legislation, civil disobedience might not have acquired the legitimacy it did in the minds of many

Americans. The civil rights movement against the legacy of slavery gave civil disobedience a higher profile than it had ever enjoyed in America.

Civil Rights, States' Rights, and Politics

The civil rights movement also compelled the federal government to become increasingly concerned in areas in which its involvement previously had been limited. Since many states either neglected the rights of African-Americans or deliberately discriminated against them, the federal government acted. In doing so it dealt a further harsh blow to the concept of *states' rights*, that is, the idea that some powers were reserved to the states rather than to the federal government. Since the states had already existed before the 1787 Constitution was written, that document permitted them to exercise certain powers over their citizens. Southern states used the concept of states' rights to justify segregation laws, just as southerners one hundred years earlier had used the states' rights doctrine to justify secession.

Indeed, it is quite likely that without slavery there would have been no Civil War on the scale of the one that actually occurred. Doubtless there would have been sectional animosity and conflicts, perhaps even military skirmishes between sections over boundaries, economic questions, and the movement of populations across state lines. But the divisions would not have been so sharply drawn, nor would the moral question have been so deeply etched. Probably most of the issues that provoked the Civil War would have been dealt with over time, but the solutions would have evolved piecemeal and a number of questions would not have been settled so definitively or so abruptly.

For example, the Civil War settled permanently the question of whether a state could leave the union of its own volition. Without slavery, the main cause of the Civil War, the indivisibility of the Union might not have been settled definitively, at least not in the 1860s. The Civil War, however, did not settle all aspects of which issues should be dealt with by the states and which ones handled by the federal government. But in the 1950s and 1960s states' rights came to be identified as a subterfuge for racism. The civil rights movement stimulated the national government, particularly the judiciary, to become far more active than previously in personal liberties issues. Presidents reluctantly moved to enforce court orders with federal troops. Congress enacted a series of civil rights laws, beginning in 1957, which changed human rights in the United States. Doubtless some human rights legislation would have been enacted anyway. But just as the emergency of the Great Depression compelled the federal government to play a larger role in the economy, the crisis of the civil rights movement and the inactivity or intransigence of the state governments compelled the federal government to enter social questions on a scale not contemplated previously. President Eisenhower was a reluctant champion of civil rights and respected the idea of states' rights. But the flagrant violation of the desegregation edicts of federal courts forced his hand. In 1957 he ordered federal troops to Little Rock, Arkansas, to desegregate Central High School over the resistance of the governor, Orval Faubus, a white supremacist. This action was the first use of federal troops to enforce the *Brown* decision, and it doomed the resistance of white southerners to court edicts. The issue of civil rights persuaded Eisenhower that presidential activism was necessary on a scale he found personally distasteful. It also compelled him, and the Congress, to seek remedial legislation. A galaxy of civil rights issues that otherwise may have been sublimated, or delayed, erupted.

The Civil Rights Act of 1957 was the first enacted by Congress since Reconstruction. The law created a new Civil Rights Division in the Department of Justice, headed by an assistant attorney general. It also authorized the federal government to obtain civil injunctions in federal courts against actual or threatened interference with the right to vote.

The Eisenhower administration proposed and the Congress enacted a second Civil Rights Act in 1960. This act authorized federal district courts to appoint referees to enroll qualified voters for all state as well as federal elections where local officials systematically denied them the right to register or to vote. President John F. Kennedy, like his predecessor, became an activist because of the forces unleashed by the civil rights movement. Like Eisenhower, he was reluctant to use force or propose civil rights legislation, but like Eisenhower he did both. In the fall of 1962 Kennedy dispatched twenty-five thousand federal troops to compel the admission of James Meredith, an African-American, to the University of Mississippi despite the opposition of Governor Ross R. Barnett. Eight months later Kennedy used the Alabama National Guard when George C. Wallace defied a federal court order to admit two African-American applicants, Vivian Malone and James Hood, to the University of Alabama at Tuscaloosa.

The cause of civil rights induced black activism on a scale that would have been otherwise unlikely. In February 1960, four African-American freshmen at North Carolina Agricultural and Technical College began the first *sit-in* demonstration of the decade at the lunch counter of F. W. Woolworth's dime store in Greensboro. Sit-ins were demonstrations in which black and white students would sit down at segregated lunch counters and wait to be served. Other sit-ins followed, mounted largely by CORE. There were also *freedom rides* in which blacks and whites boarded legally segregated buses and took seats wherever they chose in an effort to desegregate interstate bus transportation. In the summer of 1963 King led the massive, peaceful, biracial March on Washington. He used the forum to call for racial harmony and to urge passage of the civil rights bill Kennedy had introduced several months earlier.

In November 1963, President Kennedy was assassinated in Dallas. His assassination in the South while his civil rights bill was pending led to a plea by his successor, Lyndon Johnson, to enact the bill to honor the slain president. Johnson used Kennedy's martyrdom, his own southern origins, and his renowned persuasive powers to have Congress enact the Civil Rights Act of 1964. The law was far stronger than the legislation of the Eisenhower administration. It forbade racial discrimination by employers or labor unions and prohibited discriminatory literacy tests, providing that anyone with a sixth-grade education be presumed literate. It outlawed discrimination in public accommodations and facilities that affected interstate commerce and authorized the withholding of federal funds from any program, public or private, which practiced racial discrimination. In the following years Johnson persuaded Congress to enact the Voting Rights Act of 1965 and the Open Housing Act of 1968. Both laws proved a boon to other minorities as well as to African-Americans.

Radicalization of the Civil Rights Movement and the White Backlash

President Johnson also launched a War on Poverty that provided unprecedented economic aid to the poor, especially minorities. Economic problems proved difficult to eliminate by legislation, however. Moreover, the consensus fashioned by Johnson after the death of Kennedy began to erode. Black leadership was radicalizing, and the biracial civil rights movement began to disintegrate. Radical black leaders joined other dissidents to oppose the policies of the Johnson administration. A large factor in their radicalization was the war in Vietnam, which Johnson was prosecuting concurrently with the War on Poverty. The civil rights movement, the rising youth culture of the 1960s, and the antiwar movement overlapped. Many civil rights leaders opposed the war, and antiwar activists borrowed tactics such as civil disobedience from the civil rights movement.

Many whites became frustrated. Some saw the demands of African-Americans and other minorities as understandable but impossible to fulfill. A *white backlash* occurred, pitting conservatives and advocates of slow change against proponents of faster, even revolutionary change. The events of the 1960s had polarized America, and much of the polarization was derived directly or indirectly from the direction and pace of the civil rights movement. In 1968 Americans elected a conservative Republican, Richard Nixon, to succeed the liberal Democrat, Lyndon Johnson. Johnson did not run for reelection, driven from office largely by the political climate polarized by race and the Vietnam War, and Nixon narrowly defeated Johnson's handpicked successor, Vice-President Hubert Humphrey. Without the divisiveness of race and Vietnam, Johnson's fate might have been different.

Busing

The civil rights issues of the 1970s differed from those of the 1950s and 1960s. *De jure segregation*—based on law and institutions—had been largely eliminated. But *de facto segregation*—not mandated by law but derived from patterns of housing and personal preference—remained. By the end of the Nixon administration more southern than northern schools were fully integrated, but racial imbalances in school systems persisted in all regions. In 1969 the Supreme Court ruled in the *Holmes County* case that "The obligation of every school district is to terminate dual school systems at once and to operate now and hereafter only unitary school systems." This decision meant busing students from predominantly black to predominantly white schools and vice versa.

In 1971 the Supreme Court delivered one of its last unanimous decisions on racial matters in the *Swann v. Charlotte-Mecklenburg Board of Education*, which mandated busing. The court proceeded to extend the use of busing as a tool in racial integration. In 1975, Judge W. Arthur Garrity, Jr., ordered extensive busing to desegregate South Boston, an area populated heavily by white ethnic groups, with few African-Americans. The program encountered heavy resistance from whites. Busing became an inflammatory political issue. In 1976 George C. Wallace won several Democratic presidential primaries by making it the center of his campaign.

However unpalatable busing may have been to many whites, the Supreme Court continued to uphold its constitutionality. In 1980, Justice Byron White, who authored the court's sweeping decisions in Dayton and Columbus, Ohio, cases argued that there is an "affirmative duty" to eliminate the effects of past discrimination even if there is no longer any discrimination practiced.

Affirmative Action

Busing addressed the problem of racial imbalances in schools, and the Court ruled that setting racial quotas for the composition of classrooms was a permissible tool in integration. (Integration implies the association of the races whereas desegregation implies only the freedom to associate.) It remained to be seen whether racial quotas were permissible in the workplace. The issue revolved around the question of whether affirmative action policies could be used to remedy the effects of past discrimination. Under affirmative action policies, employees or universities could reserve places for minorities to rectify the effects of past preferential treatment. Many who did not belong to the groups aided by affirmative action argued that this constituted reverse discrimination based on double standards in ranking, hiring, and promotion.

Affirmative action addressed not present discrimination but the history and effect of discrimination in America, another legacy of slavery. Even its advocates admitted it was not an ideal solution. But the effects of past racism were so pervasive, they argued, that harsh medicine was necessary to cure the disease. In 1978 Allan Bakke, a white applicant to the University of California's Medical School at Davis, sued the school for failing to admit him. Davis had set aside sixteen positions in the medical school for minority students. The university admitted that Bakke was more highly qualified than any of the students admitted under the affirmative action program. The Supreme Court issued a decision in which neither the plaintiff nor the defendant won every point. It ruled that the university must admit Bakke, but also ruled that while rigid racial quotas were unacceptable, race could be used as one factor in determining admissions.

A year later the court ruled on a similar case, this one involving affirmative action in the workplace. Brian Weber, a worker for the Kaiser Aluminum and Chemical Corporation in Gramercy, Louisiana, sued the company and the union over preferential job advancement. Kaiser and the United Steelworkers had devised an affirmative action plan that made at least one-half of the available thirteen positions in an on-the-job training program reserved for African-American employees. Weber claimed this constituted a violation of the Civil Rights Act of 1964, which banned racial discrimination in employment. His suit was upheld by two federal courts but overturned by the Supreme Court. The majority held that the law had been enacted to remedy past discrimination against African-Americans, and it would be ironic to turn it against them.

In 1988–89, in his first term as chief justice of the Supreme Court, William Rehnquist fashioned a tenuous conservative majority and joined in a series of decisions with fellow conservatives appointed by President Ronald Reagan. In *Martin v. Wilks*, the Court permitted white fire fighters in Birmingham, Alabama, to challenge an affirmative action settlement that had been in effect since 1981. In *City of Richmond v. J. A. Croson* the court rejected a Richmond, Virginia, program that had set aside 30 percent of city contracts for minority-owned construction companies on the grounds that it violated the rights of white contractors to equal protection of the laws.

The Legacy of Slavery

The racial lines drawn by slavery still resonate throughout the American political system. Not courts, nor legislators, nor executives have proved infallible on racial issues. If the history of slavery teaches anything, it teaches that humanity is imperfect. Even without slavery and its bitter legacy, that imperfectibility would exist. Laws may be developed to mitigate this legacy, but mitigation is not likely to satisfy everyone. A society in which slavery had never existed in America would be no utopia, but it might be quite different from the present one.

On the other hand, it is possible that some problems perceived as racial in reality have other roots. Poverty, illiteracy, unemployment, and crime are not determined by race, though they affect minorities disproportionately. But it is also true that when education and class are held constant, many of the apparent racial disparities decline if not disappear.

A society seeking solutions must first delineate causes. Public policy is often based on perceptions of past history. It is therefore relevant to ask the extent to which racial polarization and the elusive goal of equality is a vestige of institutionalized racism emanating from slavery. Furthermore, if slavery is the origin of many contemporary problems, would the problems exist if slavery had not? In addition, the present concept of civil rights in the United States is so linked to race that we might consider how the civil rights of all Americans might have evolved without slavery.

An Alternative Scenario

We have already shown how certain issues were placed on the agenda because of the heritage of slavery, or at least became more prominent. But beyond attributing certain developments largely to remnants of the institution of slavery, let us sketch an alternative scenario. Let us postulate an America in which slavery never existed. To do so, we must make several assumptions. Assume, for example, that blacks emigrated to America from Africa not as slaves but as free persons, seeking the same economic opportunity and religious freedom that brought immigrants from Europe. Assume that free black immigrants came in approximately the same numbers as the slaves had come. It is of course, unlikely that African-Americans would have come to America in large numbers if they had not been imported as slaves, but such an assumption is necessary to play the game.

Let us stretch our imaginations. What would such an America be like? What would be the economic and political status of the white and black citizens of such an America, and the dimensions of their civil rights? To what extent was slavery a factor in the development of social, political, and economic institutions?

The South Without Slavery

Even if slavery based on race had not existed in the seventeenth century, the African-Americans who came to America would have brought different skills and a different background to America than other immigrants because Africa was quite different from Europe, which supplied most of the early immigrants to the United States. African-American immigrants would not have spoken English and their skills would have been predominantly agricultural. Like most immigrants, they probably would have settled in the area of the New World most like the region from which they came. Thus many would have settled in the southern colonies, but settlement would have been more widely dispersed than that which actually occurred. The southern economy would have developed differently because the cheap labor that made plantation agriculture profitable would have been unavailable or at least more expensive. Many African-Americans, like other settlers, would have become small farmers rather than plantation laborers because they would have had access to free or cheap land. Those who chose to work for others would have demanded higher wages, making labor-intensive crops like tobacco, cotton, sugar cane, and indigo far less profitable. Southern agriculture thus would have become more diversified, and the South would have developed industry more quickly, though it lacked the waterpower available in the North.

As the southern economy actually developed, much of its capital was invested in slaves. Without slavery, where would the capital have gone? Like northerners, southerners would have invested in industry and commerce, particularly the latter. The South had good ports and a river network available for transportation. Without tidewater plantations as a magnet for capital, the interior would have developed more rapidly and industries based on raw materials would have been created. The South would still have been more agriculturally oriented than the North because its soil and climate were better, but the type of agriculture would have been far more diverse than the plantation South. Many different crops rather than a few cash crops would have been grown. It is likely that corn, livestock, and vegetables would have been produced in larger quantity. These would have been traded with the north. Tobacco, the most labor intensive, would have been rare; thus the smoking of tobacco probably would not have developed on a large scale, or at least not until mechanization.

It is likely that an economy more geared to commerce would have generated cities; the South would have been more urban. The Old South was built on three principal features: a rural environment, a one-crop economy, and the plantation system. None of these would have existed on a large scale without the cheap labor available through slavery. A more urban South would have offered both African-Americans and whites wider options for employment and education. Slavery isolated African-Americans, prevented them from obtaining an education, and limited them to rudimentary agricultural skills. Free African-Americans living in cities could have become merchants, wholesalers, and operators of a host of service industries, as only a few free blacks already were. They could have worked in factories, on ships, and on railroads. They would have attended schools in the cities and obtained educations that would have permitted them to become teachers, lawyers, doctors, and white-collar professionals. Since African-Americans would not have been so concentrated in one region of the country, they would not have been perceived as a major threat to the existing political order.

There would doubtless have been segregated housing patterns, as all ethnic groups tended to congregate. But institutionalization of housing segregation probably would not have developed. African-Americans would have lived in enclaves, especially in cities, but would not have been isolated from commerce or access to political news or current events. They would have voted if they owned property; some would have run for office.

African-Americans like other immigrants would have improved their economic standing with each succeeding generation. Saving money, which was not possible under slavery, would have occurred. Property and businesses would have been acquired and bequeathed to offspring. Thus succeeding generations would have started with advantages they did not have under slavery.

Race, Society, and Politics

The society would *not* have been color blind; no society ever has been. African-Americans may have been considered inferior like many other minorities, but their race would have been less of a stigma. If they reached the middle class, as did the second generation of many immigrant groups, some of the prejudice against them would have dissipated, but not all of it. The reason is that African-Americans are distinguishable from many other minorities by their skin color. One cannot readily identify a Jewish-American, Italian-American, or German-American by ethnic characteristics. But those groups that are readily distinguishable (even where slavery is not a factor) are more often stigmatized—Asians and Native Americans, for example. Skin color is the most overpowering identifying characteristic in a diverse population. It is possible that African-Americans and whites would have intermarried en masse and racial identity assimilated. But given the predilection of American colonists to marry within their own groups, and given the different religious and cultural backgrounds of African-Americans, large-scale intermarriage would have been unlikely. There would have been some intermarriage, but African-Americans would have remained racially identifiable.

On the other hand, many of the legal distinctions based on race would not have arisen. African-Americans would have developed an identity, but not as a distinct oppressed minority. Their identity would have been tied to the cultural associations they brought from Africa, doubtless transmuted into something quite different in America. Slavery compelled African-Americans to repudiate or at least to eventually lose their culture. Freedom might have permitted a more gradual, less pronounced transformation. Distinctions would have been cultural and racial but not legal and institutional. African-Americans would have been more dispersed in their memberships in religious denominations and political parties.

Political parties would have evolved differently. African-Americans would have been free to join any party as parties began to develop in the period when the Constitution was drafted and ratified. The early parties were largely based upon economic and regional interests. There would have been regional, cultural, and economic variations in the nation, but the South would not have been unique, and the culture and economy that made it politically monolithic would have been altered. The abolition movement and the sectional conflict based on slavery would not have occurred, but there would have remained political differences among the regions. The South would not be readily identifiable as the states of the Old Confederacy; it would have a much looser, vaguer identity.

The factors that gave rise to the Whig and Republican parties would have been less pronounced. The Whigs relied heavily on support from southern planters who used slaves, and the Republican party was organized in the 1850s largely to oppose the extension of slavery into territories seeking to become states. Without slavery, the Whigs would have been deprived of economic interests that supported them, while the Republicans would have lost their major issue. These parties might not have developed at all or at least they would have had to find other supporters and different issues. The Republicans would not have been so much a force for change, nor the Whigs such defenders of the status quo. Abraham Lincoln, deprived of the issue that made him the first Republican president, would have remained an obscure Illinois politician.

Without the issue of slavery in the territories, which arose when Missouri, and later Kansas and Nebraska, sought admission to the Union, new states would have been added more rapidly. As it was, the South opposed the admission of additional free states where slavery was prohibited, while the North opposed admitting more slave states.

Race would have been a factor in politics to the extent that all ethnic groups seek a slice of the economic pie and the spoils of victory. But without the experience of the Civil War and Reconstruction, race would not be a dominant theme in politics. A variety of issues, rather than a few definitive ones, would have led to looser, less ideological alignments based on regional, economic, and cultural differences. The nation might have several regional parties, or perhaps only a conservative and liberal party. The terms *conservative* and *liberal* would not include the emotional baggage of race. Defense of the status quo would mean something entirely different if slavery and segregation were never institutionalized.

The welfare state still would have evolved out of the Great Depression. In the economic crisis of the 1930s President Franklin D. Roosevelt introduced the welfare state as a system of government services and grants, providing social security and assistance in education, job training, and unemployment benefits. Roosevelt's New Deal made the Democrats the majority party because his Republican predecessors were blamed for causing the Depression and then dealing with it ineffectively. African-Americans, who were poor, benefited from New Deal programs and overwhelmingly supported the Democrats. These developments would still have transpired, but since African-Americans would have been less impoverished in a society that never experienced slavery, they would have become Democrats in smaller numbers. They would simply be another cog in the Democratic coalition of minorities along with the Jews, the Italians, and the Irish. Given the fact that they would have brought less wealth to America, and fewer technical skills, African-Americans might have been somewhat poorer than average, but the disparity would be less pronounced than it actually became.

There would be a larger African-American middle class and more wealthy African-Americans, which would affect their political affiliation.

Minority Rights in Modern America

The movement for civil rights might have taken an entirely different direction. Certainly if such a movement developed, race would not have been so dominant an issue in American political life. Rather it is likely that African-Americans, women, gays, the disabled, the indigent, and disadvantaged ethnic groups would have created a coalition pitting the *have nots* against the *haves*. There would still be civil rights laws, and the Supreme Court would still rule on discrimination, but its decisions would be broader and less tied to racism specifically.

There would, of course, have been no need for the Thirteenth Amendment, which freed the slaves. It is possible that there would have been no compelling demand for the Fourteenth (defining citizenship) or Fifteenth (defining voting rights) Amendments, at least not in the late nineteenth century. It is likely that the movement for increased civil rights would have been more gradual and less dramatic. Sit-ins, bus boycotts, freedom rides, and mass marches might not be a part of our history. At the least, they would not be linked to a distinct era or a specific race.

Today all Americans enjoy greater civil liberties because of the predominantly black civil rights movement. Some of these rights might not be written into law without the stimulus of a racially oriented civil rights movement. It is likely that the civil rights laws of the 1960s would have taken a different form and been passed sporadically rather than periodically.

The denial of rights to African-Americans, when questioned, raised a number of questions about denials of rights to other minorities. The civil rights movement raised the consciousness of all disadvantaged groups. The feminist movement and the gay liberation movement derived inspiration and tactics from the civil rights movement. Minority rights in general became public issues. Many of the court cases that tested discriminatory laws arose from the question of rights for African-Americans. Most of these decisions, of course, were applied to other minorities as well. Such cases and issues may not have been raised otherwise, or at least not so many of them so rapidly.

Some white complaints about the civil rights movement might be irrelevant if the movement had not been identified so closely with African-Americans. It is unlikely that welfare would be viewed as a racial issue or that affirmative action or busing would have been proposed. It is unlikely that black martyrs or white bigots would be so prominent in our history.

With a more dispersed, economically self-sufficient African-American community, segregated schooling probably would not have developed, at least not as a legal principle. The economy would have operated more efficiently without dual school systems and job discrimination. This situation would have produced an African-American population that perceived of itself as a part of mainstream America, not an isolated entity. Neither African-Americans nor whites would be so race conscious, although they would not be entirely oblivious to race. There might have been small African-American separatist movements, but they would have little attraction to most blacks. Armed groups like the Black Panthers probably would not have existed, nor would there be separate courses in African-American studies in universities. The history of African-Americans would be taught like that of other major ethnic groups, as a distinct but not unique fragment of the American kaleidoscope.

America Without Slavery

Problems such as unemployment, drugs, and lack of education would still exist but not as facets of racial stigma. There would be economic inequities, but they would be associated with the population generally, not with racial characteristics.

Ironically, African-Americans might be less rather than more politically involved. African-American politicians would not have been recruited from the ranks of civil rights leaders but from the same vocations as white politicians, largely attorneys, businessmen, and labor leaders. They would have to deal with apathy, not outrage, among their constituents. As the most identifiable minority, African-American candidates would still face prejudice when running for office, much as Catholics once did. Without concentrated black populations in their districts or precincts, they would encounter difficulties in winning elections. Their platforms would be quite different from those of black politicians today, focusing less on civil rights and demands for funds for a racially designated group, and it is likely they would represent varied interest groups in their constituencies like other politicians.

An America without the experience of slavery would be neither color-blind nor problem-free. Many contemporary problems would still exist, but proposed solutions might differ because such problems would not be linked specifically to race. There would still be racial friction, occasional riots, demonstrations, and racially motivated crimes. Some three thousand lynchings of African-Americans in the South occurred between 1865 and 1968, when *lynching* (a killing by a mob) became a federal crime. Such killing, sometimes by groups such as the Ku Klux Klan, would not have been widespread, nor would there have been legal obstruction to African-American rights by such organizations as the White Citizens' Council; but extremism would persist if not flourish.

It is wrong to assume that race is the root of all problems or that slavery is the root of all racism. Nations without a history of racially designated slavery still discriminate, and racial prejudice flourishes where slavery never existed. Prejudice exists, for example, against Jews, Hispanics, and Asians, though none of these groups was subjected to slavery in America. The United States is not unique in experiencing racial problems, but without the history of slavery the irony of discrimination in a democracy might not be so apparent. But an America without slavery would not necessarily be an America without racial prejudice. The bitter edge might be removed, and the dramatic confrontations might not have occurred, but America would be no utopia.

Throughout history slavery has existed without racism and racism without slavery. It is overly simple and naive to assume that slavery alone dictated American racial attitudes, although it was no doubt the greatest single influence. But racial attitudes are complex, scapegoating exists in all societies, and no society ever, no matter how democratic, has been entirely free of discrimination of one type or another.

African-Americans would not have been just another minority without slavery, but the dimensions of their distinctiveness would be mitigated. Skin color is too overpowering an element, and the cultural background of Africa so profoundly different from that of Europe that blacks would remain the most identifiable minority. But both African-American self-perceptions and the stereotyped images of them in the minds of whites would differ in degree even if they did not vanish.

Civil rights would have sprung from different motivations; appeals for broadening them would have arisen from different situations.

We cannot, of course, change or ignore history. We must live, work, play, and think, in a real, not an ideal world, a world with a past and present that is not uniformly pleasant. But perhaps imagining things as they might have been has a practical side if it inspires us to reevaluate our assumptions and rethink stereotypes. John and Robert Kennedy often quoted George Bernard Shaw's reflection: "Some men think of things that are, and ask 'why?' I dream of things that never were and ask 'why not?' "

Sources and Suggested Readings

The literature on racism, prejudice, and the civil rights movement is extensive. For an introduction to theories of prejudice see Gordon Allport, *The Nature of Prejudice* (published originally in 1954) (Reading, Mass.: Addison-Wesley, 1987). For racism and discrimination in the United States, see Gustavus Myers, *History of Bigotry in the United States* (New York: Random House, 1943); Gunnar Myrdal, *An American Dilemma: The Negro Problem and Modern Democracy* (New York: Harper and Bros., 1944); and C. Vann Woodward, *The Strange Career of Jim Crow* (New York: Oxford University Press, 1966). The institutionalization of racism is discussed in Joe R. Feagin and Clairece Booher Feagin, *Discrimination American Style: Institutional Racism and Sexism*, 2nd ed. (Malabar, Fla.: R. E. Krieger, 1986). Thomas F. Gossett, *Race: The History of an Idea in America* (Dallas, Texas: Southern Methodist University Press, 1963) is an excellent introduction to the development of racial stereotypes in the United States. Stanley Feldstein has edited a useful book of documents, *The Poisoned Tongue: A Documentary History of American Racism and Prejudice* (New York: Morrow, 1972).

More theoretical works include Joel Kovel, *White Racism: A Psychohistory* (New York: Columbia University Press, 1984); and Joel Williamson, *The Crucible of Race: Black-White Relations in the American South since Emancipation* (New York: Oxford University Press, 1984).

The best single-volume history of black Americans is John Hope Franklin, *From Slavery to Freedom: A History of Negro Americans*, 5th ed. (New York: Knopf, 1980). The civil rights movement is described in Juan Williams, *Eyes on the Prize: America's Civil Rights Years, 1954-1965* (New York: Penguin, 1987); and Rhoda Lois Blumberg, *Civil Rights: The 1960s Freedom Struggle*, rev. ed. (Boston: Twayne, 1991). Richard Kluger, *Simple Justice*, 2 vols. (New York: Knopf, 1975), is the definitive account of the *Brown* decision. Francis M. Wilhoit, *The Politics of Massive Resistance* (New York: G. Braziller, 1973), describes resistance to desegregation in the South, and J. Harvie Wilkinson, III, *From Brown to Bakke: The Supreme Court and School Integration: 1954-1978* (New York: Oxford University Press, 1979) is the best account of the Supreme Court's racial rulings under Earl Warren and Warren Burger.

JUDITH F. GENTRY

8 | What If the 1787 Constitution Had Provided for Equal Rights?

Should men and women be fully equal before the law? Should they have equal rights and equal responsibilities as citizens of the United States? This was the question posed in the 1970s and early 1980s by consideration of the Equal Rights Amendment (ERA) to the Constitution. Under the rules for amending the United States Constitution, a two-thirds vote by both houses of Congress and ratification by three-fourths of the states are required. Although public opinion polls suggested that the ERA was supported by a majority of the American people, it fell three states short of ratification. And so, in federal law women and men in America do not now have equal rights, nor do they have equal responsibilities.

Since the early 1960s, however, several major laws have been passed at the federal level providing for more nearly equal rights for men and women than had ever been the case before. In addition, major changes have taken place in most states through the passage of legislation attempting to reduce discrimination based on sex or gender in state law.* A few states have even added strong equal rights amendments to their constitutions.

The question therefore arises whether these changes have been suf-

---

*In this discussion, the terms *sex discrimination* and *gender discrimination* will be used interchangeably.

ficient to accomplish the purpose of the proposed ERA. When considering this question, it is important to understand that *statute laws*—laws enacted by Congress or state legislatures—generally pass by a simple majority and can be repealed by a simple majority. A provision for equal rights for women in the United States Constitution would be much more difficult to overturn, since two-thirds of Congress plus three-fourths of the states would have to agree on a repeal.

Of course, the Constitution is subject to interpretation by the federal courts, ultimately the Supreme Court. The Supreme Court generally attempts to discern the intent of the framers of the Constitution or of Congress at the time the constitutional provision or the amendment was debated. There is a very large record of congressional intent in connection with the ERA, so in most cases it is possible to anticipate how the Supreme Court would interpret it.

What if the framers of the Constitution had included a provision for equal rights more than two hundred years ago? And what if the Supreme Court had interpreted that provision of the Constitution in the same manner we can anticipate that it would interpret the ERA? How would the American political system be different from what it is today if the following provision had become a part of the Constitution in 1789?

> Equality of rights under the law shall not be denied or abridged by the United States or by any State on account of sex.

If the framers of the Constitution had included an equal rights provision two hundred years ago, Congress would have had to take care that all the laws it passed be gender neutral. The states would have had to revise their laws to make them gender neutral, or a series of lawsuits over time would have resulted in court decisions eliminating sex discrimination in state laws. Societal attitudes and practices, of course, would not have changed immediately. Custom and tradition would have stood in the way of rapid change. But, over the ten generations that have intervened, major change would slowly have taken place, and we would likely have a society today in which men and women actually have equal rights.

For our analysis we will examine the status of women today and then consider how an equal rights provision in the Constitution would have affected that status. Specifically, we will look at the civic order, government, the private sector, and state laws.

The Civic Order

Citizens have responsibilities and duties in democratic governments. But for most of American history, women have been denied the opportunity to exercise the rights of citizenship and to perform their civic responsibilities. They have been denied participation in voting, officeholding, jury duty, and military service.

Voting

Until the adoption of the Nineteenth Amendment in 1920, women were not permitted to vote in most elections. Like most newly enfranchised groups, women were slow to develop the habit of voting. It was not until 1980, a delay of about sixty years, that women voted in equal proportions to men.

For the first forty or so years, women tended to vote similarly to their husbands. They saw their interests as identical to the interests of their husbands. They usually shared with their husbands membership in the same social and economic class, the same religious organization or orientation, and the same ethnic or racial group. These affiliations rather than their condition as a woman affected their voting choices. After about forty years, however, a *gender gap* in voting behavior was noticeable. In other words, in the 1960s women began to vote differently from men on some issues.

Economic developments in the early nineteenth century were probably responsible for the eventual development of the gender gap. Industrialization had caused changes in work habits that affected men and women dramatically and in different ways. Before industrialization began, wives and husbands both worked in or near their home. They spent long periods of time together, and they both participated in the informal training of their children. In the nineteenth century, however, larger and larger numbers of husbands took jobs in factories or offices that kept them away from the home ten to twelve hours a day for six days a week. The work atmosphere for men was highly individualistic, competitive, and impersonal. To survive in the business world, men had to abandon traditional values of emphasis on community and extended family, sharing, visiting, and dealing primarily with people known personally. Few women entered the paid work force in the nineteenth century, so they were not required to abandon these traditional values. In fact, husbands encouraged their wives to retain traditional values, for they wanted a respite from the business world when they came home at night. These different value systems persisted into the twentieth century. Eventually, these different value systems began to affect how women voted. Also, when additional economic changes after World War II brought larger and larger numbers of women into the paid work force and when social changes resulted in more women losing the security of marriage because of the increasing number of divorces, women began to perceive their interests as women as being sometimes different from their interests as a member of their family. Eventually, these different perceptions were reflected in small but significant differences in the way that men and women voted on some issues.

The gender gap has been most visible on issues related to war and peace. Women have been less supportive of military intervention in other countries than men have been, and women have been less supportive of military spending than men. Women also support gun control and oppose capital punishment in proportions greater than men. Women support spending for social programs—like infant and child nutrition programs and medical care for the poor—in greater proportions than men. Larger proportions of women than men want to end the construction of nuclear energy plants. Women have also been slightly more likely than men to support passage of the Equal Rights Amendment, federal appropriations for day care centers, and other legislation promoting an equal role for women in American society. On the other hand, there are many issues about which there is no significant gender gap, including taxes and the economy.

The gender gap became highly visible in the 1980s. Women favored Ronald Reagan over Jimmy Carter in 1980, but they favored Walter Mondale over Reagan in 1984 and Michael Dukakis over George Bush in 1988. Politicians are not at all sure, yet, how to respond to the gender gap in a way that will enhance rather than harm their chances for election or reelection.

Had there been an equal rights provision in the Constitution, women would have begun voting in small numbers from the beginning of the Republic, and their rate of participation would have slowly increased until it was roughly equal to that of men. At first, women would probably have voted similarly to their husbands, since they shared the same economic and ethnic interests. During the nineteenth century, the attitudes of men and women would have diverged on many issues, since men entered the paid work force in large numbers and relatively few women entered the paid work force at that time. By the late nineteenth century, and perhaps earlier, a gender gap in voting would have developed. Women would have been less likely than men to support American involvement in foreign wars. Women would have been more likely than men to support government assistance to the needy, government efforts to help people find jobs, and the introduction of unemployment insurance, worker's compensation laws, safety regulations in the workplace, assistance to the disabled, pensions for the elderly, and health care programs for all. In summary, women would have been more likely to support the development of a welfare state than men. In all likelihood the United States would have moved more quickly to develop a welfare state and would now have a more extensive one similar to those in the Scandinavian countries. The gender gap might also have resulted in federal support for child care centers.

Officeholding

Although women have the legal right to hold elected office, they are, in fact, underrepresented in national, state, and local positions. There has never been a woman vice-president or president, although there was a woman vice-presidential candidate of a major political party— Geraldine Ferraro for the Democratic party in 1984. In 1990, there were three women state governors (6 percent of the total), two female U.S. senators (2 percent), and twenty-five women out of 435 members of the House of Representatives (6 percent). Women constituted 17 percent of state legislators, 14 percent of city council members, 8 percent of county council members. Women legislators often find themselves with at most one or two other women in the same legislative body and are frequently excluded from the informal "old boy" network that exercises much of the power in politics. There was only one woman justice on the Supreme Court—Sandra Day O'Connor. Women constituted only 12 percent of federal judges and approximately 6 percent of state and local judges.

Had there been an equal rights provision in the Constitution in 1789, women would have been holding political office for two hundred years. The number of women elected at first would have been rather small, because customs and behavior change more slowly than the law.

Long before now, however, women would have gained the necessary habit of participation, experience, and role models to be active participants in the political process. Support from the women's movement that emerged in the mid-nineteenth century would have advanced officeholding by women. In 1843, the transcendentalist and feminist author Margaret Fuller wrote, "We would have every arbitrary barrier thrown down. We would have every path laid open to women as freely as to men." Women would have entered politics in roughly the same proportion as they entered the paid work force. Today women would constitute approximately 45 percent of the senators, representatives, judges, governors, state legislators, school board members, members of economic development commissions, and members of regulatory boards. And there would have been women vice-presidents and presidents.

Jury Duty and Military Service

Until the 1970s, women were automatically excused from jury service in some states. Now, in all jurisdictions, the jury lists are designed to include all adult citizens. There still persists, however, a tendency on the part of judges to excuse women jurors with children from service on juries without careful inquiry about whether the family already has younger children in day care or the older children could be provided for after school by some other means.

If there had been a provision in the Constitution for equal rights for women, there would now be a long tradition of women serving on juries. Most jurisdictions would excuse from jury service the parent (male or female) of pre-school children who is the primary caretaker of those children, unless the family already had those children in day care. Yet more families would likely have chosen to have the mother as primary caretaker of the children, and so more women than men would be excused under this rule.

Another responsibility of citizenship is to serve in the armed forces. Today, there is real discrimination against both men and women in military service. Although the law authorizes the drafting of both men and women in an emergency, only young men are required to register with their selective service boards, because there is no current plan to draft women.

At present, the armed services are an entirely voluntary force.

Women volunteers are excluded from serving in jobs that are classified as combat positions. They are allowed to serve in jobs, however, that will bring them very close to the front lines and will subject them to long-distance artillery fire. Indeed, some women in the U.S. military were killed or wounded in the war against Iraq in 1991. Yet, by being excluded from combat positions, women are much less likely than men to be in battle. The exclusion from combat harms women service personnel by preventing them from receiving both valuable training (as jet pilots, for instance) and leadership experience, which are important for promotion to high-level officer ranks. The officer corps of the military services is heavily dominated by men. The nation is failing to take advantage of the ability that highly qualified women would bring to the leadership of the military. There are, of course, no women on the Joint Chiefs of Staff, which heads the military establishment.

Each service has a quota for women. Thus, many women are deprived of opportunities to receive employment, training, leadership responsibilities, and veterans' benefits. Excluding a large portion of women from veterans' benefits has a significant impact, for they include programs helping veterans attend trade schools or college and assisting veterans to become homeowners. Denial of veterans' benefits, moreover, also seriously affects the ability of women to obtain the high-paying civil service jobs in those states that offer preferences to veterans or give them bonus points on qualifying examinations.

Today women are excused from their duties as citizens to contribute equally to the defense of their country. And they are deprived of the real benefits that can come from full participation in the armed services.

Had there been an equal rights provision in the Constitution, women would be accepted into the armed services on an equal basis with men. Both male and female recruits would be required to have the same educational and mental capabilities and to be physically able to perform the duties of their jobs. Since relatively few women would be qualified physically for jobs that require lifting or carrying heavy weapons or equipment, few women would be doing that kind of work. Since relatively few men would be qualified for jobs that require working in small places, like the interior of tanks, submarines, gun turrets on ships, and space capsules, few men would be doing those kinds of work. But women and men could equally well perform the vast majority of jobs in the armed services. As is the case now, women, of course, would be admitted to the Naval Academy, West Point, and Air Force Academy and become officers. They would, however, become jet pilots, command warships, and lead soldiers into battle. Women as well as men would serve in combat, be wounded, suffer the indignities of capture by the enemy, and sacrifice their lives for their country.

The military today as in the past serves as an important economic opportunity for young people from poor families. Those who have little education and no training often find it difficult to get civilian jobs. Many volunteer for the armed services, so that they will have jobs and receive training. With an equal rights provision in the Constitution, young men and women would have an equal opportunity for this employment and training. These veterans would have an advantage over nonveterans when applying for positions as airline pilots, helicopter pilots, sailors on merchant vessels, and technicians in the electronics and nuclear energy fields, as well as in many other positions where civilian and military skills are interchangeable.

Having performed the duties of military service, women as well as men would be eligible for veterans' benefits. In the past, these benefits have included free or reduced tuition, reimbursement for books and equipment, and monthly support while they pursued an education in college or trade school. There are also programs that assist former servicepersons with borrowing money for their first home. Moreover, many state and local governments as well as the federal government give preferences to veterans when hiring civil servants. Men and women would have equal opportunity to qualify for these benefits and would use them to build better lives for themselves and their families after they have left military service.

If conscription becomes necessary and the Constitution provided for equal rights, women would be required to serve. All young persons— women and men—would be required to register with their draft boards when they reach the age of eighteen. There would likely be a provision of the draft law exempting the parent of minor children who has been and is the primary caretaker of those children. In most families, the mother is the primary caretaker and thus would be awarded the exemption.

Government

Government makes laws that are binding on its citizens. Government has an enormous impact on the lives of women as well as men. Here we examine that impact in government programs, government employment, and public educational institutions.

Government Programs

Today there are many government programs designed to help the unemployed, those who have been hurt on the job, the elderly, and those who cannot afford adequate food, medical care, housing, or college education. Government provides welfare assistance for families with no wage earner present, assistance to middle-income people through guaranteed low-interest loans for their children's education, and aid to farmers and small businesses.

These government programs are relatively free of gender distinction, but they are not totally gender neutral. Unemployment rules, for instance, do not allow a married woman to collect unemployment insurance benefits who has quit her job because her husband has been transferred. Unemployment rules also do not allow benefits to be collected if a worker leaves his or her job to care for a sick child or elderly parent, and these rules work to the detriment of women, for it is usually women who are called upon to perform these family duties.

Social security old age benefits rules are becoming more gender neutral on their face (there are no longer different provisions for widows and widowers, for example). The entire program, however, was based on the concept of a male breadwinner and a full-time female homemaker whose marriage persisted until the death of one of them. Therefore, both the woman who works for pay and the woman who has divorced before her marriage lasted ten years are disadvantaged under the present system. The woman who works for pay must make contributions to the system but earns so little that the widow's benefit is larger than what she would receive from her own account; in effect, all her social security contributions are for nothing. The woman who has been a full-time homemaker but whose marriage breaks up after nine years has no claim to social security.

The rules of the welfare system were also designed with the assumption that the full-time caretaker of young children will be the mother, and there are gender-based applications of these rules as a matter of course. It is almost impossible for an indigent single father of young children to get on welfare, whereas indigent single mothers qualify relatively easily.

An equal rights provision in the Constitution would have a profound impact on these many government programs. The design and the administration of the program would be gender neutral. The single parent—male or female—of young children would be provided welfare payments if the other parent could not or did not provide adequate support. If single parents of children age three or older are required to participate in Workfare, a program that requires welfare recipients to take jobs, these provisions would apply whether the single parent is the mother or the father.

The social security old age benefits system is an interesting example. The most likely mechanism for making it gender neutral would be a system of shared contributions and benefits. To provide equally for the spouse who contributes to the family income by taking care of the home and children, wages earned by either spouse would be divided in half, with half going into the account of the employed spouse and half going into the account of the homemaker spouse. Similarly, if both spouses are employed but one earns twice as much as the other, the contributions to their social security old age credits would be equal, for the wages of each would be divided in half, with half going into the account of each spouse. This arrangement would eliminate any need for special provisions for widows and widowers. And it would provide an equitable and administratively easy way to provide for homemakers who divorce and perhaps remarry.

Government Employment

At present, sex discrimination in employment is prohibited by federal statute—the Equal Pay Act of 1963 and Title VII of the Civil Rights Act of 1964—and by executive order of the president. Federal workers (except those employed directly by Congress), workers employed by state and local government, and all employees in private firms that have fifteen or more workers are covered by the statutes. The Equal Pay Act requires equal pay for men and women doing similar work. Title VII of the Civil Rights Act of 1964 prohibits discrimination based on sex in any aspect of employment. It allows an employer to establish occupational qualifications related to strength or other physical characteristics only if those characteristics are directly necessary to job performance. It requires employers to refrain from and prevent their employees from sexually harassing any employee.

There are, however, persisting patterns of sex discrimination within the government work force at all levels of government. Many states and local governments still have job titles that are gender specific. Even if job titles have been changed, there is very little opportunity for women to be hired into traditionally male-dominated areas of state and local civil service. Veteran-preference rules have resulted in men dominating many of the higher-paying civil service positions because the armed forces have many more men than women. Finally, the attitudes of those who do the hiring are the biggest hurdle for a woman who wishes to be employed in a state civil service position traditionally reserved for men.

The discriminatory practices in hiring have a major impact on the existing large pay differentials for female and male civil servants. The areas of work in which women predominate (secretary, clerk, schoolteacher, lunch worker) are paid considerably less than the areas of work in which men predominate (police officer, truck driver, garbage collector, maintenance worker). The federal government and state and local government (with only a very few exceptions) have made no effort to require that pay be related to the skills required for the job.

Although in theory, promotion in government jobs is not based on sex, there are relatively few women in middle-management jobs in the various civil services and even fewer in upper-level management positions. Many women, of course, have interrupted their careers to devote their full energies to child care when their children are young, and these women are disadvantaged when they later return to government service. Yet large numbers of women have accumulated the necessary years of service, and these women have not been promoted in proportion to their presence in the work force. There is slow improvement in this area, as evidenced by the slowly growing number of women as school principals. At current rates of improvement, it will take at least two to three generations (forty to sixty years) before women are represented at the higher levels of government employment in proportion to their participation in the government work force.

Discriminatory practices in fringe benefits persist. Since 1983, newly hired employees are entitled under federal law to have gender-free pension plans. But female workers hired before 1983 may be required to make larger contributions or may receive smaller monthly checks under their pension plan than their male co-workers. All workers may still encounter gender-based discrimination in the life insurance policies that are offered to them as a fringe benefit of employment. Since men do not live as long as women (on average), men are often charged higher premiums than their female co-workers for the same insurance coverage.

Had there been an equal rights provision in the Constitution, it would apply to all workers employed by any government unit. Government workers, from nuclear energy technicians to schoolteachers or garbage collectors, would be hired, trained, paid, provided fringe benefits, and promoted without regard to sex. As in the military service, physical requirements for jobs could be established if they are actually related to the duties of the position. Agencies would be required to design equipment, however, so that physical strength and height would be deemphasized as job requirements. There would be some government jobs that impinge on the personal privacy of others—such as attendants in public rest rooms and police officers and prison guards who do body searches or supervise prisoners while they are disrobing, bathing, or sleeping. In these cases, the sex of the officer or guard would be an allowable occupational classification.

Training opportunities for government jobs or promotions would be available equally to both women and men. This training and the experience attained by government workers would in some instances have been carried over into the private work force, as persons would move from the public to the private sector. Similarly, promotions would be without reference to the gender of the applicant. Women would thus be found in numbers roughly proportional to their presence in the government work force in such positions as high school principals, presidents of public universities, directors of public works, and directors of public health agencies.

Women and men would probably receive equal pay for comparable work in government jobs. *Comparable work* is work that has similar skill levels and responsibility. Pay scales for different positions would be determined by a system that awards points to a position based on the number of years of education and training required for the position and the amount of responsibility exercised in it. On this scale, schoolteachers are higher than secretaries, and secretaries are higher than truck drivers, and truck drivers are paid more than garbage collectors.

All provisions related to pensions, insurance benefits, and leaves would be gender neutral. Women and men would make equal contributions to pension plans and receive equal monthly pension payments when they retire. Women and men would also make equal payments to life insurance carriers and receive equal coverage. Leaves—for military reserve service, for infant bonding, for care of sick children or elderly parents, or for other purposes—would be provided without reference to the gender of the government worker.

Government workers constitute 15 percent of the work force and would be entitled under the equal rights provision of the Constitution to equal treatment. Another third of the work force is employed by government contractors and also probably would be protected. The rest of the work force—those working for private companies that are not government contractors—would be indirectly affected, since private companies would have to compete to hire the best workers. Currently, persisting sex discrimination by governments with regard to their employees legitimizes continuing sex discrimination by private employers. In contrast, the elimination of sex discrimination by public employers that would exist with an equal rights provision in the Constitution would serve as an example and provide economic pressure on private employers to eliminate sex discrimination.

Public Educational Institutions

Today, primarily because of Title IX of the Educational Amendments Act of 1972, there is something approaching equal educational opportunity in public schools and universities and private schools and universities that receive public funding, except in admissions, physical education and athletics, and vocational counseling. All academic courses, including physical education and vocational education, are open to all students, except for physical education courses in contact sports.

Single-sex public schools and universities are allowed only when equally good single-sex public schools and universities are provided for the other sex; the requirement of equally good schools has proved impossible to achieve in practice, however. This *separate but equal* approach in public education has thus far been acceptable to the federal courts. Private schools and universities receiving federal funds are free to discriminate on the basis of sex in admissions policies.

Schools and universities covered by Title IX (i.e., public schools and universities and private schools and universities receiving federal funds) are required either to offer athletic opportunities to girls on separate teams or to allow them to try out for any sport in which there is only one team, with an exception for contact sports. There is no requirement of equal spending in support of women's athletics, but there is a requirement that women students have equal athletic opportunity with men students. The law requires that girl and women athletes be provided equal equipment, facilities, practice time, and similar conditions, but compliance with this provision is very spotty. Despite the exceptions and limitations in athletics, a dramatic expansion of opportunity for girls and women in interscholastic and intercollegiate sports has developed since the mid-1970s. Scholarship money, numbers of teams, and numbers of female athletes have increased many times over.

The penalty for noncompliance with Title IX is withholding of all federal funds from the school or university in noncompliance. Although there is considerable noncompliance, in no case have federal funds actually been withheld. Institutions are aware that the law has not been enforced and in many cases are no longer engaged in an effort to comply.

If there were an equal rights provision of the Constitution, there would be no single-sex public schools. The educational programs would be fully gender integrated. Physical education classes would include both boys and girls. All would participate in contact sports like football, basketball, or wrestling according to categories determined by the weight or height of the participants. Changing areas and rest rooms would, of course, be for only boys or only girls. All extracurricular activities, including interschool athletics, would be open to both sexes and would not be sex segregated. Instead of sex-segregated teams, there would be several levels of competition based on the weight or height of the athletes.

Public colleges and universities would be similarly affected. There would be no public universities just for women or just for men. Physical education classes, vocational and technical classes, and counseling programs would be free of gender discrimination. Intercollegiate athletics would exclude no one from a team based on gender; they would instead be organized according to weight or height classes. Dormitories, rest rooms, and areas where students change clothes would be separate for men and women. Dormitories could provide no facilities—like washing machines and dryers or air conditioning—for one sex and not for the other. All extracurricular activities would be open to both male and female students.

The Private Sector

The equal rights provision of the Constitution would not apply directly to private associations, private employment, and private business practices. The only time that the equal rights clause would apply would be if a government—federal, state, or local—were involved in some way; that government involvement is called *state action*. The example of equal rights in the public sector would also have an indirect impact on the private sector.

Entirely private organizations and individuals could continue to discriminate on the basis of gender if they wished to. Individuals, private clubs, private sports organizations, private businesses (cocktail lounges and bars, for instance) could prohibit women from becoming members, refuse to serve women customers, or sell insurance with premiums based on gender-based tables, so long as the organization was entirely private.

But certain private sector organizations might be affected by an equal rights constitutional provision. The federal court system has a well-developed set of case law on the concept of state action, developed primarily with regard to the Fourteenth Amendment. It has held that private sports organizations, like Little Leagues in some areas, have accepted so much aid from local government that they come under the state action requirement and must allow girls to try out for teams. In other locales, Little League has no special privileges from local government; in these cases, Little League has been ruled private and so does not have to allow girls to try out. With regard to private schools and colleges, the federal courts have consistently ruled that even though they receive large grants of money from federal and state government, they are still essentially private institutions and do not come under the state action concept. The Constitution allows them, if they wish, to discriminate on the basis of sex.

Private Associations

Today private associations and individuals may discriminate on the basis of gender if they wish to unless they have accepted so much assistance from government that they come under the concept of state action. Men can hold doors open for women if they wish to. Boy Scouts can be for boys only. A women's center can exclude men from membership and activities if it wishes to. A church can form a men's softball team or a men's Bible study class if it wishes to. None of this would change if there were an equal rights provision in the Constitution.

Private Employment

Discriminatory employment practices penalizing women persist in the private sector today, despite the protections afforded women by the Equal Pay Act and Title VII. Women working full time are paid, on average, only about 65 percent of what full-time male employees are paid. Part of this pay differential can be explained by the average lower seniority of women workers. The single largest explanation for the pay differential is the concentration of women in a small number of low-pay jobs—office worker, domestic service, food and laundry service, and schoolteaching, for instance. About 15 percent of the pay differential is not explained by seniority or the concentration of women in traditionally low-pay women's work. Women doing the same job as men with as much seniority are paid less. Women in the private sector are seldom promoted into the higher levels of management, and only a very small percentage exercise power on the governing boards of major corporations. There also persists discrimination in fringe benefits. Finally, a serious weakness of Title VII is that workers in firms with fewer than fifteen employees are not protected. No federal law prohibits the owners of these small businesses from discriminating against their female employees.

If the 1789 Constitution had included an equal rights provision for women, there would have been no direct impact on private sector employment unless the concept of state action applied. Purely private employers would have remained free to discriminate based on sex, if they wished to, unless and until Congress passed laws like the Equal Pay Act and Title VII. It is likely that the federal courts would have interpreted federal contractors to be covered under state action, and so employees of government contractors would have the same constitutional protections as government workers. All other employees in the private sector would have only the protections that Congress might have extended.

However, two hundred years of government employees' and government contractors' employees' having equal opportunity would have indirectly affected private sector employment. Private employers would have to compete in a marketplace where women received equal treatment with men if they worked for the government, so private employers would have had to treat women more equally to obtain their services. In addition, the example of two hundred years of equal treatment of women in government service would have had a subtle impact on attitudes toward women and on the expectations of women. Girls and women would have seen women exercising responsibility and enjoying adequate pay and benefits, and many would have aspired to do the same.

Private Business Practices

Today women experience discrimination in their everyday business. No better examples illustrate these injustices than insurance and credit matters.

Congress passed an Equal Credit Opportunity Act in 1974 to provide for gender-free bases for determining whether to extend credit to an individual. There are two serious remaining problems, however, with regard to credit opportunity. Most women are paid less than men and so are less credit worthy. This situation might also exist for private sector workers under an equal rights provision of the Constitution, but large numbers of female government workers and women who work for government contractors under an equal rights provision would probably receive equal pay for comparable work and so be more credit worthy. The second problem is that lending institutions are allowed to consider the impact of state laws that discriminate against married women with regard to property rights (explained below), and on this basis many women are deemed not to be credit worthy.

Congress has not acted on discrimination in insurance. Insurance companies are free to charge young men more than young women for automobile insurance since women are safer drivers. Insurance companies are also free to charge men more than women for life insurance since women live longer.

With an equal rights provision in the Constitution, private insurance companies could still discriminate on the basis of gender. Similarly, nothing in the equal rights provision of the Constitution would prevent banks and credit companies from discriminating on the basis of gender in deciding whether to extend credit to an individual.

Recognition by politicians that women exercise political power would, however, probably have resulted in the passage of federal laws that would prohibit such discrimination by insurance companies and credit providers and also extend protections against discrimination in employment. If women had begun voting their gender interests in the late nineteenth century instead of the mid-twentieth century, politicians would have responded then. Women's political power would probably have also resulted in a federal law requiring equal pay for comparable work. Federal law would also probably require all employers to provide on-site day care facilities for the children of both male and female employees. In these indirect ways, then, the equal rights provision of the Constitution would have affected private businesses.

State Laws

In the U.S. political system, state governments play the most important role in family law and criminal justice. In both areas, women have been adversely affected.

Family Law

Some states have adopted nearly gender-free laws, regulations, and practices in family law, and many have taken steps in that direction, but in most states there still remains serious discrimination on the basis of sex. Many states have marital property laws by which the property is owned by the spouse in whose name it is registered or whose earnings paid for it—nearly always the husband. This leaves the spouse who is a homemaker with no claim to this property during the marriage and unable to obtain credit on the basis of it. Most states still require that the husband support the family and that the wife serve her husband. However, no court will require a husband to spend more on his family than he wants to, and no court will force a woman to serve her husband. When the husband or wife dies, most states currently have a requirement that the widow (or in some states either surviving spouse) receive a minimum of one-third or one-half of the husband's (or deceased spouse's) property, but a few still give the widow only the use (not the ownership) of one-third of the husband's property. In most states, if the wife dies, she can bequeath by will only property she owned before the marriage, inherited, received as a gift, or bought with her own wages. Most homemakers, consequently, do not have the right to bequeath very much.

Most states require that the wife's domicile be the family home and provide that the husband has the right to determine where the family home will be located. This requirement causes extra expense for managing any property the wife might own in the place where she lived before she married and prevents her from qualifying there for in-state tuition for state colleges. Some states still have requirements that the wife use her husband's surname when applying for a driver's license and that the children use the father's surname.

The causes of action for a divorce are now gender free in many states. Many states attempt to divide the marital property equitably; the judge has wide discretion in these states to do whatever he or she thinks is fair. A few states divide the marital property equally at the time of the divorce. Many states award the property to the spouse in whose name the property is registered or whose money paid for it, although this practice is declining. Some states still allow only the woman to receive alimony. In most cases, which parent receives custody of the children in divorce proceedings is determined by the principle of the best interest of the children. When applying this principle, consideration of the material well-being of the child often favors the father, who generally owns more property and has a higher income than the homemaker or even the wife who has been in the paid work force. The standard for most of the twentieth century, known as the *tender years doctrine* and holding that when the child is young the mother should be given preference for custody, is now being applied less regularly. Preference is sometimes given to the primary caretaker of the children. Most often, the mother still gets custody of the children, but the trend is in the direction of more fathers getting custody.

In summary, there is no such thing today as equal rights for women in family law except in those few states that have strong equal rights provisions in their state constitutions. In all the rest of the states, discrimination based on sex is pervasive in laws on marital property, marital responsibilities, domicile, and divorce.

If the framers had put an equal rights provision in the Constitution, the states would have altered their laws two hundred years ago so as to remove all distinctions based on gender. One important area of family law is marital property—property accumulated by the couple during the marriage. All the states would have established property laws requiring that the couple share equally all wages, salaries, rents, profits, dividends, and other income earned by either husband or wife. Both husband and wife would have to contribute to the economic well-being of the family, either by earning income or by tending house and taking care of children. Either husband or wife could take the name of the other spouse, retain surnames, or choose a new surname for both to use. Both would share decision-making about the lives of their children. Both would meet the same minimum age requirements for marriage. Either could establish a domicile (legal address) separate from their home if he or she wished to.

Either spouse could bequeath by will his or her half of the marital property to whomever desired. The surviving spouse would retain ownership of his or her half of the marital property without restriction.

If a divorce occurs, each spouse would get half the marital property. The grounds for divorce would be gender neutral, as would be the bases upon which alimony might or might not be awarded. Generally, alimony would be awarded to the spouse who had sacrificed his or her earning power by maintaining the home and caring for the children. Custody of minor children would generally be awarded to the parent who was the primary caretaker of those children. Child support would be shared by the parents, with the custodial parent contributing primarily time and energy and the noncustodial parent contributing primarily money.

Criminal Justice

Today there is a great deal of discrimination based on sex in the criminal justice system. The exact situation varies from state to state. Juvenile girls, for instance, may be imprisoned for years for being sexually active, but juvenile boys are not imprisoned for this offense. This practice derives from society's double standard regarding the acceptability of sexual activity by boys and girls plus the fact that in most states juveniles can be imprisoned for "incorrigibility" or as "persons in need of supervision." Girls who are sexually promiscuous are often considered to be "in need of supervision" by the state, yet sexual promiscuity is almost never the reason why boys are deemed to be "in need of supervision."

In some states women are given indeterminate sentences for crimes for which men are given set terms. The time served under indeterminate sentences is consistently longer. On the other hand, judges tend to give shorter sentences to women than to men for the same crime if set terms are given. Most jurisdictions have applied the equal rights concept to rape and now punish rape whether the victim is male or female. Most jurisdictions punish only female prostitutes, and in some jurisdictions the prostitution laws are written in gender-specific language (i.e., a *prostitute* is by definition female).

Prisons now are segregated by sex. Women's prisons generally have inferior libraries, recreational facilities, and training programs. Men's prisons generally have more stringent restrictions and rules. Clearly girls and women who violate the criminal laws do not today have equal rights with boys and men who do so.

Had there been an equal rights provision in the Constitution, the states would have made all criminal laws gender neutral two hundred years ago. The penalties for crimes would be the same whether the crimes were committed by a female or a male. Rape would still be a crime, whether the perpetrator was male or female and whether the victim was male or female. If homosexual acts were a crime for men, they would also be a crime for women. Prostitution could still be a crime if it includes both male and female prostitutes. Prisons would be integrated, except for areas where privacy is important such as areas for disrobing, body searches, bathing, and sleeping.

Conclusion

The above discussion has highlighted several principles with regard to an equal rights provision in the Constitution. First, there would be large areas of American life that would not be directly affected. These would be the private areas of society—interpersonal relations, private clubs and associations, private schools and colleges, and private businesses that are not government contractors. Second, there would be areas of American society in which the impact would be direct—government programs, government jobs, public schools and universities, the military, family law, criminal justice, and other areas of law that have in the past treated one sex differently from the other. In addition, there would be a significant indirect impact on the private sector of the economy and on attitudes. This indirect impact would not have been immediate. It would have taken decades or even generations to work its effect fully.

In some areas, the future impact of an equal rights provision has been anticipated (at least partially) by legislation. Recent changes in family law and practice in some states, the recent requirement that women as well as men be required to serve on juries, the increased role of women in the armed services, changes in the social security system equalizing the benefits due widowers and widows, equal employment legislation, and more nearly equal opportunity for girls and women in education fit this category. These laws were changed in most cases by simple majorities in the legislature. These laws could also be repealed by simple majorities in the legislature. If there were an equal rights provision, it would take a constitutional amendment requiring two-thirds of Congress and three-fourths of the states to take those rights away.

In some areas, federal court decisions have resulted in practices that an equal rights provision in the Constitution would have assured. The most important steps taken by the courts on equal rights for women have come under the equal protection clauses of the Fifth and Fourteenth Amendments. The *equal protection clauses* prohibit the federal government and the states from denying any person equal protection of the laws. However, from the earliest decisions the courts have acknowledged that states often do, and under the Constitution may, treat different groups of people differently. For instance, the federal government may provide pensions to persons over age sixty-five and not to persons under age sixty-five. Categorizing people by age, income level, and sex have been acceptable under the equal protection clauses so long as the category was *reasonable.*

In the mid-twentieth century, as the nation decided that racial discrimination was unacceptable, the test for acceptable categorization by race was made much more severe. Any law that categorizes by race is now subject to *strict scrutiny.* For such a law to be constitutional, it must be for a *compelling* purpose and there must be no other way for the government to achieve its compelling purpose. Under this test, virtually all laws categorizing persons by race have been declared unconstitutional. This is the same test that would apply to sex if there were an equal rights provision in the Constitution.

In the 1970s, the Supreme Court considered applying *strict scrutiny* to laws categorizing by sex, but in the end it did not do so. Instead, it developed a test somewhere between *reasonableness* and *strict scrutiny.* Under this test, laws categorizing people by sex must be *reasonable* and must have an *important* state purpose. This is the constitutional standard that now applies. Under this standard, the courts have ruled unconstitutional some laws discriminating on the basis of sex and have allowed other laws discriminating on the basis of sex to stay in effect. Women today have no constitutional right to fully equal treatment under the law.

The fact that women are not now equal under the law is a signal to society that it is acceptable to discriminate against women. It will take considerable time to bring society to a place where it is unacceptable to discriminate on the basis of sex. The process is slowed when our Constitution, one of the cornerstones of the American democracy, allows discrimination on the basis of sex.

Even at this late date, we can adopt an Equal Rights Amendment. Assuming that this step is taken and that we keep or strengthen our laws prohibiting gender discrimination by private individuals and firms in employment and the granting of credit, women will eventually find themselves with incomes roughly equal to men and with an equal share of the marital income. Women will begin to exercise economic and political power on an equal basis with men. Women will be represented in the higher echelons of the military services and government bureaucracies. There will come to be a more nearly equal representation of women in Congress, state legislatures, local government, the judiciary, and the presidency of the nation. The gender gap may become, at least temporarily, a more powerful determinant of national policy. Women will lose the privileges that the law now gives them; they will have to fulfill equally the responsibilities of citizenship. None of these changes will take place immediately upon ratification of an Equal Rights Amendment. It will take decades and perhaps generations for the new legal reality to change customs, traditions, and habits of thought.

Since governments would treat men and women the same if there were an equal rights provision, whether in family law, criminal law, or the military, there would be a fundamental impact on women's experience, demonstrated ability, and self-concept. Women would become more effective citizens than they would otherwise have been. Women would trust in their capacity to make decisions and would participate energetically in the civic process.

Sources and Suggested Readings

For commentary on the interpretation of the Equal Rights Amendment, U.S. Citizens' Advisory Council on the Status of Women, *Interpretation of the Equal*

Rights Amendment in Accordance with Legislative History (Washington, D.C.: Government Printing Office, 1974), is central. See also Thomas I. Emerson et al., "The Equal Rights Amendment: A Constitutional Basis for Equal Rights for Women," *Yale Law Journal* 80 (April 1971): 871–985; and U.S. Citizens' Advisory Council on the Status of Women, *The Equal Rights Amendment-Senator Ervin's Minority Report and the Yale Law Journal* (Washington, D.C.: Government Printing Office, 1972). For the impact of the Equal Rights Amendment on state laws, see Barbara A. Brown et al., *Women's Rights and the Law: The Impact of the ERA on State Laws* (New York: Praeger, 1977); and Anne K. Bingaman, *A Commentary on the Effect of the Equal Rights Amendment on State Laws and Institutions* (Sacramento, Calif.: California Commission on the Status of Women, 1975). For the current status of women under the law without an Equal Rights Amendment, see Carol H. Lefcourt, *Women and the Law* (New York: Clark Boardman Company, 1989). See also Susan Deller Ross and Ann Barcher, *An American Civil Liberties Union Handbook: The Rights of Women* (New York: Bantam Books, 1983).

For background on the status of women's civil and political rights in 1963 and 1970, see President's Commission on the Status of Women, *Report of the Committee on Civil and Political Rights* (Washington, D.C.: Government Printing Office, 1963); and President's Task Force on Women's Rights and Responsibilities, *A Matter of Simple Justice* (Washington, D.C.: Government Printing Office, 1970).

For analysis of the political debate over ratification of the Equal Rights Amendment, see Janet K. Boles, *The Politics of the Equal Rights Amendment: Conflict and the Decision Process* (New York: Longman, 1979). For arguments opposing ratification of the Equal Rights Amendment, see Sam J. Ervin, Jr., "The Question of Ratification of the Equal Rights Amendment: Con," *Congressional Digest,* 56 (June 1977): 171, 173, 175, 177; and writings by Phyllis Schlafly. For discussion of women's political participation and the gender gap, see Ethel Klein, *Gender Politics: From Consciousness to Mass Politics* (Cambridge, Mass.: Harvard University Press, 1984).

JOHN J. PITNEY, JR.

9 | What If There Were No Welfare State?

Americans receive a wide array of educational and social services from every level of government. The organizations that devise and deliver such services make up the American welfare state. During Franklin Roosevelt's New Deal of the 1930s and Lyndon Johnson's Great Society of the 1960s, the federal government expanded its contributions to the welfare state. And throughout the century, states and localities have also been increasing their own social spending, sometimes in response to federal programs but often ahead of them.

To grasp how much the welfare state has grown in recent years, we can compare social spending by all levels of government in 1960 and 1987. To factor out the effects of inflation, we use *constant dollars* (adjusting 1960 dollar figures to 1987 levels). And to allow for population change, we use *per capita amounts* (dividing total spending by population). After making these calculations, we find that 1987 social welfare spending came to $3,364 for every woman, man, and child in America, more than *three times* the 1960 level of $1,037.[1]

Despite this growth, the American welfare state remains smaller than those of most Western democracies. The United States has limited its national health insurance mainly to veterans, senior citizens, and the poor, while countries such as Britain and Canada have comprehensive health programs for all their citizens. That contrast reflects our unique outlook: Americans have accepted the welfare state more reluctantly than people in other countries. When a public opinion survey asked people in various countries whether the government should provide everyone with a guaranteed basic income, only 21 percent of Americans agreed, compared with 56 percent of West

Germans, 61 percent of Britons and 67 percent of Italians.[2]

Nevertheless, some American political leaders seek greater social spending on the Canadian or British model. Others argue the opposite, saying that the welfare state has already grown too large and has defeated its own purposes by fostering dependency. These debates about the proper size and role of the welfare state commonly focus on specific programs. Too often, people neglect a more basic and illuminating question: What if America had no welfare state at all? A close look at that question will not only help you evaluate social policy, it will also show the extent to which the welfare state has shaped American politics and society.

Social Consequences

Welfare is a fighting word. To most Americans, it means government payments to poor people—and it usually carries ugly overtones. The old Country and Western song "Welfare Cadillac" exemplifies the widespread belief that most welfare checks go to buy luxuries. And to American ears, the use of the term *state* in the sense of "society" connotes totalitarianism, as in "police state."[3] In this context, a *welfare state* is a government that bullies hard-working taxpayers for the benefit of derelicts. The term is often used by those who oppose greater social welfare spending, while those who support it prefer to speak of *human services.*

The term *welfare state* has a broader meaning, however. Public policy experts apply it to all programs aimed at providing economic security and opportunity. To be sure, this concept includes food stamps and Aid to Families with Dependent Children, the programs that most people associate with "welfare." But in addition, the welfare state includes social security, which provides pensions for most elderly Americans, rich and poor. It also includes public education. If you are attending a state university or using a government-backed student loan, then *you* are benefiting from the welfare state.

That should hardly come as a surprise—even if you think of yourself as fairly well off. Most welfare state spending is not set aside for the needy. Each year, the federal government spends more than half a trillion dollars on *entitlement* programs, which give benefits (usually checks) to all who meet eligibility standards set by law. Only one dollar in six goes to programs that make recipients prove need; the rest goes to programs that help the middle class as well as the poor.[4]

That is no accident. Although the founders of the modern welfare state were concerned mainly with the needy, they knew that their social programs would have a better chance of getting passed and funded if they also gave benefits to the more numerous and powerful middle class. By linking programs such as social security and medicare to *earmarked* taxes (set aside for those specific purposes), policy makers sought to convince people that they were *earning* benefits. Social security manuals refer to recipients as *claimants* and stress that the government *owes* claimants their pensions.[5] Through these and other devices, most people came to dissociate most social welfare spending from *welfare*.

The welfare state touches everybody—and its absence would have far-reaching consequences:
- No free public schools
- No state universities or tuition assistance from the government
- No social security or medicare
- No government-funded disability or unemployment insurance
- No veterans' hospitals or pensions.

Taxes

Before jumping to the conclusion that everyone would lose out, remember a huge offsetting benefit: lower taxes. As we shall see, non-welfare-state spending might be somewhat greater, so it is hard to pin down how much lighter the tax burden would be. But you would surely notice the difference. In the late 1980s, the average person's federal, state, and local taxes amounted to his or her earnings through May 4 of each year—the so-called Tax Freedom Day. In 1941, defense took about the same share of *gross national product* (GNP, the total value of all goods and services produced by Americans) as in 1989, but the welfare state was much smaller. Tax Freedom Day of 1941 fell on March 17.[6] In other words, today you work more than a month and a half longer to support the welfare state than you would have in 1941.

In one respect, low-income earners would get a special break if there were no welfare state. Without social security programs, there would be no social security taxes—which currently place a disproportionate burden on the working poor. Low-income earners must pay more than seven cents on every dollar they make. High-income Americans pay social security tax only on earnings up to a specified amount (about $61,000 in 1993); every additional dollar of earnings above that amount is free from social security taxes.[7]

Lower taxes would mean greater economic growth, because people would have more money to save and invest. At this point, you might be asking: How can this be? Ronald Reagan cut taxes in 1981, but the economy grew slowly during the decade. The answer is that the overall tax bite actually stayed about the same. The 1981 tax cut was wiped out by subsequent increases in other levies—especially the social security tax. In 1979, federal revenues took 18.9 percent of gross national product. In 1989, they took 19.2 percent.[8]

If the welfare state were gone and your taxes were lower, you could not spend all your extra take-home pay on compact discs and pizza. Americans would have additional expenses because they would have to seek substitutes for public education, medicare, and other benefits of the welfare state. To some extent, these substitutes already surround us. Americans already spend more than $500 billion a year on pensions, health insurance, and schooling. As a share of gross national product, this spending rose from 7.7 percent in 1972 to 12 percent in 1987.[9] Relieved of the welfare state's tax burden, middle-income Americans could increase these outlays even more.

Under completely private control, social services would work much differently: some people would benefit, while others might suffer. It is time to look at specific examples.

Education

No public schools. The very thought may conjure up scenes of mass ignorance and illiteracy, the American version of the Dark Ages. You might be tempted to dismiss the proposal at once.

Wait a minute. Remember that educating children and putting huge sums of tax dollars into public schools are not the same thing. With inflation discounted, public elementary and secondary schools are now spending *twice* as much per pupil as they did in the 1959–60 academic year.[10] Yet between 1959 and 1989, average combined Scholastic Aptitude Test (SAT) scores plunged by seventy points.[11]

Today's public system is marked by monopoly, bureaucracy, and failure. A reporter who spent a year teaching in a New York City public high school tells how the education bureaucracy treats teachers and students: "I found a system where excellence is rarely rewarded and incompetence is rarely punished or helped. Even a simple thank you is rarely uttered by an administrator to a teacher. . . . Ultimately I saw a system that often does not have the time nor the inclination to care about the kids inside it." The harshest verdict on public education has been rendered by the people who know best: public school teachers themselves. A survey of nine major cities found between one-fifth and one-third of public school teachers send their children to private schools.[12]

All other things being equal, private schools work better because they must compete in the marketplace, which discourages bureaucracy and fosters effectiveness. And they nurture educational diversity because their curricula are not reduced to the lowest common denominator by political pressures. *Privatization*—moving toward a completely private system of education—would multiply schools of every stripe: Jewish, Catholic, Protestant, and atheist schools; schools that specialize in the arts, the sciences, or public affairs; schools that use traditional classroom lectures and schools that use the Socratic method of teaching. Parents could choose which kind of education they wanted for their children, and they would exercise far greater control over the schools. Having to pay the full cost, they would have a great financial incentive to keep an eye on school performance. And they would "vote" on that performance with their tuition dollars: schools that satisfied them would flourish, while those that disappointed them would go out of business.

Only one out of every eight elementary and secondary students attends a private school.[13] To accommodate the rest, private schools would have to be bigger and more numerous—and therein lies an objection. Some contend that private schools do better only because of their small size and selectivity. If they had to take on the load that now falls on public schools, they would end up suffering the same problems. The counterargument is that private schools tend to outpace public schools even in poor, crowded urban areas. School organization affects student achievement independently of the students' background.[14]

Opponents of a private system say that "diversity" could lead to schools that teach racism or lure children into religious cults.[15] They also argue that the market would throw education into chaos. The absence of a standard curriculum would hurt students whose schools went under, as they would have a tough time transferring to other institutions. Supporters of a private system foresee order in diversity: private accrediting organizations, much like those in higher education, would emerge to help parents judge elementary and secondary schools. The "privatizers" add that public education endures more chaos than any marketplace. Many urban schools have become ill-managed prison camps where learning takes second place to surviving. And by shutting out religiously based ideas of right and wrong, say some critics of the current system, public education has done far more moral damage than could a few private schools run by fringe groups. Those who favor maintaining the current system argue that public schools can teach generally accepted "secular values" without violating the separation of church and state.

Another basic objection is that educational opportunity would shrink. The goal of free public education is to give all Americans an equal chance to develop their talents. Although a totally private system would allow for charity admissions, most poor children would get only a short, rough schooling. As a result, they would have little chance to gain the skills necessary to thrive in a technological society. A number of middle-income Americans would also lose ground. A couple with many children could ill afford to school them all; the prospect of multiple tuition bills for kindergarten and upward would hasten the trend toward smaller families. Parents of handicapped or gifted children would face huge bills for additional educational services.

Even the strongest champions of private education acknowledge that needy children would miss out on educational opportunity without some sort of government support. As we shall see, tax credits or *vouchers* (certificates that can be redeemed for services such as schooling) could prevent this problem without restoring an educational bureaucracy. The critics of privatization respond that such a system would do little to reduce inequality, as rich parents could send their children to better schools by supplementing vouchers with their own funds. This criticism falters. Under the current system, affluent families already have the choice of paying for private education or moving to pricey neighborhoods with good schools. Poor families have no such choice.

As for higher education, a totally private system is easier to picture. Private institutions have always made up a large share of American colleges and universities, and it takes no great imagination to see how they could expand if government stayed out of the business. But students would have to finance their education in different ways. Today a majority of students attend tax-subsidized public institutions, and more than half of the students at private colleges receive government aid.[16] Without a welfare state, lower taxes would mean that more students could pay tuition at private schools and more alumni could make voluntary donations to support scholarships.

Still, many would-be students could not afford college. In the past quarter-century alone, the average tuition at private colleges has increased by more than one-third after inflation. Before large-scale government aid to higher education started in the 1940s, less than 5 percent of American adults had finished four years of college, compared with more than 20 percent today.[17]

Social Security

Many Americans think of social security as a system of government-run savings accounts: you contribute to the program during your working years and then withdraw the money when you retire. In reality, social security has never worked that way. For most of its history, the system operated on a "pay-as-you-go" basis: each year's taxes went to pay each year's benefits. Because the number of taxpayers greatly exceeded the number of beneficiaries, social security could provide good benefits at low tax rates. In 1955, for instance, the social security tax amounted to just 2 percent of covered earnings. People who spent most of their working lives paying such low rates now receive far more in benefits than they contributed in taxes. In the mid-1980s, it took only twenty-three months for average retirees to get back all their social security taxes.[18] As mentioned earlier, however, policy makers succeeded at portraying social security as a savings plan, so beneficiaries bitterly resented any suggestion that the government was giving them something that they did not earn.

If you are now in your teens or twenties, forget about any social security bonanza. The number of retired people is growing in comparison with the number of working people, so something has to give. To keep the system afloat, Congress has raised taxes and made benefit adjustments so that outlays grow more slowly than in the past. As a result of these changes, you may never recover all your tax payments—unless you live to be very old. Indeed, according to some projections, the system will go into the red in another forty or fifty years—just when today's college students are getting ready to retire. All told, you would probably get more return on your money if you could put it into a private investment account instead of social security taxes.[19]

So, if social security had never existed, today's college students could look forward to lower taxes during their careers and higher income during retirement. And many of today's senior citizens would still be living fairly well, since they would have put more money into savings and annuities while they were working.

So far so good. But some elderly people would face a drastically worse fate. Those who earned meager wages between the 1940s and 1980s enjoyed an especially high ratio of benefits to taxes, so they gained far more from social security than they could from private plans. Without social security, a life of low wages would have ended in an old age of destitution.

Make no mistake: social security has been crucial in improving the lives of today's senior citizens. More than 40 percent of their income derives from social security. Since the late 1960s, the (inflation-adjusted) median household income among the elderly has grown by more than half, compared with a mere 7 percent increase for all households. In the late 1950s, when many retirees still received no social security benefits, more than one-third of the elderly lived in poverty. By the late 1980s, less than one-eighth of the elderly fell below the poverty line, a rate lower than the population as a whole. And because social security benefits do not rise and fall with the business cycle, they have provided the elderly with a stable, predictable income.[20]

In the absence of social security, the poverty rate for the elderly would now be much closer to the level of the 1950s. The shadow of destitution would reach far beyond the elderly poor themselves, for many people in late middle age would live in fear of want and humiliation lying ahead. Social security was intended as much to quell this anxiety as to meet economic needs. That is why it is called social *security*.

Health Care

Unless you are old or poor, you probably gain little direct benefit from government health insurance programs. Even so, these programs may be making a big difference in your life.

The largest government health program is medicare, which pays for medical care for the elderly and disabled. Just under 1.5 percent of your paycheck goes directly to medicare's Hospital Insurance Trust Fund. Medicaid is a joint federal-state program that provides assistance to poor people. This and other health programs annually cost more than two hundred dollars for every American, a sum that is reflected in your total tax bill.[21]

When Congress enacted the original medicare legislation, it let hospitals charge medicare for the *reasonable cost* of treating the elderly and allowed physicians to charge *reasonable and customary* fees for their services.[22] This vague language encouraged hospitals and physicians to raise their rates. Together with costly new technologies and other factors, government health policies have thus helped drive medical price increases to twice the general rate of inflation.

The United States now spends a greater share of its gross domestic product (GNP minus income from foreign assets) on health care than any other industrialized country. Yet Americans do not enjoy better health than the people of Japan or Europe. We rank twenty-second in infant morality among developed nations. And our life expectancy rate is below the average of the seven countries with the largest market economies.[23]

Government has tried to make the health care system more efficient through tighter regulation. Many doctors and hospital administrators argue that the complex new rules have backfired: complying with government paperwork requirements has itself become a major cost that they must pass on to patients.[24]

If government had never gotten involved in health insurance, medical prices might be lower. And with more take-home pay, people at all income levels would be better able to afford private health insurance and out-of-pocket medical expenses. In many respects, the health-care system could deliver services more efficiently, because it would not be distorted by government subsidies, which have sometimes encouraged physicians and hospitals to buy unnecessary equipment and carry out needless and risky procedures.

Supporters of government health insurance argue that any price benefits resulting from a totally private system would be greatly outbalanced by increased problems of access. What is more, they argue, a more extensive public system of medical care could actually reduce costs instead of raising them. They point to the example of Canada, which has had lower medical price inflation than the United States even though it has a more far-reaching program. The Canadian system allows greater cost control than the fragmented, decentralized American system. According to Theodore R. Marmor, Jerry L. Mashaw, and Philip L. Harvey: "The perceived trade-off between accessibility and cost in American health politics offers a false choice that is largely detached from the realities of medical care. In this corner of the American welfare state, the most pressing problems are ones of uneven provision and the absence of unified public control."[25]

Those who back a private system respond that, as with education, problems of access could be remedied with vouchers or tax breaks that would enable people to take care of themselves. (But until the concluding part of this chapter, we will continue to assume no governmental substitutes for the welfare state.) They point out that countries with national health insurance force people to wait a long time for hospital services. Nearly 800,000 Britons are awaiting surgery at any time; and in Newfoundland, the average waiting time for a mammogram (a procedure that detects breast cancer) is two and a half months.[26]

Poverty Programs

To repeat: taxes would be lower if America had no welfare state. Lower taxes could mean more economic growth and employment, which in turn could result in less poverty. Even if this tidy scenario actually worked out—and many deny it—an expanding economy would still leave a large number of people in need. How would they get by without poverty programs?

For one thing, they might be living in better homes. Community development policies, purportedly designed to improve poor people's lives and put roofs over their heads, have often had the opposite effect. During its heyday, federal urban renewal tore down four times as many homes as it built, so it ended up aggravating the housing shortage for those with the greatest trouble finding a suitable dwelling.[27] What is worse, many of the neighborhoods destroyed by urban renewal were safe and stable in spite of their poverty.

Instead of providing clean and secure places to live, public housing projects have often turned into vertical slums. In 1976, the St. Louis housing authority stopped trying to salvage a project called Pruitt-Igoe and instead just blew it up. A 1987 report on the Washington, D.C., local housing authority described an agency with employees "who just are not capable of doing their jobs," property managers "who just sat in their offices all day," engineers who were "creating havoc in our boiler rooms," and administrators who turned in reports full of misleading information.[28]

If urban renewal and public housing programs had never started, many poor people would be living in older, privately run buildings instead of housing projects. The buildings might be run-down, but they would often be located in neighborhoods where people felt a sense of rootedness and community.

Critics of the welfare state argue that homelessness stems in part from misguided housing policies. They also point out that the problem is most severe in cities with rent control, which squeezes the housing market by making it unprofitable to supply rental housing. Supporters of the welfare state dismiss such arguments, noting that while many rent-control laws were enacted a long time ago, homelessness has surged only in recent years.

According to Charles Murray's influential *Losing Ground*, income-support programs (e.g., Aid to Families with Dependent Children, food stamps, unemployment insurance) have actually worsened poverty by encouraging dependency over honest work. Murray cites data showing that progress against poverty stopped just as federal spending on public assistance hit new highs. Without these programs, he says, poor people would act in different ways. The government would neither support out-of-wedlock children nor subsidize abortions, so teenagers would be more likely to think twice about early sexual relations. Whereas government benefits currently make it easier to drop out of the labor market, the prospect of starvation would encourage poor youths to accept the discipline of the workplace and gain the skills necessary to get better jobs. The upshot: fewer children would be born into the poverty cycle, and fewer able-bodied adults would be hanging out on streetcorners.[29]

A number of scholars have attacked Murray's analysis, saying that his evidence fails to show that welfare benefits have led many youths to leave the work force. While they acknowledge that some programs have worked poorly, they point to various job-training and early education efforts as success stories. They also dispute Murray's conclusions about the moral effects of welfare. According to Marmor, Mashaw, and Harvey:

Decisions about childbearing, marriage and living arrangements are very complex. They surely are not unaffected by economic incentives, but they are affected by a host of other factors as well. If those other factors—for example, the general societal perception of out-of-wedlock births or of single parenting—are also shifting, they may dwarf the effects of the economic incentives.[30]

Both sides agree that a large number of poor people cannot easily find work: teenage mothers, the disabled, and the handicapped. If they could not turn to government, they would first turn to family members. Much more than today, poor people would have to ask their better-off relatives for financial help. Extended families would be proliferate, as several generations would save on expenses by living together. "The Waltons" notwithstanding, such arrangements would usually involve discomfort and loss of privacy.

Many poor people either would have no close relatives or could find none willing and able to help. In these cases, the poor would have to rely on voluntary organizations—which have always played a central role in American social life. Alexis de Tocqueville noted more than a century and a half ago: "Americans of all ages, all stations in life, and all types of disposition are forever forming associations. . . . Americans combine to give fetes, found seminaries, build churches, distribute books, and send missionaries to the antipodes. Hospitals, prisons, and schools take shape in that way." Today, America has an enormous web of such organizations, of all sizes, purposes, and levels of formality: shelters for the homeless, soup kitchens, food banks, and groups of mothers who share babysitting duties so all can take part-time jobs. About 45 percent of American adults do volunteer work to help others.[31]

Voluntary associations have been particularly important to the economic development of the black community. Black churchgoers annually give more than $1 billion to their parishes, and the Congress of National Black Churches has used some of these funds to set up credit unions and insurance programs. Local black churches have been increasingly active in providing day care, health care, low-income housing, and other social services.[32]

Without a welfare state, voluntary associations would have a much greater workload, but they would also have greater resources. More disposable income would probably mean more private charitable giving. Some analysts argue that the expanding welfare state has crowded out such donations. According to one study, every additional dollar of social welfare spending will cut private contributions by thirty cents. Yet even under the current welfare state, charitable contributions top $100 billion a year.[33] If taxes were low enough, one might expect this figure to climb.

In spite of all this goodwill, however, the poor would have a harsher life. (Again, for the time being, we assume no voucher plans.) Voluntary efforts could scarcely fill in for all the services provided by the welfare state, and many people would fall through the cracks. The elderly poor would face a particularly terrible lot. Too proud for charity and too frail for work, many would spend their last years in shacks, doing without basic necessities of life. This is no thought experiment: this is the way many old people lived before social security and other programs for the aged were enacted.

Political Consequences

Contemporary politics revolves around the welfare state. Most debates about domestic policy focus on education, health, social security, and programs for the poor. Politicians can often win elections by simultaneously denouncing "welfare" and supporting social programs that benefit their constituents. While sometimes disagreeing about marginal changes in policy, politicians of both parties accept a large government role in promoting social welfare. Although Republicans have tended to take more conservative stands than Democrats—particularly since the Reagan presidency—the 1988 national GOP platform failed to call for the abolition of a single social program. Indeed, it repeatedly *endorsed* key elements of the welfare state:

• "We pledge to preserve the integrity of the social security trust funds."

• "We led the way to enacting landmark legislation for catastrophic health insurance under medicare."

• "We will reach out to these children [in poverty] through Head Start and targeted education."

• "We support the FHA [Federal Housing Administration] mortgage insurance program, the Government National Mortgage Insurance Association, the VA [Veterans Administration] guarantee program, and other programs that enhance housing choices for all Americans."[34]

Such language from the party of Ronald Reagan suggests the extent to which the welfare state has shaped our political life. Without it, the content and tone of American politics would be radically different.

Size and Cost of Government

Social welfare takes 50 percent of federal spending and 60 percent of state and local spending.[35] Minus these outlays, much of government's current machinery would either be much smaller or entirely absent.

Which federal agency has the largest budget? Although some might think the Defense Department, the answer is the Department of Health and Human Services (HHS), which runs social security, medicare, and other social programs that form the core of the welfare state.[36] No welfare state, no HHS. The oblivion list would also include the Departments of Education, Veterans' Affairs, and Housing and Urban Development, as well as independent agencies such as ACTION, which runs the Literacy Corps and other volunteer programs. Other bureaucracies would go on with fewer functions. The Agriculture Department would still work on programs such as soil conservation but would lack one of its current major activities, the food stamp program.

The legislative branch would look different, too. Congress does much of its work in committees and subcommittees, each of which deals with particular policy areas. The House Ways and Means Committee each year puts out a handbook on social programs within its jurisdiction: in 1990, that book was two inches thick and 1,495 pages long.[37] Reflecting the size and complexity of the welfare state, committee jurisdictions are intricate and overlapping. In the House of Representatives, for instance, health care policy is handled by the:

- Labor-HHS Subcommittee of the Appropriations Committee
- Budget Committee Task Force on Human Resources
- Health and Safety Subcommittee of the Education and Labor Committee
- Health and Environment Subcommittee of the Energy and Commerce Committee
- Human Resources and Intergovernmental Relations Subcommittee of the Governmental Operations Committee
- Hospitals and Health Care Subcommittee of the Veterans' Affairs Committee
- Health Subcommittee of the Ways and Means Committee

• Health and Long-Term Care Subcommittee of the Select Aging Committee.

Every other major welfare policy area involves an equally long list. Without a welfare state, Congress would have fewer panels, and those that remained would often have less authority.

The difference would be even more dramatic in statehouses and city halls. Nearly two-thirds of state and local employees work in health, education, and social services, with schoolteachers alone accounting for more than a third of local government payrolls. Many elective offices have been directly created by the welfare state. The United States has some fourteen thousand school districts, most of which are governed by elected school boards. And one-third of state education chiefs are chosen by the voters.[38] None of these positions would exist in the absence of a welfare state.

Critics of the welfare state argue that its main beneficiary is the bureaucracy itself. Says Robert L. Woodson of the National Center for Neighborhood Enterprise:

> The fact is that most of the money going to the poverty programs does not go to the poor but to those who ''serve'' the poor. For instance, the City of New York did a survey of the $14.8 billion that flows into the city to meet the needs of 1.2 million poor people—one fifth of that city's population. They found that about 68 cents of every dollar goes not to the poor but to social workers, counselors, and all the people who serve the poor.[39]

But if the welfare state were gone, public spending might remain larger than advocates of limited government would like. Each bureaucracy's appetite for larger budgets is curbed by other bureaucracies that vie with it for scarce tax dollars. If social programs were removed from the competition, other areas of government would probably be bigger than they are today. On the federal level, the Defense Department would pick up much of the slack. In 1960, the Pentagon got 59 percent of federal spending, not counting social security. During the next two decades, that share fell as social welfare spending rose. Despite the 1980s military buildup, defense got only 31 percent in 1990.[40] If the Pentagon's portion of the budget had been restored to its 1960 level, it would have had an additional $277 billion.

On all levels of government, likewise, the other bureaucracies

would gain from the welfare state's nonexistence. Certainly, more resources would go to agencies that build public works: roads, bridges,
buildings, parks, and water projects. Public works create many construction jobs and provide permanent, tangible evidence of politicians'
achievements; that is why elected officials like to spend money on
them.

The Power of Government

The welfare state not only provides benefits to Americans; it enables
the government to influence their behavior. If the welfare state were to
vanish, so would this influence.

Social control has often taken the form of public education. When
policy makers seek to solve problems such as drug abuse and the
spread of AIDS (acquired immune deficiency syndrome), they call
upon public schools to educate young people about the risks of misbe-
havior. Especially during wartime, schools work to instill patriotism
and encourage military enlistments. More recently, some people have
suggested that public schools should teach tolerance of various sexual
orientations.

With a completely private educational system, government would
have a harder time getting its lessons across. Schools might often shrug
off the government's position; indeed, they might sometimes fight it.
Those affiliated with liberal religious denominations might bar military
recruiters, while fundamentalist Christian schools would denounce the
idea of tolerating certain sexual practices. The government might try to
force private schools to teach certain ideas but could hardly keep them
from teaching others and could not exert control over how they were
taught. Teachers who disagreed with the government position could
always tell their classes, "This is what Uncle Sam wants you to hear,
but this school has a different point of view."[41]

Another source of influence is the ability to tie strings to government assistance. If you are a male college student, for example, you
cannot legally receive federal scholarship or college loan aid unless
you have registered for the draft. And if a college has any students who
receive such aid, then it must comply with federal civil rights regulations.

The welfare state also gives the federal government more say over
the states and localities. A good deal of social spending consists of

categorical grant programs, which require states and localities to perform specific tasks in order to qualify for federal aid. Although recent administrations have talked about converting these programs into "no-strings-attached" grants, nearly all federal aid to states and localities still carries stringent conditions.

In each specific instance, federal rules have a praiseworthy goal, such as the advancement of civil rights. But put together, federal mandates and requirements gives Washington enormous control over everyday life in the United States. If Washington could offer no aid to individuals or units of government, it would have far less leverage over their behavior.

The strong arm of the government is more than a matter of broad policy; often it takes concrete, personal forms. People who rely on government aid are at the mercy of bureaucrats who can make their lives very difficult. Poor people often resent social workers and public housing managers, and old people sometimes have frustrating experiences with social security administrators. But unlike customers in a marketplace, recipients of government assistance cannot take their business elsewhere.

Elections

Elected officials also like the welfare state because it enhances their political fortunes in several ways.

First, backing the welfare state can boost their overall popularity. Although most voters dislike the idea of welfare, they favor most of the elements of the welfare state. According to a public opinion survey, a majority of Americans think that the federal government should increase spending on social security, medicare, medicaid, and day care programs.[42] In particular, it is hard to name any politicians who lost elections because they supported social security. It is easy to think of a number who sustained damage or defeat because they voted to trim it.

Second, they can win the support of interest groups that have a big stake in the welfare state. Through campaign contributions and other political resources, these groups can reward their friends and punish their adversaries. In 1976, the National Education Association (NEA), the largest teachers' union, rallied its members behind the presidential candidacy of an obscure former governor of Georgia named Jimmy Carter. NEA's support tipped crucial primary elections to Carter, who won the Democratic presidential nomination. Once elected, Carter returned the favor by helping NEA reach its top legislative goal: the establishment of a separate U.S. Department of Education.[43] Likewise, veterans' groups got Presidents Ronald Reagan and George Bush to support the creation of a Department of Veterans' Affairs.

Third, the welfare state multiplies politicians' chances to perform good works for their constituents. As social services have expanded, more and more people have had more and more dealings with the bureaucracy—and consequently, they have had more and more bureaucratic problems for which they need solutions.[44] Enter the friendly city councilor, state legislator, or member of Congress, who can help the harried citizen get the grant or find the lost social security check. And in the process, the politician just happens to win the gratitude of the citizen, who then praises the politician to everyone in the neighborhood. Many politicians actively drum up such business, traveling around to say to their constituents, "I'm your champion in the government. What can I do to help you?" From the politicians' standpoint, the beauty of such *casework* is that even if they oppose the enactment of a particular program, they can still milk it for their constituents if and when it passes.

Fourth, politicians can use grants and staff appointments to build cadres of political propagandists. The expansion of legislative committees has been accompanied by mushrooming staff payrolls; and many aides who purportedly work on welfare state issues actually spend their time writing speeches and press releases to make their bosses look good. While the law forbids public funds to go directly to partisan organizations, politicians of both parties have channeled grants to "nonpartisan" groups that support their point of view.

These advantages have accrued to politicians at all levels, and particularly to members of the U.S. House of Representatives, whose average reelection rate has steadily risen:

$$1946–66: 88\%$$
$$1968–82: 93\%$$
$$1984–90: 97\%[45]$$

Although it is difficult to prove cause and effect, the expansion of social programs in the 1960s and 1970s probably contributed to incumbent protection. Members of Congress also enjoy free mail and other benefits that help them win popularity.

Deprived of the welfare state, elected officials would have less of an edge. While the bureaucracy would no longer be providing social services, it would no longer be causing problems requiring a politician's helping hand. Lawmakers would lack opportunities to vote for popular social programs. And they would have nothing to offer interest groups such as the NEA, which would have no material incentive to support politicians. Ironically, groups that now *oppose* a larger welfare state would also stay out of the game. If socialized medicine had no chance, the American Medical Association would not have to spend millions to beat it.

Public works programs might make up for part of this political shortfall. More than ever, elected officials would try to win votes by bringing home the concrete, but this strategy would yield less support than working the welfare state. For one thing, you can get only so many harbors and public beaches into your home town—particularly if it is located in Arizona. For another thing, public works are less personal than constituent services. When you go to the local park, you may not always know who got it built, and you certainly do not need that person's help in using it.

Currently, the incumbency advantage reinforces itself because it tends to scare away opponents: Who wants to spend so much effort against a foe who will probably win anyway? Many incumbents have weak challengers: in some recent elections, a fifth of House incumbents have had no major-party opposition at all. Without the advantages resulting from the welfare state, however, officeholders would face greater risk of defeat. Not only would they have fewer occasions to gain popularity and interest group backing; their increased vulnerability would itself attract stronger challengers. Races would be closer, campaigns more exciting, results less predictable, reelection rates lower, and turnover higher.

And voters would turn out in greater numbers. When an election campaign has a foregone conclusion, people are less likely to take the trouble to go to the polls because they sensibly conclude that their votes will make no difference. The current drop in voter turnout began in the mid-1960s, just when the Johnson expansion of the welfare state was starting to help incumbents quash competition. Although a causal link is again hard to prove, other explanations for the decline in turnout are much less convincing. For instance, those who blame voter registration requirements have a weak case because these requirements have been greatly relaxed since 1960.[46] In all likelihood, declining competition has helped turn people away from the voting booth; greater competition would reverse the turnout trend.

Some might argue that turnout would *fall* without the welfare state, because fewer people would have any direct stake in government. The evidence suggests otherwise. The 1932 election produced higher turnout than the 1988 election, even though most of the modern welfare state did not even exist yet. This difference is all the more remarkable because a large part of the 1932 voting age population—southern blacks—could not go to the polls because of racial discrimination.

Compared with the current political balance, the absence of a welfare state would disadvantage Democrats more than Republicans. In part, that difference would simply result from a smaller incumbency advantage, since Democrats make up the vast majority of House members and state legislators. Other differences would also tip the scales, however. As described earlier, the welfare state creates many government jobs; because Democrats tend to be more attracted to government service than Republicans, they have taken a disproportionate share of these posts. In many cases, legislative staffs or executive bureaucracies have supplied training grounds for future Democratic candidates. According to the Democratic leader of the Wisconsin State Senate: "People get out of college, go to work in the capitol, back home to run for office, and then back to the capitol as legislators. They are good candidates because they have connections with the establishment up here, and they have access to finances."[47]

Thanks both to that training and their party's long-standing affinity for social welfare, Democrats have exhibited more skill in supporting popular programs and helping constituents get benefits from the welfare state. Once more, recent decades show a revealing pattern: the expansion of the welfare state has coincided with extended Democratic ascendancy in state legislatures and the longest stretch of one-party control in the history of the U.S. House of Representatives.

Legislative, Executive, and Judicial Authority

According to James Madison in *The Federalist* 51, "In republican government, the legislative authority necessarily predominates."[48] In addition to strengthening the political security of individual lawmakers, the expansion of the welfare state has increased the institutional power of Congress and the state legislatures. As suggested before, legislative committees and staffs proliferated along with social programs. This increased institutional capacity enables the legislative branch to keep a tight rein on the administration of laws.

Supporters of legislative authority laud this *oversight* function, pointing out that lawmakers have rooted out executive branch corruption and inefficiency. Critics damn it as *micromanagement* and argue that it has *increased* corruption, as lawmakers have tried to steer bureaucratic decisions in favor of their campaign contributors. Both sides point to the 1980s scandal concerning the Department of Housing and Urban Development: congressional investigations uncovered the scandal—in which lawmakers had helped get contracts for their financial patrons.

Without a welfare state, much of this power would be gone. The contrast would be particularly vivid at the federal level, where the remaining functions of government would consist largely of foreign policy and national security. Much as it does today, Congress would try to oversee or micromanage these areas, but it would have less success than in social policy. The executive branch has traditionally had a stronger hand in these fields. To borrow Alexander Hamilton's words, defense and foreign affairs require "decision, activity, secrecy, and dispatch." Congress seldom displays these characteristics—precisely because the framers kept them from the legislative branch's reach. By dividing Congress into two chambers, the framers deliberately slowed down the legislative process: it takes time to get the House and Senate to agree on the precise wording of a bill. And by providing for numerous representatives, they meant "to guard against the cabals of a few."[49]

The executive branch can usually act more quickly and quietly than Congress. And in times of trouble, the people will rally behind the president as a symbol of national unity. To the extent that national politics would revolve around international politics, the president would usually prevail.

The framers considered the judiciary the "least dangerous" branch of government. Yet the judiciary has become ever more important, not just because of *judicial activism*—the purported tendency of judges to read their own preferences into the law—but also because of increased litigation. Between 1980 and 1987, the civil caseload of U.S. district courts increased 42 percent.[50] And in a modern society without a welfare state, the judiciary would assume still greater authority because lawsuits would abound even further. Today, people are protected by social "safety-net" programs such as workers' compensation for those who are injured on the job and disability insurance for those who can no longer work. Without the safety net, people who suffered such harm would try to recover their losses in court. Much of the public would spend much of its time suing, being sued, and testifying in other people's suits. To handle all the cases, the states and the federal government would set up many more judgeships.

In many states, voters elect judges. With some notable exceptions, these races have tended to get little attention, and judges have often won reelection without contest. But in a society where so many more people would confront legal entanglements, everyone would have a much greater personal stake in the outcome of judicial elections. Voters would pay closer heed to the records and philosophies of people running for judgeships. Proplaintiff and prodefendant groups would spring up to back their own candidates. Indeed, judicial campaigns might become as costly and prominent as legislative campaigns are today.

The Political Agenda

If America had no welfare state, would the people be clamoring for one?

At first glance, the obvious answer seems to be yes. The major elements of the welfare state—public education, social security, medicare—did not start via immaculate conception. Each came as a result of a widespread belief that some problem needed solving, and each enjoyed widespread support. And the expansion of such programs has not occurred in the dead of night. When lawmakers increased benefits or pegged them to the inflation rate, it was because such action was sought by a large and vocal constituency. If America had no welfare state, Americans would notice that every other major country has one. While an unfettered market would leave many Americans better off, others would have hard times—and they would seek relief.

And yet the clamor might ring softer than we might imagine. Widely shared troubles do not automatically become national issues. For a problem to reach the national political agenda, somebody has to define it, articulate it, measure it, and propose solutions. It may take years for policy activists to carry out these tasks—and even then, they have no guarantee of success. But if they get the government to attend to the problem and launch a policy, then they have crossed a key threshold. It is much easier to *sustain* a policy than to start it. Once a government program is in place, it develops its own constituency of bureaucrats, lawmakers, staffers, and interest groups. The members of the constituency have an interest in keeping the issue alive by seeking out new facets of the problem that demand further attention.

Poverty is a good example. In 1950, most Americans simply did not think of poverty as a major national problem, even though the ranks of the poor were enormous by today's standards.[51] The government lacked a poverty policy; in fact, it even lacked a fixed definition of poverty. In the late 1950s and early 1960s, a number of activists worked to bring poverty to America's attention. Congress passed laws, a poverty bureaucracy grew, and interest groups emerged to call for more action. By the 1980s, activists had moved beyond the general issue of poverty to focus on more specific aspects of the problem, such as homelessness.

But if this issue had never crossed the threshold into policy, poverty activists might have lost their momentum over time. Debates about poverty policy are fueled largely by poverty statistics. With no poverty programs, the government would gather no data about poverty, so welfare rights activists would have a weaker argument to present to Congress and the public. In addition, if they had no allies on congressional staffs or executive agencies, activists would have difficulty getting official attention.

So while some people would be calling for a welfare state, many Americans might dismiss the idea as foreign or utopian. Instead, they would focus on what they considered as the *real* political issues: foreign affairs, highways, water projects, and tort liability.

For Better or for Worse?

If America had no welfare state, would it be a better place?

In purely material terms, most people would probably come out ahead. Greater growth and lower taxes would enable them to buy the goods and services that the welfare state now provides. Furthermore, government would be smaller, more efficient, more comprehensible, and more responsive.

But as the conservative activist Paul Weyrich puts it, "While a free market is preferable to other forms of economic organization, its benefits are not equally felt. Poverty, especially among working people, is the Achilles' heel of the free market."[52]

With no free schools, people barely scratching out a living could not offer the hope of economic opportunity to their children. Without social security, some elderly Americans could face wretched poverty. Without health programs, infant mortality might rise even higher. And without income support programs, people who could not work would have to rely on the kindness of strangers. Voluntary organizations would help, but if history is any guide, they would not quite close the gap.

At this point, the choice seems grim: a bureaucratic welfare state or a free-market society marred by tragic destitution. But this is a false dichotomy: there are other paths for public policy.

A number of public policy analysts—including Democrats and Republicans, liberals and conservatives— have been searching for ways to achieve the welfare state's goals without resorting to the welfare state's current methods and structures. This emerging philosophy embraces several principles.

First, government programs should foster individual choice. Instead of maintaining a huge educational bureaucracy or completely turning its back on education, government should give parents a voice in which schools their children attend. One version of this idea is simply to allow parents to choose among public schools. A more fundamental reform is to provide families with scholarships or vouchers, which they could redeem at the public or private school of their choice. (Public schools would no longer receive their operating expenses directly from the government. To stay afloat, they would have to compete with private schools for students.) In the field of health care, a "choice" approach would replace government-supplied health insurance with tax credits, which would let people shop for the private health policy best suited to their particular needs. Some analysts have suggested a highly controversial plan under which working people could opt out of social security and medicare. The sums that they would otherwise remit in payroll taxes would instead go to tax-sheltered savings accounts, which they could tap during retirement.

Second, government policies should stress the empowerment of citizens rather than government officials. Instead of having paid administrators run public housing projects, why not turn the management over to the residents themselves? This idea has already worked in several places, and it points the way toward a more basic change: allowing poor people to buy their residences from public housing authorities. This reform would help transform poor people from passive recipients of government aid into property owners.

Third, to the extent that government must continue to provide social services, the management and delivery of those services should be decentralized. Specifically, the federal government should cut the strings on a number of categorical grant programs and instead allow the states and localities to carry on their own experiments in public policy. Centralized institutions lack flexibility. Government works better when managers on the scene can make their own decisions.

Fourth, policy makers should appraise programs not by how much they spend but by how well they perform. While this idea may seem self-evident, even trivial, current bureaucracies often fund according to *inputs*: how many job slots are allotted, how many students sign up, how many poor people can qualify.[53] Governments should instead fund according to *outcomes*: how many children learn, how many people get off welfare rolls and onto payrolls.

More than two hundred years ago at the Constitutional Convention, Gouverneur Morris of New York was assigned to write the preamble to the Constitution. He wrote that a primary purpose of American government is to "promote the general Welfare." As he used the term, *welfare* referred to the country's general well-being. The programs of the American welfare state have indeed served that end—sometimes admirably, sometimes passably, but never as well as they should. During the last decade of the millennium, the welfare state needs reform— for ourselves and our posterity.

Notes

1. U.S. Department of Commerce, Bureau of the Census, *Statistical Abstract of the United States, 1990* (Washington, D.C.: Government Printing Office, 1990), p. 350.

2. "America: A Unique Outlook?" *American Enterprise*, March/April 1990, p. 113.

3. William Safire, *Safire's Political Dictionary* (New York: Ballantine, 1978), p. 785.

4. U.S. Congressional Budget Office, *The Economic and Budget Outlook: Fiscal Years 1991–1995* (Washington, D.C.: Government Printing Office, 1990), p. 128.

5. Theodore R. Marmor, *The Politics of Medicare* (Chicago: Aldine, 1973), pp. 21–22.

6. The Tax Foundation, *Facts and Figures on Government Finance* (Baltimore, Md.: Johns Hopkins University Press, 1990), p. 19.

7. U.S., Congress, House of Representatives, Committee on Ways and Means, *1990 Green Book* (Washington, D.C.: Government Printing Office, 1990), p. 71.

8. U.S., Congressional Budget Office, *Economic and Budget Outlook* 1991–1995, p. 123.

9. U.S. Bureau of the Census, *Statistical Abstract, 1990*, p. 349.

10. Calculated from U.S. Department of Education, *Digest of Education Statistics* (Washington, D.C.: Government Printing Office, 1989), pp. 10, 30; U.S. Office of Management and Budget, *Historical Tables: Budget of the United States Government, Fiscal Year 1990* (Washington, D.C.: Government Printing Office, 1989), pp. 19–20.

11. "Education Performance," *The American Enterprise*, March/April 1990, p. 108.

12. John E. Chubb and Terry M. Moe, *Politics, Markets and America's Schools* (Washington, D.C.: Brookings Institution, 1990), pp. 182–83; Emily Sachar, "Teaching Doesn't Count," *Washington Monthly*, September 1990, p. 25; Warren Brookes, "Education Choice Tide Rising," *Washington Times*, August 30, 1990, p. G3.

13. Calculated from U.S. Bureau of the Census, *Statistical Abstract, 1990*, p. 138.

14. Chubb and Moe, *Politics, Markets and America's Schools*, p. 129.

15. Bill Honig, "School Vouchers: Dangerous Claptrap," *New York Times*, June 29, 1990, p. A25.

16. U.S. Bureau of the Census, *Statistical Abstract, 1990*, p. 158.

17. U.S. Department of Education, *Digest*, pp. 281–82; U.S. Bureau of the Census, *Statistical Abstract, 1990*, p. 133.

18. Geoffrey Kollmann and David Koitz, *How Long Does It Take for New Retirees to Recover the Value of Their Social Security Taxes?* (Washington, D.C.: Congressional Research Service, 1986), p. 11.

19. Peter Ferrara, *Social Security Rates of Return for Today's Young Workers* (Washington, D.C.: National Chamber Foundation, 1986).

20. Brian W. Cashell, *Economic Status of the Elderly* (Washington, D.C.: Congressional Research Service, 1989); U.S. Department of Commerce, Bureau of the Census, *Money Income and Poverty Status in the United States: 1988* (Washington, D.C.: Government Printing Office, 1989), pp. 58, 60.

21. U.S. Bureau of the Census, *Statistical Abstract, 1990*, p. 350.

22. Stuart Butler and Anna Kondratas, *Out of the Poverty Trap: A Conservative Strategy for Welfare Reform* (New York: Free Press, 1987), p. 197.

23. U.S. Office of Management and Budget, *Budget of the United States Government, Fiscal Year 1991* (Washington, D.C.: Government Printing Office, 1990), pp. 184–85.

24. Sidney Marchasin, "One Hospital Tells the Cost of Regulation," *Wall Street Journal*, June 26, 1990, p. A18.

25. Theodore R. Marmor, Jerry L. Mashaw, and Philip L. Harvey, *America's*

Misunderstood Welfare State: Persistent Myths, Enduring Realities (New York: Basic Books, 1990), p. 212.

26. John C. Goodman, "An Expensive Way to Die," *National Review*, April 16, 1990, pp. 30–32.

27. Martin Anderson, *The Federal Bulldozer: A Critical Analysis of Urban Renewal, 1949–1962* (Cambridge, Mass.: MIT Press, 1964), pp. 7, 67.

28. David Osborne, "They Can't Stop Us Now," *Washington Post Magazine*, July 30, 1989, p. 16.

29. Charles Murray, *Losing Ground: American Social Policy, 1950–1980* (New York: Basic Books, 1984), pp. 56–68, 230–31.

30. John E. Schwarz, *America's Hidden Success: A Reassessment of Public Policy from Kennedy to Reagan*, rev. ed. (New York: Norton, 1988), pp. 42–48; Marmor, Mashaw, and Harvey, *America's Misunderstood Welfare State*, p. 220.

31. Alexis de Tocqueville, *Democracy in America*, 1835, trans. George Lawrence, ed. J. P. Mayer (Garden City, N.Y.: Anchor, 1969), p. 513; Butler and Kondratas, *Poverty Trap*, p. 72; U.S. Bureau of the Census, *Statistical Abstract, 1990*, p. 371.

32. Gerald David Jaynes and Robin M. Williams, Jr., eds., *A Common Destiny: Blacks and American Society* (Washington, D.C.: National Academy Press, 1989), p. 176.

33. John C. Goodman and Michael D. Stroup, *Privatizing the Welfare State* (Dallas, Tex.: National Center for Policy Analysis, 1986), p. 33; U.S. Bureau of the Census, *Statistical Abstract, 1990*, p. 372.

34. Republican National Convention, *An American Vision: For Our Children and Our Future* (New Orleans: Republican National Convention, 1988), pp. 15, 24, 28, 52.

35. U.S. Bureau of the Census, *Statistical Abstract, 1990*, p. 352.

36. In 1989, the Defense Department spent $318 billion, compared with $400 billion for the Department of Health and Human Services. U.S. Office of Management and Budget, *Budget 1991*, p. A298.

37. U.S. House of Representatives, *1990 Green Book*.

38. U.S. Bureau of the Census, *Statistical Abstract, 1990*, pp. 291, 300; Council of State Governments, *State Elective Officials and the Legislatures, 1989–90* (Lexington, Ky.: Council of State Governments, 1989).

39. Robert L. Woodson, "The Poor and Conservative vs. the Poverty Industry," address to the Heritage Foundation, Washington, D.C., August 13, 1987.

40. Calculated from U.S. Office of Management and Budget, *Historical Tables*, p. 48; U.S. Office of Management and Budget, *Budget 1991*, p. A303.

41. David Friedman, *The Machinery of Freedom*, 2d ed. (LaSalle, Ill.: Open Court Press, 1989), pp. 56–57.

42. ABC News Poll, August 17–21, 1989, cited in *The Polling Report*, September 4, 1989, p. 4.

43. Michael Barone, *Our Country: The Shaping of America from Roosevelt to Reagan* (New York: Free Press, 1990), p. 631.

44. Morris Fiorina, *Congress: Keystone of the Washington Establishment*, 2d ed. (New Haven, Conn.: Yale University Press, 1989).

45. Calculated from Norman J. Ornstein, Thomas E. Mann, and Michael J. Malbin, *Vital Statistics on Congress, 1989–1990* (Washington, D.C.: Congres-

sional Quarterly Press, 1990), p. 56; "Election '90 Results," *Congressional Quarterly Weekly Report*, February 21, 1991, pp. 493–500.

46. Walter Dean Burnham, "The Turnout Problem," in *Elections American Style*, ed. A. James Reichley (Washington, D.C.: Brookings Institution, 1987), pp. 109–10.

47. Joe Strohl, quoted in Alan Ehrenhalt, "How a Party of Enthusiasts Keeps Its Hammerlock on a State Legislature," *Governing*, June 1989, p. 33.

48. James Madison, *Federalist* 51, 1788, in Alexander Hamilton, James Madison, and John Jay, *The Federalist Papers*, ed. Clinton Rossiter (New York: Mentor/New American Library, 1961), p. 322.

49. Alexander Hamilton, *Federalist* 70, James Madison, *Federalist* 10, both 1788, in ibid., pp. 424, 82.

50. Hamilton, *Federalist* 78, in ibid., p. 465; Harold W. Stanley and Richard G. Niemi, *Vital Statistics on American Politics*, 2d ed. (Washington, D.C.: CQ Press, 1990), p. 282.

51. Murray, *Losing Ground*, pp. 3–5.

52. Paul Weyrich, "Conservatism for the People," *National Review*, September 3, 1990, p. 25.

53. David Osborne, "Ten Ways to Turn D.C. Around," *Washington Post Magazine*, December 9, 1990, p. 22.

Sources and Suggested Readings

Charles Murray, *Losing Ground: American Social Policy, 1950–1980* (New York: Basic Books, 1984), argues that social programs have worsened the poverty problem. An earlier and more specific form of this argument can be found in Martin Anderson, *The Federal Bulldozer: A Critical Analysis of Urban Renewal, 1949–1962* (Cambridge, Mass.: MIT Press, 1964). Stuart Butler and Anna Kondratas offer an equally conservative but more hopeful view in *Out of the Poverty Trap: A Conservative Strategy for Welfare Reform* (New York: Free Press, 1987).

For a superb analysis of the welfare state from a liberal viewpoint, consult Theodore R. Marmor, Jerry L. Mashaw, and Philip H. Harvey, *America's Misunderstood Welfare State: Persistent Myths, Enduring Realities* (New York: Basic Books, 1990). Marmor, *The Politics of Medicare* (Chicago: Aldine, 1973), provides a concise introduction to health politics and policy. John E. Schwarz looks at both social and economic policy in *America's Hidden Success: A Reassessment of Public Policy from Kennedy to Reagan*, rev. ed. (New York: Norton, 1988).

For general reference on federal entitlement programs, a comprehensive (if somewhat slanted) guide is U.S. Congress, House of Representatives, Committee on Ways and Means, *1990 Green Book* (Washington, D.C.: Government Printing Office, 1990). The social problems of black Americans are discussed in Gerald David Jaynes and Robin M. Williams, Jr., eds., *A Common Destiny: Blacks and American Society* (Washington, D.C.: National Academy Press, 1989).

Michael Barone, *Our Country: The Shaping of America from Roosevelt to Reagan* (New York: Free Press, 1990), is not specifically about the welfare state, but its sweeping political history emphasizes the importance of such programs as the GI Bill.

HERBERT M. LEVINE

10 | What If There Had Been No Cold War?

On April 25, 1945, American military forces fighting the German army from the west met up at the Elbe River in Germany with Soviet forces advancing against the Germans from the east. The conquering armies expressed the friendship that comes when comrades engage in a long war against a common enemy.

Within two weeks, World War II in Europe ended. The meeting of the American and Soviet forces seemed both an affirmation of the wartime unity of the two countries as well as an omen of enduring cooperation. In the jubilation of victory many people forgot that the friendship between the governments and peoples of the United States and the Soviet Union was only a few years old. It was an alliance of convenience, since both countries had political systems, economic structures, and interests that had often been in conflict.

Soviet–U.S. Relations, 1917–1945

From November 1917, when a communist government took power in Russia (reorganized as the Soviet Union in 1922), relations with the United States were strained. Communist leader V. I. Lenin had built a reputation as a radical committed to promoting revolution throughout the world. He advocated a theory based on the principles of the German philosopher and revolutionist Karl Marx but with some important modifications. Marxism-Leninism, as the communist theory was called, advocated class struggle and world revolution. It urged and predicted the destruction of *capitalism*, the economic system based on private property and market forces that prevailed in the United States and other Western countries. It also held that political democracy was a sham and should be replaced by *communism*, a system of one-party rule and government command of the economy.

The Bolshevik Revolution, named after Lenin's radical political faction, had major consequences for World War I, since Russia had been allied in the war with Great Britain, France, and the United States. When Lenin made a separate peace with Germany, thus taking Russia out of the war, he alienated the country's former allies.

In 1918, President Woodrow Wilson sent two battalions of U.S. troops to Russia to support anti-Bolshevik forces as part of an Allied effort to keep Russia in the war. The expedition failed but further soured relations between the two nations.

Relations deteriorated even more in 1919, when Lenin set up the Third International (the Comintern), committed to fostering world revolution. Socialists in every country were called upon to promote revolution and to undermine noncommunist governments.

The Comintern angered many Americans. Business leaders viewed communism as a threat to capitalism. Liberals interpreted it as a challenge to democracy. Many socialists, who, like the communists, opposed capitalism, split with the communists because they revered political democracy.

In America, anticommunism combined with bigoted antiforeigner sentiments to create a Red Scare in 1919. Suspected communists, anarchists, and socialists were spied upon and rounded up; some were deported. The authorities' actions demonstrated an American fear of communism even when there was really no communist threat—domestic or foreign—to American political and economic institutions.

The Red Scare fizzled by 1920. Although the United States and the Soviet Union engaged in extensive trade relations after World War I, it was not until 1933 that they established formal diplomatic relations.

The Soviet Union experienced significant changes in the 1920s and 1930s. Within a few years of the death of Lenin in 1924, Joseph Stalin became the Soviet leader. Far more than Lenin, Stalin established totalitarian rule based on rigid adherence to communist orthodoxy as interpreted by him and his underlings in the Communist party. The full horror of Stalin's atrocities was difficult to grasp for many years, in part because the Soviet government maintained total control over communications and strictly limited travel within the country. Today, Soviet officials admit that Stalin may have killed more than 20 million people in a network of prison camps known as the *gulag*.

The common enemy of Nazi Germany brought the United States and the Soviet Union together. The Soviet Union and Germany had signed a nonaggression pact in 1939 in which both sides agreed on territorial conquests and pledged peace with each other. But in June 1941, Adolf Hitler attacked the Soviet Union, thus forcing it into an alliance with Great Britain.

In December 1941 the United States entered the war after Japan attacked American forces at Pearl Harbor in Hawaii. Germany, an ally of Japan, quickly declared war on the United States. The United States had already begun shipping supplies to the Soviet Union and Britain under the Lend-Lease Act of March 1941.

Lend-Lease marked the beginning of wartime cooperation with the Soviets. The United States and the Soviet Union were now allied nations, and American policy makers promoted Soviet-American friendship. Stalin became known in the United States as "Uncle Joe" and was given stature as one of the Big Three, with President Franklin Roosevelt and British Prime Minister Winston Churchill, the three leaders who made the major wartime decisions.

During the war and just after Germany surrendered, the United States and the allies concluded a number of agreements, among them the Yalta Agreement and the Potsdam Agreement. In August 1945, a few months after the defeat of Germany and two days after the United States dropped an atomic bomb on the Japanese city of Hiroshima, the Soviet Union entered the war against Japan in accordance with the Yalta Agreement.

There was hope that the unity among the Allied powers would continue. The major powers had agreed during the war to establish a world organization committed to the maintenance of peace—the United Nations (UN). The UN Security Council received primary responsibility for maintaining security. It was composed initially of five permanent and six nonpermanent members. (Today, there are ten nonpermanent members.) Each of the permanent members—the United States, the Soviet Union, Great Britain, France, and China—had a veto power over the Security Council's decisions. The veto was intended to assure that no decisions for international peace and security could be made unless the big powers agreed. The permanent members were to serve as a world police force to meet threats to world security. For the UN to work, the wartime unity of the major powers had to continue in peacetime.

The Cold War

Allied harmony, however, was not to be. In the years following the end of World War II, relations between the Soviet Union and its wartime allies—particularly the United States—became increasingly rancorous.

Early Postwar Years

The United States and its noncommunist allies in the West made a number of accusations, especially that the Soviet Union was not living up to its international wartime agreements to allow free elections in the European countries it had liberated from German rule. Instead it was installing totalitarian communist dictatorships under the control of Stalin, and elsewhere it was encouraging revolutionary activities by Communist parties aiming to subvert existing governments.

The noncommunist nations were alarmed about other developments in Europe, too. They objected to Soviet intransigence in concluding a peace treaty with Germany. The supposedly temporary military division of Germany by the United States, Great Britain, France, and the Soviet Union persisted. In 1948, a coup in Czechoslovakia put a Stalinist regime in power there. In the same year, the Soviets began the Berlin blockade—an effort to prevent the West from furnishing food and supplies to West Berlin, which was located within the Soviet zone of Germany. An airlift successfully broke the blockade. Worry increased when, in 1949, the Soviet Union detonated a nuclear device, demonstrating that it was now a nuclear power.

The United States was troubled not only about conditions in Europe but about developments in Asia as well. In 1949, communist forces in China under Mao Zedong defeated the Nationalists of Chiang Kai-shek and established a communist government. Many Americans believed that a victory for communism in China was a victory for the Soviet Union. In 1950, when North Korea attacked South Korea, many Americans concluded that the Soviet Union was behind the attack.

For its part, the Soviet Union regarded its wartime allies as responsible for the ill will. The Soviets believed they were pursuing a defensive foreign policy, not one that threatened world peace. Of all Germany's adversaries in World War II, the Soviet Union had suffered the most, with wartime deaths estimated at about 20 million people, and so the Soviets thought they had legitimate reason to protect themselves against a resurgence of German expansionism.

Nor could the Soviets allow a return of German militarism. Hence, they believed, it was essential to have friendly governments in Eastern Europe. The Western Allies had once recognized such concerns as legitimate but were now reneging on their commitments, in the Soviet view. Moreover, before 1949 the United States had a monopoly on nuclear weapons and would not share them with the Soviet Union except on unacceptable terms, demonstrating a lack of trust that the Soviets returned.

Moscow argued that the Soviet Union was economically weak and had to devote its energies to rebuilding its economy instead of expanding its power. The Allies were suspicious unnecessarily. Western rearmament posed a serious danger to the security of the Soviet Union that no Soviet government—whether radical or moderate—could ignore.

Some left-wing Western scholars place blame for the cold war on American expansionism. At the turn of the century, they argued, the United States put down Philippine insurrections and essentially took over the islands. Marines fought in China, and throughout the twentieth century, U.S. armed forces invaded Central American countries to collect debts, suppress revolutions, and impose friendly governments. The idea of Manifest Destiny, whereby America was thought to have a moral right and duty to expand to its continental limits, was sometimes applied internationally as well. The U.S. policy of containing communism, according to the left-wing view, was nothing more than a desire for access and control over foreign markets and raw materials—in other words, imperialism.

The Cold War in Theory and Practice

Relations between the Soviet Union and the United States dominated the world political system after World War II. For more than two centuries before the war that system had been characterized by the existence of several powers, mostly European, no one of which was so powerful as to dominate the world. The European countries formed alliances of convenience to protect their security.

But the years following World War II were characterized by a two-power (bipolar) system in which the United States and the Soviet Union had so much more power than other nations that they were in effect *superpowers*. The superpowers sought allies not only in their immediate spheres but throughout the world. They built up military arsenals and prepared to take measures to protect their security. They had political, economic, and ideological differences, but they never engaged in a shooting war directly with each other. The tense relationship became known as the *cold war*.

When one speaks of war, one usually refers to military conflict. But a cold war entails hostility expressed not through combat but through the *threat* of force and other instruments of power, such as diplomacy, propaganda, and economics.

The strategy of the United States in meeting the Soviet challenge was known as *containment*. Its chief architect was George F. Kennan, an expert on the Soviet Union and later the U.S. ambassador there. Kennan argued in an article published in the journal *Foreign Affairs* in 1947 that the Soviet Union posed a danger to the United States. According to Kennan, the United States must meet that threat at various points around the world so that communism could be contained within its own borders. If the United States met the challenge, the Soviets would be forced to turn inward and eventually moderate its policies.

Kennan later said that his view of containment did not mean a military challenge to the Soviet Union. But while he foresaw political and economic means, others emphasized the military actions. They believed that any advance of communist power amounted to an expansion of Soviet power. This view proved wrong in many cases; some communist countries pursued their own agendas rather than those of the Soviet Union.

A ringing assertion of the containment policy was made by President Harry Truman in 1947. In his message to Congress he asked for aid to Greece and Turkey, both threatened by the Soviet Union. In what became known as the Truman Doctrine, he declared that "it must be the policy of the United States to support free peoples who are resisting attempted subjugation by armed minorities or by outside pressures."

Containment became the rationale for the major U.S. foreign policy initiatives in the postwar period. Among these initiatives were the Marshall Plan of U.S. economic assistance to Western Europe, the formation of the North Atlantic Treaty Organization (NATO) military alliance, and U.S. intervention in the Korean War and the Vietnam War. To U.S. presidents from Truman to George Bush, containment meant strengthening military establishments (particularly nuclear capabilities) and pursuing economic, political, and ideological conflict with the Soviet Union.

Experts differ about the chronology of the cold war. Some say it began in 1917 when the communists took control of Russia and advocated world revolution. Others say it started after 1945. Experts also differ about its conclusion. Some argue that it ended with the death of Stalin in 1953. Somewhat close to this assessment is the view that there were two cold wars: the first lasting from 1946 to 1953 and the second from the mid-1970s until the late 1980s. Still others assert that although there have been periods of less belligerent relations (also known as *détente*) between the two powers, the cold war continued until 1989–90, when the Soviet Union accepted the legitimacy of non-communist governments in Eastern Europe and showed some interest in copying the political and economic institutions of Western democracies. The most notable examples of détente came in 1953 after the death of Stalin, in 1962–63 after the Cuban missile crisis in which nuclear war between the superpowers was perceived to be a very real possibility, and in 1972 when a Soviet–U.S. strategic arms control treaty was concluded.

Although the degree of tension varied, the cold war may best be considered as having begun after the conclusion of World War II and having continued until 1990, when most of the tension dissolved following specific actions taken by both the Soviet Union and the United States.

The Impact of the Cold War

The cold war affected many aspects of American life. It influenced budgetary priorities, with many economic and social consequences; it also shaped the organization of government and relations among its government, the growth of a military-industrial complex, civil liberties, and civil rights. Let us take a close look at these aspects in light of the cold war and consider whether things would have been very different had there been no cold war.

Budgetary Priorities and Their Consequences

The cold war was responsible for a major increase in government expenditures on national security, the bulk going to the military. Immediately after World War II, the United States demobilized rapidly as the nation headed toward an anticipated era of peace. But as America's relations with the Soviet Union deteriorated, it devoted more and more funds to national security.

When Great Britain could no longer defend Greece and Turkey in 1947, President Truman asked for $400 million to aid these nations and proclaimed the Truman Doctrine. The Marshall Plan, which provided $10.25 billion in economic assistance to Europe over a three-year period, soon followed. Advocates of the Marshall Plan said it would prevent communism from taking hold in Western Europe. Other U.S. military and economic assistance programs around the world were rationalized in a similar manner.

After the USSR produced nuclear weapons, the United States embarked on an arms race in an effort to stay ahead of its rival. Altogether from 1947 to 1990, the United States spent more than $4 trillion on defense. Until 1974, defense spending constituted the largest segment of federal government expenditures. Although large in dollar terms, in terms of the nation's gross national product GNP this defense effort was relatively low compared to World War II.

Critics of this cold war spending have called it a disaster for the nation. They argue that had there been no cold war:

1. The United States would have spent much less on the military establishment.
2. The economy of the United States would have been more prosperous.
3. American science and technology would have flourished.
4. The nation could have addressed its social problems.

Defense Spending

Clearly, the United States devoted huge sums to defense during the cold war. Even in the absence of a Soviet threat, however, it is likely that the United States would have maintained a strong defense establishment costing trillions.

World War II had changed America's position in the world, and Americans accepted the new realities. By the last year of the war—*before* the cold war began—an overwhelming number of Americans believed that a return to a policy of isolationism in American foreign policy would not serve their country's interest. Both Republicans and Democrats held that it was essential that the United States join the United Nations. Many Americans felt that one cause of World War II was the failure of the United States to join the League of Nations, the international organization established largely through the efforts of President Woodrow Wilson after World War I. World War III, it was widely believed, could be avoided if the United States played an active role in postwar world politics.

Americans recognized that the conditions of world politics that once had been so favorable to the United States—a balance of power among the nations in Europe, a focus on empires in Asia and Africa rather than North and South America, the protection provided by the two vast oceans, and a level of technology that would allow America time to mobilize in case of war—had changed. The years after World War II showed that aircraft could travel across wide oceans, deliver bombs, and return safely to their home bases.

One important change in the postwar world was the rise of independence movements in the so-called *Third World*—the areas last to experience the industrial revolution, including impoverished Africa and Asia and to some extent in Latin America, too. As people sought to free themselves from European rule, civil wars erupted everywhere. American interests were often at risk in the face of the forces of nationalism, ethnic violence, and civil disorder. On occasion the United States employed its military power even though the Soviet Union was not involved. The use of U.S. air power against bases in Libya in 1986 to thwart terrorist activities is one example. The invasion of Panama by U.S. armed forces in 1989 to topple a dictator trafficking in drugs is another.

In the absence of the cold war, then, America would still have had vast global economic interests requiring protection. Even if a revolution had established a democratic government in the Soviet Union in 1945, the United States would still have had to meet its own national security needs, as do all nations. It would still have had political, economic, and national security interests in a world experiencing enormous change.

In these years the world economy became interdependent to the degree that countries engaged in increasing trade relations. Although international trade was not as vital to the United States as to, say, Great Britain, in dollar terms U.S. trade was extensive. The United States produced both raw materials and finished products, but it also imported raw materials from other nations. The new materials were essential to its economy and its military security.

The oil embargo of 1973, in which Arab oil-producing countries refused to send their oil to Western countries that supported Israel, highlighted the importance of oil to the economies of the developed states of the West. It started a process that quadrupled the price of oil in the United States in a few years. Even in the absence of a Soviet rival, the United States and other Western countries still have had strategic interests in the Persian Gulf region, as the U.S. response to the Iraqi invasion and occupation of Kuwait in 1990 demonstrated.

Probably even more important, the United States had—and has—a stake in a prosperous Europe apart from any rivalry with the Soviet Union. Although it emerged from World War II as the strongest economic power in the world, the United States had a selfish interest in a global economy that was back on its feet and thriving. The only way to sell abroad what America produced at home was to make certain that other countries were economically strong enough to buy its goods.

The record is clear that countries with strong economies trade with each other more than do rich countries with poor countries. The United States has more trade ties with advanced industrial societies than it has with less-developed countries. In other words, it trades today with Canada, Japan, and Western Europe more than it does with poor countries of Africa and Asia. So it was in the interest of the United States to provide some assistance to the European countries ravaged by the war as well as to the poor nations of the Third World. Possibly the level of assistance would not have been as high as it actually was during the conditions of the cold war, since the domestic U.S. political situation would not have been conducive to major aid programs.

Had there been no cold war, there would have been no Marshall Plan. There would have been no NATO, either. The countries of Western Europe would have found little need to unite against the Soviet Union, nor would they have sought U.S. involvement in such an alliance. Moreover, some European countries—in both Western Europe and Eastern Europe—would have probably been at war with each other, as they have been throughout recent centuries. As a big power, the United States would no doubt have moved to strengthen its military forces and intelligence services under such conditions.

Had there been no cold war, moreover, the possible proliferation of nuclear weapons in other countries would have posed security problems for the United States. The fact that India detonated an underground nuclear explosion in 1974 suggests that nuclear weapons development could have occurred as part of a dynamic of international politics having little or nothing to do with the cold war.

Knowledge, science, and technology have never been any country's monopoly for long. Even without the Soviet Union, the United States would have had to address the development and production of nuclear weapons by a number of nations, and to keep ahead would have required some of the enormous expenditures that the United States actually made for defense against the Soviet Union.

The Economy

Has the cold war military buildup been harmful to the American economy and American society? The popular case has been made that the United States owes its current economic and scientific difficulties to the high burden of defense expenditures it carried for more than four decades.

Specifically, critics say that money devoted to defense, which contributes nothing or little to producing wealth, could have been used to better advantage in the nondefense sector of the economy. In the nineteenth century, for example, the United States was not a world power and so could concentrate on economic development and not war. It had a small military establishment, much like Japan today. The United States, consequently, became a giant industrial power in the twentieth century, a power it has squandered in building the war machine of the cold war.

The critics overstate their case. In spite of the large U.S. defense expenditures in dollar terms, the burden of defense spending was not really great. The largest percentage of the GNP devoted to defense during the cold war period was 14 percent at the height of the Korean War. Vietnam War annual defense expenditures never reached 10 percent of GNP. And even Ronald Reagan's military buildup reached a high of only 6.5 percent of GNP in 1986 and 1987. Compare these figures to U.S. military expenditures in World War II, with its high of 39 percent of GNP. In contrast, Soviet military expenditures are estimated by some intelligence officials to have been about twice that of the United States in terms of GNP during most cold war years.

Moreover, high defense spending is not necessarily the crucial factor in a failure of economic development. There are contemporary examples. While Japan spends little on defense and has a high economic growth rate, South Korea spends much on defense and has an even higher growth rate.

Often forgotten in the discussion of America's economic decline are global conditions since the end of World War II. In 1945, the United States was the *only* major economic power in the world. Most of the major competitors—victors and vanquished alike—had been devastated. This situation was bound to change once these countries were able to get back on their feet. While the U.S. share of global wealth has declined, the standard of living of Americans has risen rapidly since 1945.

Scientific and Technical Leadership

Critics of America's cold war priorities maintain that the arms race directed America's scientific attention to military items that have little benefit for the nation's scientific and technical progress. The contest of war and human progress is not new to the post–World War II era. It has been argued that the major advances in scientific thinking have been made by scientists who were not concerned with solving problems of war. Isaac Newton was not working for the military when he devised his theories of gravity. Albert Einstein did not originate the theory of relativity as part of military research.

But while there is some truth to such assertions, wars and preparations for wars have often had effects that benefit societies, although there is obviously no benefit to those whose lives are shattered. Defense expenditures for the cold war were responsible for major advances in science and technology that had application for both military and nonmilitary use. Aircraft manufacturing is a case in point. Many scientists and technicians, moreover, received research grants from the Defense Department, and their work contributed to scientific knowledge.

As indicated above, the United States as a world power would have had to devote considerable economic resources to defense spending even in the absence of the cold war. Its science and technology, consequently, would have been influenced in a manner similar to the way that they have been shaped by the cold war.

And would America have embarked on its adventures in space had there been no cold war? Maybe so, but the impetus for space exploration came from the cold war. Had there been no cold war, space exploration would have proceeded but at a much slower pace.

Social Problems

Critics of U.S. involvement in the cold war argue that defense priorities interfered with solutions to the nation's social problems. Specific criticism is directed against America's inability to raise the economic standing of the nation's poor and improve its public education. But the critics often ignore the many ways in which the cold war helped to solve some of its social problems.

Wars and the military have often served as a mechanism of social mobility for groups excluded from such mobility elsewhere. The military establishment offered training, jobs, health care, and financial security for many people who would not have had access to such opportunities. And veterans' benefits had an impact on educational opportunity for minorities. Such developments do not excuse American society from closing off opportunities because of race or economic condition so that jeopardizing life and limb becomes one of the few ways that a poor person or a member of a minority group can move up the economic ladder. But the opportunities offered by military service were often beneficial to minorities. Without the cold war, then, social mobility for disadvantaged groups might have been slower.

The cold war also provided direct benefits to education. The invention of nuclear weapons demonstrated the importance of technology to America's security. America needed to have the scientific and technical skills to maintain its military strength. When the Soviet Union put its earth-circling satellite *Sputnik* in orbit in 1957, thus indicating that it had a technology that could easily be converted to long-range military missiles capable of hitting the United States, Congress enacted the National Defense Education Act. That law was of great benefit to scientific education in the United States. In the absence of the cold war, such assistance might not have been forthcoming in a country still wedded to an ideology contending that government is best which governs least.

Organization of Government

With the onset of the postwar years and the cold war, the United States established what some critics have called the *national security state*. A feature of this state was the formation of new agencies of government and the reorganization of foreign policy and national security governmental units. Had there been no cold war, would these developments have occurred?

There can be little doubt that they would. Many lessons were learned from the experience of World War II. The surprise Japanese attack on U.S. forces at Pearl Harbor on December 7, 1941, revealed the importance of military intelligence. No longer would the United States be unprepared, lest it suffer military disaster.

Had there been no cold war, then, there still would have been a need for an intelligence organization like the Central Intelligence Agency (CIA). The CIA itself was an outgrowth of an intelligence agency of World War II, the Office of Strategic Services (OSS).

World War II had also shown the need for better coordination between the armed forces. It demonstrates that cooperation among the military services, for operations, often required combined air, naval, and ground forces. The Joint Chiefs of Staff (JCS), formed in 1941 to serve as the counterpart to a British military structure, initiated strong interservice collaboration. During the war, there were two cabinet-level departments handling military operations—the Department of War and the Department of the Navy. The air force was not then a separate entity but was instead part of the army. The war demonstrated the importance of air power and gave strength to the arguments supporting an air force as a separate military service—on a par with the army and navy.

Had there been no cold war, the air force would still have become a separate military unit. The combined operations of different services, moreover, indicated the need for greater coordination. It is likely, then, that a single Department of Defense would have been created whether the Soviet Union was a military rival to the United States or the United States faced no major adversary.

The need for coordination between diplomatic and military agencies became apparent from the war, too. Accordingly, the National Security Council was formed in 1947. Its presiding officer was the president, and its members included key officials of the national security establishment, such as the secretary of state, secretary of defense, and CIA director. Its primary function is to "coordinate" policy at the highest levels. Even without the cold war, reorganization would have occurred because of the experience of the United States during World War II in which State Department input in decision making was overshadowed by the professional military leadership.

But what about the role of intelligence agencies? Would they have become so powerful without the cold war?

The cold war has been good to intelligence agencies. Their funding has been generous. In the 1980s, their budgets nearly tripled to reach slightly under $30 billion in fiscal 1990. Of these funds, money for the CIA has been plentiful, according to some accounts. It might be argued that the funding of the CIA would not have been so high in the absence of the cold war. To begin with, some might say, the United States would not have intervened in the two postwar conflicts of Korea and Vietnam. Both the attack by North Korea on South Korea in 1950 and the war in Vietnam of the 1960s and 1970s would have been considered civil wars, not threats to the security interests of the United States. Both North Korean leader Kim Il Sung and North Vietnamese leader Ho Chi Minh were concerned with local and regional matters. Neither had ambitions to conquer the world.

Following this line of thinking, it can be argued that it is unlikely that the CIA would have been permitted to play an interventionist role in shaping the character of foreign governments. In 1953, the CIA helped restore the shah of Iran to his throne. In 1954, it engineered a change of government in Guatemala. In 1961, it sent a force of Cuban exiles to invade Cuba in an attempt to topple the communist government there. During the cold war, it also intervened in Indonesia, Zaire, Ecuador, Ethiopia, Chile, Somalia, Brazil, Angola, Libya, Nicaragua, Vietnam, El Salvador, Cambodia, Panama, Lebanon, and Korea. By some accounts it used covert operations in many other places.

But the argument that the CIA would have had a minimal role in the absence of the cold war is unconvincing. It is likely that the CIA would have intervened *even more* in the absence of the cold war. First, all U.S. interventions were *always* assessed in terms of the nature and extent of the Soviet reaction anticipated. And some operations were aborted after they were under way when it became clear that Soviet reaction had been underestimated. Without the built-in constraint of Soviet reactions, the CIA would have been *more* active, especially since in the absence of the cold war the role of the regular U.S. military in foreign affairs would have been less than it actually was.

Second, the world would probably have been a more unsafe place in the absence of the cold war. Often ignored by both cold warriors and their critics is the stability that the bipolar system produced. Neither the United States nor the Soviet Union pushed too hard against the other side for fear that war—possibly nuclear war—would destroy them both. They often acted to restrain their client nations from engaging in military actions that threatened to involve the superpowers directly.

Both superpowers, moreover, played a role in mediating disputes within their alliance systems. Traditional conflicts of nationalism, for example, were muted because of superpower influence. By providing security guarantees to their allies, both sides limited nuclear proliferation.

Without the cold war, it is likely that national conflicts would have been even greater than they have become. *Balkanization*, a term derived from the countries occupying the Balkan peninsula in southern Europe, and meaning the breaking up of a country into smaller countries, often by hostile means, has its origins in pre–cold war years. It is likely that ethnic rivalries would have led to great turmoil that would have threatened U.S. security and economic interests. Eastern Europe and the Middle East are cases in point. The threats to U.S. security interests would have come from many sources. In a multipolar system, more countries would have produced nuclear weapons. And as already mentioned, the United States still would have had many economic interests that could be jeopardized, as they were by the Iraqi seizure of Kuwaiti oil fields in 1990. Within several weeks of the Iraqi move, the United States orchestrated a major military buildup in Saudi Arabia and the Persian Gulf in anticipation of hostilities with Iraq. In January 1991, the United States and its allies fought a successful war against Iraq and restored Kuwait's independence. In this case the Soviet Union supported the U.S. actions.

Finally, the bureaucratic impulse would have led the CIA to take interventionist policies. A governmental agency that is doing nothing is a prime target for budgetary cuts. In an unstable world with many nationalistic wars and many nuclear powers, the CIA would no doubt have found it easy to justify interventionist activities abroad and so strengthen its budgetary position.

The cold war did give great power to the CIA. It also was responsible for increasing the power of the national security adviser, who is an assistant to the president. In the age of strong secretaries of state, such as Dean Acheson and John Foster Dulles, the national security adviser had a subordinate position. Beginning with the administration of John Kennedy, however, the adviser became a major player in Washington's foreign policy establishment—at times more powerful than the secretary of state and secretary of defense. Without the cold war, the adviser would have been equally important in a highly unstable world system.

Relations among the Branches of the Federal Government

"The Constitution ., . is an invitation to struggle for the privilege of conducting foreign policy," wrote constitutional scholar Edward S. Corwin. Along with other writers, Corwin noted that the framers of the Constitution were afraid that power would be concentrated; consequently, they sought to divide it among the different branches of government in what is known as the *separation of powers*. Not only did they divide powers, but they established a system of *checks and balances* in which the power of each branch was in some degree constrained by the other two.

Accordingly, the Constitution gives some powers to Congress and others to the president in foreign policy. Among its powers Congress can declare war, provide for the armed forces, appropriate money, regulate commerce with foreign nations, impose taxes, and pass laws. The Senate must approve treaties and confirm most presidential appointments.

The president is the commander in chief of the armed forces. He has the power to recognize foreign governments and to execute laws. He can veto legislation. He appoints ambassadors and other federal government officials.

From the very beginning of American history under the Constitution, the powers of the president in war and foreign policy were embroiled in dispute. When George Washington issued the Neutrality Proclamation in 1793 on his own authority, he immediately became the center of a controversy that continues to this day. The proclamation stated that the United States would not take sides in the war then raging between Great Britain and France. Immediately, Alexander Hamilton and James Madison, both (like Washington) participants in the Constitutional Convention of 1787, took opposing views on the proclamation. In a series of published debates, Hamilton asserted that the framers intended the president should make decisions on neutrality, while Madison argued that the framers intended Congress to have that power.

Who has the power to commit American armed forces in military action? The President, Congress, or both? From Washington's time to the present, presidents have used armed forces without a declaration of war on more than two hundred occasions. Congress has formally declared war or recognized that a state of war existed only five times. Drawing the line to limit the power of the president as commander in chief, then, has always been a subject of contention in the American political system.

Another area of contention is the use of executive agreements rather than treaties. A treaty must be approved by two-thirds of the Senate, but an executive agreement can be made by the president without the Senate's consent. Franklin D. Roosevelt used the executive agreement power to a greater extent than any of his predecessors in 1940 when he transferred fifty destroyers to Great Britain in exchange for the lease of some British bases in the Atlantic. During the cold war, presidents relied on executive agreements to end wars, establish bases, and direct military assistance.

It is clear that during periods of national emergency presidents have extended their powers at the expense of Congress. Abraham Lincoln took drastic measures in the Civil War, blockading southern ports, spending money that had not been authorized by Congress, and freeing slaves in the states fighting the Union Army. Woodrow Wilson assumed unprecedented economic authority during World War I.

As in past emergencies, the cold war strengthened executive power. But modern military technology *necessitated* delegating great authority to the president. Nuclear missiles capable of spanning continents could be launched by an adversary with only fifteen-minute warnings before detonation. In such a situation, the president simply would not have time to consult with Congress to order a retaliatory blow.

Although Congress and the president often clashed on foreign policy matters in the years since World War II, Congress voluntarily gave the executive branch enormous powers: to use nuclear weapons, react to military crises, and direct military assistance. Still, even during the cold war, Congress was an active participant in foreign policy. For example, President Harry Truman, a Democrat, brought Congress and leading Republicans into his confidence to build support for his cold war foreign policy initiatives such as the Marshall Plan and NATO. And President Dwight Eisenhower, a Republican, asked Congress for resolutions to take whatever measures he considered necessary—including the use of armed forces—to resist communist aggression in Formosa and the Middle East. Congress obliged in both cases.

When the Korean War broke out, however, Truman did not ask Congress for a declaration of war. He claimed that he had the authority to commit U.S. forces through his power as commander in chief and through powers emanating from U.S. treaties governing responsibilities to the United Nations.

Presidential power to commit troops became a contentious issue as the Korean War dragged on. The war in Indochina, which involved the United States in military operations in Vietnam, Laos, and Cambodia, provoked similar complaints about the use of executive power to make war without a congressional declaration of war. John Kennedy launched the Bay of Pigs operation in Cuba and managed the Cuban missile crisis without congressional authorization. Lyndon Johnson sent twelve thousand troops into the Dominican Republic in 1965 without congressional authorization. Richard Nixon ordered the bombing of Cambodia in actions kept secret from the American people for more than a year. Presidents Gerald Ford, Jimmy Carter, Ronald Reagan, and George Bush all took military actions without congressional authorization.

And Congress responded to what it regarded as excessive executive power. The War Powers Resolution of 1973 limited the authority of the president to commit forces to long-term conflict on his own. Every president from Nixon to Bush has challenged the legality of the War Powers Resolution, but none has brought the matter to a contest that would require judicial determination.

U.S. involvement in the Vietnam War provoked congressional efforts to limit presidential power, not only through the War Powers Resolution but through other means as well. Congress passed laws forbidding a continuation of various kinds of U.S. military operations in Southeast Asia. It cut off funds for such operations. It instituted a system of congressional oversight of intelligence agencies and covert military activities. And it established the mechanism of the *legislative veto* (later declared unconstitutional by the Supreme Court) to disallow U.S. sales of weapons to foreign countries. The legislative veto permits one or both houses of Congress to reject an action of the executive.

How would congressional-executive relations have fared in the absence of the cold war? Even without a Soviet adversary, the United States would still have had occasions in which it used its military power. In such contingencies, the chances are that Congress and the president would have clashed at times—particularly if the military actions had proved unsuccessful. There is too long a history of executive-congressional conflict to blame recent disharmony on the cold war.

But if the same period had been marked by more harmonious foreign relations, then Congress would have played a greater role in foreign policy. Under such circumstances, economic policy and human rights would have been the principal issues in American politics, and Congress traditionally has played a central role in these areas.

The Military-Industrial Complex

Because a central feature of the cold war was military preparation, the importance of weapons research and development became widely recognized. World Wars I and II began before America participated. Because of the great distances between the United States and its adversaries, the United States had time to mobilize in both world wars. But technology made distance less important than had been the case before World War II. Once the Soviet Union developed and produced long-range bombers and intercontinental missiles in the 1950s, America became vulnerable to attack.

The invention of nuclear weapons made another difference. The United States was able to recover from the surprise attack on Pearl Harbor and go on to win the war. A nuclear bomb attack would be vastly more devastating. The United States had to be sure that it had sufficient forces ready to counterattack. It had to be equally certain that the weapons of war would be effective against any Soviet countermeasures.

The security concerns of the United States gave rise to the growth of defense industries dependent upon a perpetuation of an acute national security danger. President Eisenhower warned against what he termed the *military-industrial complex*: the network of military agencies, political leaders, and private industries engaged in research, development, and production of military items. All these entities could benefit from perpetuation of the cold war.

Some observers, such as C. Wright Mills, argue that the generals and admirals, politicians, and corporations committed to the perpetuation of the cold war constituted a "power elite" and really ran American society. One does not have to accept Mills's views about the extent of power held by these constituent elements to recognize the importance of the military-industrial complex.

Had there been no cold war, would there have been a military-industrial complex? Probably so, given the nature of America's position in the world at the end of World War II and the development of nuclear weapons and technology systems. Perhaps its power would have been less, but as indicated above, the world political scene had experienced enough turmoil that even without the cold war America would at least have been prudent to maintain a strong and modern defense establishment. And alongside such an establishment would have developed a military-industrial complex.

Civil Liberties

Civil liberties are often among the casualties of wars and national emergencies. During World War I, the Espionage Act restricted freedom of speech. The Smith Act of 1940 served a similar purpose during World War II, and American citizens of Japanese descent were placed into relocation camps as a wartime measure in clear violation of their civil liberties.

The cold war also brought attacks on civil liberties. The domestic American response to communism and the Soviet danger was more intense than anything experienced by noncommunist European powers. Anticommunist fervor in the United States was fueled by allegations (mostly false) about Communist party members in the U.S. government, the spread of communism in Europe and Asia, America's loss of its nuclear monopoly, and the Korean War.

Although the Truman administration began the hard-line policy of containment, it was accused by Republicans of being "soft on communism." Some even accused Truman, Secretary of State Dean Acheson, and Secretary of Defense George Marshall of being traitors. In an effort to blunt criticism and forestall possible congressional action, in 1947 Truman issued Executive Order 9835, establishing a federal loyalty program. Under the order, each federal government agency made initial findings about the loyalty of its employees; a Loyalty Review Board would hear appeals and coordinate procedures.

The standard for dismissal was "reasonable grounds . . . for belief that the person involved is disloyal to the Government of the United States." Such grounds included sabotage, espionage, treason, advocacy of forceful or violent revolution, and serving the interests of a foreign government. One ground for dismissal was affiliation with a group designated by the attorney general as "totalitarian, fascist, communist, or subversive."

Although a democratic government legitimately needs authority to protect itself against subversives allied with foreign powers, there are limits to how it should act if it is to retain its commitments to basic democratic principles and to civil liberties. The initial regulations of the Truman program breached these limits in that they denied a person accused of being a loyalty risk the right of confronting his or her accusers.

Moreover, the United States government established a list of subversive organizations. Government employees who had been members of any of those organizations were immediately suspected of disloyalty. People's jobs were threatened despite the fact that they had committed no crimes of disloyalty.

A central figure in what became an anticommunist crusade was Joseph McCarthy, the Republican junior U.S. senator from Wisconsin. He came to prominence in 1950 with a speech delivered in Wheeling, West Virginia, in which he said that he had in his hands a list of 205 known communists in the State Department. (In later speeches, McCarthy altered the number. He never produced the list.) McCarthy proceeded to conduct investigations of communist influence in government. He went after a variety of figures, not only suspected communists but also liberals.

James Wechsler, editor of the *New York Post*, categorized the period of fervent anticommunism as the age of suspicion. Until McCarthy was brought down in 1954 after he accused the U.S. Army of coddling communists, many Americans were afraid to assert viewpoints that could even remotely be considered to be liberal, let alone Marxist.

The anticommunist fervor pervaded all segments of American society. An anticommunist group circulated a blacklist of suspected communists in film, radio, and television, making it impossible for some people so named to get work. High school teachers and university faculty members with left-wing views were put under pressure to leave their positions. Trade unions, civil rights organizations, and civil liberties organizations purged their membership of communists or suspected communists in self-protection.

From the immediate post–World War II years through the 1980s,

American private groups that disagreed with U.S. foreign policy were placed under surveillance by the Federal Bureau of Investigation (FBI) and other intelligence organizations. Civil rights organizations were cases in point. In some cases FBI officials surreptitiously disrupted the work of these groups. People were prosecuted because of their beliefs, not because of their actions—a fundamental violation of their civil liberties.

Had there been no cold war, it is unlikely that Americans would have tolerated such violations of civil liberties. Without a perceived Soviet threat from both internal and external sources, it is likely that civil liberties would also have been better protected.

We should note, however, that even during the Vietnam War when American soldiers were fighting a communist enemy, widespread dissent was tolerated. As befits a free society, antiwar activists conducted meetings, wrote books, demonstrated, and sought, at times successfully, to defeat prowar candidates in peaceful elections.

Civil Rights

To some observers, civil rights was a casualty of the cold war. Such thinking is in accord with the views of social scientists who link war with the ending of social reform. Some argue that U.S. intervention in World War I marked the end of Progressive reforms and intervention in World War II brought an end to the New Deal.

But such a view ignores the impressive gains made by black Americans in the period between 1945 and 1989. One of the earliest gains came in the military. During World War II, black soldiers fought in segregated units. Although World War II had been conducted against Nazi Germany with its notions of racial superiority, segregation—the separation of races—continued to be practiced even in America's fighting units. The cold war required an effective American armed forces. It was also embarrassing for the United States, which claimed to be the leader of the Free World, that its black soldiers were second-class citizens. In 1948, President Truman desegregated the armed services; thus the military establishment became one of the first American institutions to end segregation. Truman had domestic political reasons for desegregating the armed services, but the cold war made such a move imperative.

The cold war pitted the United States against a nation that was critical of U.S. racial policies toward blacks. The Soviets used stories about lynching and racial discrimination as anti-American propaganda. Diplomats from Africa and Asia who visited the American South were sometimes mistaken for American blacks and subjected to local discriminatory practices. These incidents naturally embarrassed the United States in its relations with Asian and African governments. When the Supreme Court considered the major case on segregation, *Brown v. Board of Education of Topeka, Kansas* (1954), the United States government issued an *amicus curiae* (friend of the court) brief arguing among other points that segregation hurt the standing of the United States in its relations with other countries.

The civil rights movement, moreover, attracted the attention of many people in the Third World. Once the movement achieved its major political objectives through the congressional legislation enacted in 1964 and 1965, the issue of segregation could not so easily be used against the United States by Soviet propagandists.

Had there been no cold war, segregation would still have been ended. But since foreign policy was so central to the post–World War II period, legal barriers to integration would likely have ended more gradually.

Conclusion

The cold war had an enormous impact on the American political system. Without it, some aspects of American politics would have moved in different directions. National security would have had a different focus in a multipolar world. Congressional challenges to presidential power would have continued but probably would not have been so strong. The military-industrial complex would have existed, although its influence probably would have been smaller.

Without the cold war, the country's record on civil liberties would be better. The cold war—particularly in the early years—generated the idea that America's security was endangered by monumental forces at home and abroad. Without such fear, violations of civil liberties would have been fewer and would not have been tolerated by most Americans.

Had there been no cold war, segregation would still have come to an end. Domestic forces alone were moving in that direction, although as indicated, the movement toward equality would have taken more time.

But without the cold war, many things would have been the same. Given the nature of America's position in the postwar world and the character of modern technology, the United States probably would have devoted a greater part of its wealth to national security than it did in the peacetime years of the 1920s and 1930s. Still, the amount would have been less than was spent because of the cold war—but probably not too much less.

Reorganization of the national security establishment would probably have continued much the way that it did. World War II had demonstrated the necessity of better coordination and improved intelligence information. In the absence of the cold war the CIA would have probably been even more interventionist.

The president would still be the major figure in making foreign policy. No doubt the precedents established by Franklin Roosevelt and other presidents would have encouraged chief executives to use the powers of commander in chief and chief diplomat against congressional "obstruction." And it could be argued that presidents would still usually get their way in foreign policy, just as they did on major matters during the cold war.

The cold war is now over. The Soviet Union as an independent political entity ceased to exist on Christmas Day, 1991. Eleven of its fifteen republics united into a weak Commonwealth of Independent States, and the other four chose independence. East European countries previously under Soviet control or influence are now independent. Communism is discredited as a viable ideology, and the United States has lost its principal rival in the world. But even before the collapse of the Soviet Union, the euphoria produced in the United States by the visits of Soviet leader Mikhail Gorbachev gives us some idea about how the United States would have regarded a democratic Soviet Union in 1945. The United States would have said that it is ready and willing to help, to join hands in cooperation, and to resolve disputes with the Soviet Union in a peaceful manner.

The Iraqi invasion of Kuwait, the ethnic and irredentist movements in Eastern Europe, Asia, and Africa, and the increasing firepower available to nations from conventional, biological, chemical, and nuclear weapons all suggest that the United States would have needed to maintain its status as a global power even in the absence of the cold war.

Sources and Suggested Readings

Differing interpretations of the origins of the cold war are found in Herbert Feis, *Churchill, Roosevelt, Stalin: The War They Waged and the Peace They*

Sought (Princeton, N.J.: Princeton University Press, 1957); Thomas G. Paterson, *On Every Front: The Making of the Cold War* (New York: W. W. Norton, 1979); Arthur M. Schlesinger, Jr., "Origins of the Cold War," *Foreign Affairs* 46, no. 1 (October 1967): 22–52; and Walter LaFeber, *America, Russia, and the Cold War, 1945–1990,* 6th ed. (New York: McGraw-Hill, 1991).

The history of the cold war is discussed in John Lewis Gaddis, *The Long Peace: Inquiries into the History of the Cold War* (New York: Oxford University Press, 1987); Miroslav Nincic, *Anatomy of Hostility: The U.S.-Soviet Rivalry in Perspective* (San Diego, Calif.: Harcourt Brace Jovanovich, 1989); and Joseph L. Nogee and John Spanier, *Peace Impossible—War Unlikely: The Cold War between the United States and the Soviet Union* (Glenview, Ill.: Scott Foresman, 1988).

Relations between the president and Congress are considered in Cecil V. Crabb, Jr., and Pat M. Holt, *Invitation to Struggle: Congress, the President and Foreign Policy,* 3d ed. (Washington, D.C.: CQ Press, 1989); Louis Fisher, *The Politics of Shared Power,* 2nd ed. (Washington, D.C.: Congressional Quarterly, 1987); and Edward S. Corwin, *The President: Office and Powers, 1787–1984: A History and Analysis of Practice and Opinion,* 5th ed., revised by Randall W. Bland, Theodore T. Hindson, and Jack Peltason (New York: New York University Press, 1984).

U.S. domestic aspects of the cold war are examined in David Caute, *The Great Fear: The Anti-Communist Purge under Truman and Eisenhower* (New York: Simon and Schuster, 1978); Mary L. Dudziak, "Desegregation as a Cold War Imperative," *Stanford Law Review* 41, no. 1 (November 1988): 61–120; Alonzo L. Hamby, *Beyond the New Deal: Harry S. Truman and American Liberalism* (New York: Columbia University Press, 1973); Seymour Melman, *Our Depleted Society* (New York: Dell, 1965); and Murray Weidenbaum, "Why Defense Spending Doesn't Matter," *National Interest,* no. 16 (Summer 1989): 91–96.

Index